# Implementing VMware Horizon 7

## Second Edition

A comprehensive, practical guide to accessing virtual desktops, applications, and services through a unified platform

**Jason Ventresco**

BIRMINGHAM - MUMBAI

# Implementing VMware Horizon 7

*Second Edition*

First published: May 2013

Second edition: June 2016

Production reference: 1240616

Published by Packt Publishing Ltd.
Livery Place
35 Livery Street
Birmingham
B3 2PB, UK.
ISBN 978-1-78588-930-1

www.packtpub.com

# Credits

**Authors**

Jason Ventresco

**Reviewer**

Mario Russo

**Commissioning Editor**

Pratik Shah

**Acquisition Editor**

Divya Poojari

**Content Development Editor**

Prashanth G

**Technical Editor**

Shivani K. Mistry

**Copy Editors**

Safis Editing

**Project Coordinator**

Ulhas Kambali

**Proofreader**

Safis Editing

**Indexer**

Hemangini Bari

**Graphics**

Disha Haria

**Production Coordinator**

Arvindkumar Gupta

# About the Author

**Jason Ventresco** is a 17 year veteran of the IT field, and currently works for $EMC^2$ as a Consultant Solutions Engineer. In that role he architects, builds, and tests the latest end user computing solutions to validate their performance and provide guidance to $EMC^2$ customers and partners.

Jason previously worked as a member of the Global Infrastructure team for FHI 360, and as an IT consultant for WorkSmart and Xerox Global Services. Jason previously published the books Implementing VMware Horizon View 5.2, VMware Horizon View 5.3 Design Patterns and Best Practices, and VMware Horizon View 6 Desktop Virtualization Cookbook.

Jason lives in Raleigh, North Carolina with his wife, Christine, and daughter, Amanda. He holds two degrees, a Master of Science in Information Assurance from Norwich University, and a Bachelor of Science in Information Technology from the University of Phoenix. In his free time, he likes to travel, go boating, and attend Carolina Hurricanes games.

*I would like to thank my wife, Christine, and daughter, Amanda, for their ongoing support. Writing books requires sacrificing family time, and without their support none of this would be possible.*

*I would also like to thank my parents, Richard and Linda Ventresco, for providing me with the opportunities they did when I was growing up; they helped make me what I am today. I love you Mom and Dad!*

*I would also like to thank my fellow EMC Solutions co-workers both here in the US and in China. Working with them has helped provide me with the experience and knowledge required to write multiple books like this.*

# About the Reviewer

**Mario Russo** has worked as an IT architect, senior technical VMware trainer, and in the pre-sales department. He has also worked on VMware technology since 2004.

In 2005, he worked for IBM on the first large project consolidation for Telecom Italia on the Virtual VMware Esx 2.5.1 platform in Italy with the Physical to Virtual (P2V) tool.

In 2007, he conducted a drafting course and training for BancoPosta, Italy, and project disaster and recovery (DR Open) for IBM and EMC.

In 2008, he worked for the Project Speed Up Consolidation BNP and the migration P2V on VI3 infrastructure at BNP Cardif Insurance. In 2014 Customize Dashboard and Tuning Smart Allert vCOPs 5.7 POSTECOM Italy Rm. He was a VCI Certified Instructor 2s Level of VMware and is certified VCAP5-DCA, VCP3-4, VCP5-DV VCP5-DT, VCP-Cloud, NPP Nutanix – ZCP Zerto, and other. He is the owner of Business to Virtual, which specializes in virtualization solutions.

He has also contributed as a technical reviewer for various other books by Packt Publishing, such as *Implementing VMware Horizon View 5.2, Implementing VMware vCenter Server, Troubleshooting vSphere Storage, VMware Horizon View 5.3 Design Patterns and Best Practices, Instant Getting Started with VMware Fusion, Implementing VMware vCenter Server, VMware vSphere Security Cookbook, Mastering vRealize Operations Manager,* and *Getting Started with VMware Virtual SAN.*

*I would like to thank my wife, Lina, and my daughter, Gaia. They're my strength.*

# www.PacktPub.com

For support files and downloads related to your book, please visit www.PacktPub.com.

Did you know that Packt offers eBook versions of every book published, with PDF and ePub files available? You can upgrade to the eBook version at www.PacktPub.com and as a print book customer, you are entitled to a discount on the eBook copy. Get in touch with us at service@packtpub.com for more details.

At www.PacktPub.com, you can also read a collection of free technical articles, sign up for a range of free newsletters and receive exclusive discounts and offers on Packt books and eBooks.

https://www2.packtpub.com/books/subscription/packtlib

Do you need instant solutions to your IT questions? PacktLib is Packt's online digital book library. Here, you can search, access, and read Packt's entire library of books.

## Why subscribe?

- Fully searchable across every book published by Packt
- Copy and paste, print, and bookmark content
- On demand and accessible via a web browser

## Free access for Packt account holders

If you have an account with Packt at www.PacktPub.com, you can use this to access PacktLib today and view 9 entirely free books. Simply use your login credentials for immediate access.

# Table of Contents

# Preface

Implementing VMware Horizon 7 is meant to be a hands-on guide on how to deploy and configure various key features of Horizon, including App Volumes and User Environment Manager. The examples provided in this book focus on 14 different topics, and it instructs you on their purpose, configuration, and administration. Using the examples provided in this book, you will be able to implement and manage these features in your own VMware Horizon environment.

There are many places in this book that refer to the official VMware Horizon, App Volumes, and User Environment Manager documentation. You are encouraged to review this documentation as it complements the material in this book and contains additional information that can provide a deeper understanding of the technical details and capabilities of the entire VMware Horizon platform.

## Why virtualize our end user computing resources?

There are a number of different reasons why an organization may decide to implement VMware Horizon in their own environment. Many organizations are already familiar with the benefits of virtualization, such as the following:

- Server consolidation: Less physical hardware is required to service the same quality of workload
- Simplified management: Fewer physical resources to manage
- More energy efficient: Less power and cooling required
- Hardware independence: Virtual machines can run on almost any hardware platform without any changes required
- Enhanced capabilities: Deploy new virtual servers much faster than physical ones, and with less effort

These are just a small sample of the benefits of virtualization. If you have already implemented virtualization in your organization, you likely have additional reasons of your own.

Virtual desktops and applications can provide an organization with additional advantages beyond those of virtualization itself. Using VMware Horizon, we can do the following:

- Roll out a new Windows desktop OS across your enterprise without making any changes to the existing desktops, although eventually you will want to retire or repurpose these machines.
- Horizon desktops are live in the data center, and they can be accessed from almost anywhere from a variety of clients. Horizon desktops, as well as the data stored on them, can't be left in airports, stolen from cars, or accidentally left on your desk at the office. Horizon offers the ability to control it and how data can be copied between the client endpoint and the desktop or application being accessed.
- Stop caring about endpoint hardware. Use existing Windows PCs as desktops if you want or move to a zero client and do away with common endpoint management tasks. Better yet, have users bring their own device and let them use it to access their Horizon desktop. Worry about what's in the data center, not on the desk.
- Microsoft *Patch Tuesday* redefined. With Horizon Instant and linked clones, you patch once and then quickly update the desktops with a whole new master image. No more testing patches across 15 different hardware platforms. No more monitoring patch status across hundreds or thousands of desktops. The same technique can be used to roll out new applications as well.
- Stop troubleshooting *random* desktop problems. Problems with Windows? Provide the user a new or refreshed desktop in minutes with linked clones, or even seconds with instant clones. With features such as User Environment Manager to manage Windows profiles and App Volumes to deliver applications on demand, the individual desktop doesn't have to matter. If a problem with a persistent desktop will take more than a few minutes to fix, refresh the desktop instead. If using nonpersistent desktops, simply ask the user to log off and on again, which will assign them a brand new desktop to use.

These are just some of the advantages of using VMware Horizon, vSphere, App Volumes, and User Environment Manager to move your desktops and applications into a data centre. While reading this book, I encourage you to think of ways that Horizon can change how you provide end user computing resources to your organization. These are just a few examples:

- Don't just simply forklift your desktops into the data center as full virtual machines, consider the benefits of linked or instant clones.

- Rather than create large numbers of master images for different departments or worker types across your organization, create a basic image that you can layer applications on top of using App Volumes.
- Investigate software that is optimized for virtual desktops, such as the vShield Endpoint antivirus platform. Software that is optimized for virtual desktop platforms typically requires less per-desktop resources, which may enable you to run more desktops on a given vSphere host.
- Horizon Enterprise has features that make the individual desktop less important, you just need to use them. Use User Environment Management to manage your users' Windows profiles, App Volumes to centrally manage and deliver applications independent of the desktop, and suddenly the individual desktop won't matter as much. This allows you to focus on the only things that actually matter: user data and applications.

VMware Horizon, App Volumes, and User Environment Manager can provide you with much more than just a means of virtualizing your desktops and applications. The more familiar you become each product's features and capabilities, the more you will realize that you can rethink a lot of what you do concerning application and desktop management and delivery, and eventually provide a higher quality experience to your end users.

I certainly hope this is the case.

# What this book covers

Chapter 1, *VMware Horizon Infrastructure Overview*, provides a broad overview of VMware Horizon and discusses topics that will influence the design, implementation, and assessment of a VMware Horizon infrastructure.

Chapter 2, *Implementing Horizon Connection Server*, covers the infrastructure requirements, sizing, limits, high availability, deployment, configuration, backup, and recovery of Horizon Connection Server.

Chapter 3, *Implementing Horizon Composer*, covers the infrastructure requirements, deployment, configuration, backup, and recovery of Horizon Composer. The capabilities of Horizon Composer and benefits of using linked clone desktops are also discussed.

Chapter 4, *Implementing Horizon Security Server*, covers the infrastructure requirements, limits, high availability designs, deployment, configuration, backup, and recovery of Horizon Security Server.

Chapter 5, *Implementing VMware Horizon Access Point*, covers the infrastructure requirements, limits, high availability designs, deployment, configuration, and troubleshooting of Horizon Access Point.

Chapter 6, *Implementing a Horizon Cloud Pod*, covers how to deploy, configure, and administer a Horizon Cloud Pod, which enables the creation of global client entitlements to resources in multisite, multi-pod Horizon environments.

Chapter 7, *Using VMware Virtual SAN with Horizon*, provides an overview of how to architect VMware Virtual SAN for a Horizon infrastructure, walks through the deployment process, and identifies what must be done when creating Horizon pools in order to use Virtual SAN.

Chapter 8, *Implementing VMware User Environment Manager*, covers the implementation and management of the VMware User Environment Manager profile management platform and provides an overview of the capabilities of some of the product's advanced features.

Chapter 9, *Implementing VMware App Volumes*, covers the infrastructure prerequisites, deployment, configuration, and administration of VMware App Volumes. Topics include the deployment and configuration of the App Volumes Manager appliance, the installation and configuration of the App Volumes Agent and AppCapture program, the App Volumes AppStack creation, update, and assignment process, the Writable Volume assignment and creation process, and App Volumes backup and recovery procedures.

Chapter 10, *Creating Horizon Desktop Pools*, covers how to configure Microsoft Windows Remote Desktop Services for use with Horizon, how to configure and manage a Horizon Application Pool, and how to manage and monitor the status of Windows Remote Desktop Services hosts and Horizon clients who are streaming applications.

Chapter 11, *Implementing Horizon Application Pools*, covers how to configure Microsoft Windows Remote Desktop Services for use with Horizon, how to deploy and manage Remote Desktop Services farms and Horizon Application Pools, and how to manage and monitor the status of Windows Remote Desktop Services hosts and Horizon clients who are streaming applications.

Chapter 12, *Performing Horizon Desktop Pool Maintenance*, covers how to perform maintenance on Horizon pools that contain linked clone or instant clone desktops. Topics include an overview of the different maintenance operations including linked clone refresh, recompose, and rebalance, instant clone push image and recovery, and how to manage the optional linked clone persistent disks.

Chapter 13, *Creating a Master Horizon Desktop Image*, covers the techniques that should be used when creating a master Horizon desktop image. Topics covered include the importance of optimizing the desktop operating system; sample optimization results; examples of how to disable native application update features; and how to optimize the Windows filesystem, Windows Operating System, and Windows user profiles.

Chapter 14, *Managing Horizon SSL Certificates*, covers how to replace the default SSL certificates on each of the Horizon components including Connection Server, Composer, Security Server, and Access Point, as well as the App Volumes appliances. This chapter also discusses how to create the SSL certificate requests and obtain new certificates using a Microsoft Active Directory Certificate Services server.

Chapter 15, *Using Horizon PowerCLI*, covers the different PowerCLI commands that you can use to configure and administer nearly all aspects of the Horizon platform, and provides examples of how those commands are used.

# What you need for this book

The reader should have a basic understanding of the following concepts that are integral to the implementation and management of View.

- Microsoft Windows Server
- Microsoft Active Directory
    - Certificate services
    - DNS
    - Group policies
- VMware vSphere
    - vCenter Server
    - Virtual machine snapshots
    - Virtual machine templates
    - VMware tools
    - vSphere administration
- Networking
    - DHCP
    - Protocol and port types
    - Basics of LAN and WAN networking

The following software is required to implement the solutions described in this book:

- VMware Horizon installation media including all optional components
- VMware App Volumes installation media including all additional components
- VMware User Environment Manager installation media including all additional components
- vSphere 6 Update 2 installation media including vCenter Server and vSphere
- Windows Server 2012 R2 installation media
- Installation media for a supported Windows desktop OS

The installation media for the required VMware products can be obtained from the VMware.com website. If you do not have a current license for the products, you can register for a trail to obtain access to the software.

# Who this book is for

If you are a newcomer to system administration and you wish to implement the Horizon environment, then this book is for you. Prior knowledge of Horizon is beneficial.

# Conventions

In this book, you will find a number of text styles that distinguish between different kinds of information. Here are some examples of these styles and an explanation of their meaning.

Code words in text, database table names, folder names, filenames, file extensions, pathnames, dummy URLs, user input, and Twitter handles are shown as follows: "Decrypt the AD LDS database backup titled `backup.LDF` to a file titled `decrypted.LDF`."

**New terms** and **important words** are shown in bold. Words that you see on the screen, for example, in menus or dialog boxes, appear in the text like this: "Click on the **Backup** tab and make any desired changes."

Warnings or important notes appear in a box like this.

Tips and tricks appear like this.

# Reader feedback

Feedback from our readers is always welcome. Let us know what you think about this book-what you liked or disliked. Reader feedback is important for us as it helps us develop titles that you will really get the most out of.

To send us general feedback, simply e-mail `feedback@packtpub.com`, and mention the book's title in the subject of your message.

If there is a topic that you have expertise in and you are interested in either writing or contributing to a book, see our author guide at `www.packtpub.com/authors`.

# Customer support

Now that you are the proud owner of a Packt book, we have a number of things to help you to get the most from your purchase.

# Downloading the color images of this book

We also provide you with a PDF file that has color images of the screenshots/diagrams used in this book. The color images will help you better understand the changes in the output. You can download this file from `https://www.packtpub.com/sites/default/files/downloads/ImplementingVMwareHorizon7_ColorImages.pdf`.

# Errata

Although we have taken every care to ensure the accuracy of our content, mistakes do happen. If you find a mistake in one of our books-maybe a mistake in the text or the code-we would be grateful if you could report this to us. By doing so, you can save other readers from frustration and help us improve subsequent versions of this book. If you find any errata, please report them by visiting `http://www.packtpub.com/submit-errata`, selecting your book, clicking on the **Errata Submission Form** link, and entering the details of your errata. Once your errata are verified, your submission will be accepted and the errata will be uploaded to our website or added to any list of existing errata under the Errata section of that title.

To view the previously submitted errata, go to `https://www.packtpub.com/books/content/support` and enter the name of the book in the search field. The required information will appear under the **Errata** section.

# Piracy

Piracy of copyrighted material on the Internet is an ongoing problem across all media. At Packt, we take the protection of our copyright and licenses very seriously. If you come across any illegal copies of our works in any form on the Internet, please provide us with the location address or website name immediately so that we can pursue a remedy.

Please contact us at `copyright@packtpub.com` with a link to the suspected pirated material.

We appreciate your help in protecting our authors and our ability to bring you valuable content.

# Questions

If you have a problem with any aspect of this book, you can contact us at `questions@packtpub.com`, and we will do our best to address the problem.

# 1

# VMware Horizon Infrastructure Overview

This chapter will discuss a number of topics that play a critical role in our Horizon design. We will discuss the different components of a Horizon installation, examine the different license levels, and outline the core requirements of a Horizon infrastructure. We will also discuss how to measure the resource requirements of a desktop, and how those requirements impact all layers of our infrastructure including the storage design, network design, and virtual desktop VMware ESXi server configuration.

By the end of this chapter we will learn:

- The individual components of a VMware Horizon installation
- The role of different components of VMware Horizon
- VMware Horizon license options
- Core infrastructure requirements for VMware Horizon
- An overview of several key VMware Horizon design and pilot project considerations

Throughout this book you may see references to components or features of VMware Horizon View made without the word *View* being included in the name. While this book focuses heavily on components of VMware Horizon View itself, it does include other components that are now part of the larger product known as VMware Horizon. So, while these names may be slightly different than you are used to seeing, know that my goal was to try and match the terms VMware wants us to use for their products, and not necessarily those that we are most familiar with (or that VMware themselves always uses for that matter).

# VMware Horizon components

VMware Horizon is a family of desktop and application virtualization solutions designed to deliver end user computing services from any cloud. The following section will provide a high-level overview of those components of the Horizon family of products that we will cover in this book, which includes:

- VMware Horizon Connection Server, Security Server, and Access Point
- VMware Horizon Composer
- VMware Horizon Agent
- VMware Horizon Client
- VMware vSphere including vCenter Server
- VMware App Volumes
- VMware User Environment Manager
- VMware ThinApp

 Refer to the VMware Horizon product page for a list of all of the products that are part of Horizon (`https://www.vmware.com/products/horizon-view`).

The following figure shows where each of the components of a typical Horizon installation resides within the IT infrastructure. The only components not shown that are discussed in this book are the VMware App Volumes servers and Windows-based files servers used for hosting VMware User Environment Manager data. If shown, both of these components would be located on the internal network along with the Horizon Connection Server, vCenter Server, and virtual desktops and Microsoft Windows **Remote Desktop Session (RDS)** Servers.

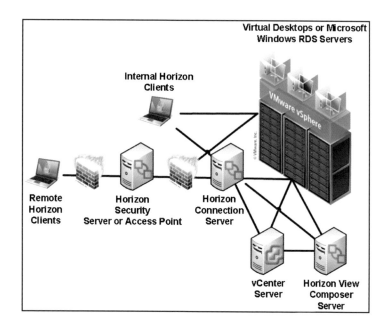

# Horizon Connection Server

VMware Horizon Connection Server is a software service that serves as the broker for Horizon client connections. In this role, it authenticates user connection requests, verifies the desktops or Microsoft Windows **RDS Servers** that the user is entitled to access, and then directs the connection to the appropriate resource. Horizon Connection Server is installed on a dedicated server that is required to be a member of an **Active Directory** (**AD**) domain that is trusted by all Horizon clients. Horizon Connection Server also hosts the Horizon Administrator console, an Adobe Flex-based web application that is used to manage the Horizon environment and perform tasks, such as:

- Deploying virtual desktops
- Creating desktop or Microsoft Windows RDS-based pools
- Controlling access to desktop pools
- Creating and managing Horizon Cloud Pods
- Examining Horizon system events

The Horizon Connection Server is one component that is required in every Horizon environment owing to the role it plays as the connection broker and management console. Chapter 2, *Implementing Horizon Connection Server*, provides the information needed to install and configure a VMware Horizon Connection Server. Chapter 6, *Implementing a Horizon Cloud Pod*, provides information about the configuration of the Cloud Pod feature that is used to provide Horizon clients access to desktops across multiple Horizon Pods, each Pod representing a standalone installation of VMware Horizon. The following chapters provide information about the deployment of Horizon desktops and management of desktop pools:

- Chapter 10, *Creating Horizon Desktop Pools*
- Chapter 11, *Implementing Horizon Application Pools*
- Chapter 12, *Performing Horizon Desktop Pool Maintenance*

# Horizon Security Server

VMware Horizon Security Server is a custom instance of the Horizon Connection Server that is designed to be installed in a datacenter **demilitarized zone (DMZ),** to provide strong authentication and secure access for Horizon clients connecting from outside the organization's private network. Multiple Security Servers may be installed to provide load balancing and high availability to these external clients. The following figure shows the placement of a Horizon Security Server, or Access Point (described next), within a DMZ.

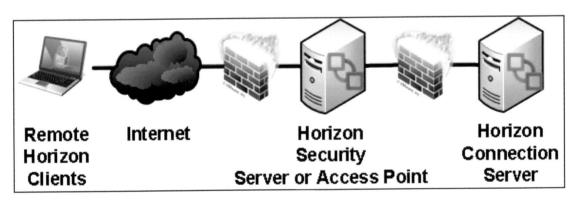

Horizon Security Server is installed on top of a supported version of Microsoft Windows' Server using the same installation package used for Horizon Connection Servers. Horizon Security Server is only required if providing access to Horizon clients residing outside of the company network. Chapter 4, *Implementing Horizon Security Server*, provides the information needed to install and configure a VMware Horizon Security Server.

# Horizon Access Point

VMware Horizon Access Point was first introduced in **VMware Horizon 6.2**, although it was previously used with the VMware Horizon Air cloud-hosted desktop and application offering. Like Horizon Security Server, Access Point is designed to provide strong authentication, and secure access, for Horizon clients connecting from outside the organizations private network. The figure in the previous section shows the placement of a Horizon Access Point within a DMZ environment, as is typical, since it performs similar functions to Horizon Security Server.

Access Point is packaged in **Open Virtualization Format** (**OVF**) and is deployed on vSphere as a hardened, pre-configured Linux-based virtual appliance. Horizon Access Point is provided as an option on Horizon Security Server, and like Security Server, it is only required if providing access for external clients, it is designed to be installed in a *DMZ*, and multiple appliances may be installed to ensure high availability and load balancing. Chapter 5, *Implementing VMware Horizon Access Point*, provides the information needed to install and configure a VMware Horizon Access Point.

VMware recommends that customers using Security Server today should continue to do so, but they have also indicated that Access Point is their primary focus moving forward. New deployments may wish to future-proof their Horizon installation by selecting Access Point, as VMware has indicated that Security Server will be deprecated or possibly even phased out in a future Horizon release. I recommended at least trying Access Point, if for no other reason than it can work with multiple connection servers at once, while Security Servers can only be paired with one connection server at a time. Additionally, Access Point can be deployed or redeployed very quickly and with minimal effort.

# Horizon Enrollment Server

**VMware Horizon Enrollment Server** is new to version 7, is installed as a standalone service and integrates with VMware Identity Manager to enable true **Single Sign-On** (**SSO**) for Horizon clients that are using non-AD-based authentication methods such as **RSA SecureID**. SSO means that, when using non-AD-based authentication methods, users will only need to log into Horizon once to reach their desktop or streamed application. The VMware blog post **Introducing True SSO (Single Sign-On) in VMware Horizon 7** (http://blogs.vmware.com/euc/2016/03/true-sso-single-sign-on-view-identity-manager-authenticate.html) provides an overview of this new Horizon feature.

This feature is only used when Horizon clients use non-AD-based methods for authentication. Implementing solutions, such as SecureID and VMware Identity Manager, is outside the scope of this book, which is why the Enrollment Server will not be covered. Consult the Horizon documentation (`https://www.vmware.com/support/pubs/view_pubs.html`) for additional information about the deployment and configuration of Horizon Enrollment Server.

# VMware vSphere

VMware vSphere, also referred to as ESXi or even ESX for earlier versions, is a Type 1 hypervisor that is the virtualization platform used for the vSphere suite of products. Type 1 hypervisors are designed to run directly on the host hardware, whereas Type 2 hypervisors run within a conventional operating system environment.

ESXi is the only hypervisor that is fully supported by VMware for hosting Horizon virtual desktops, as it fully integrates with Horizon for full desktop lifecycle management. All of the primary desktop provisioning and maintenance tasks are performed using the Horizon Administrator console; the vSphere Client is not used. Horizon supports multiple versions of vSphere, but **vSphere 6.0 Update 1** and newer are required to leverage many of the latest features of the platform, and **vSphere 6.0 Update 2** is required when you want to use the latest version of **Virtual SAN** (**VSAN**). Refer to the *VMware vCenter Server* requirements section for examples of some Horizon features that require a specific version of both vSphere and vCenter Server.

VMware vSphere also includes the **VSAN** feature that uses local ESXi server storage to build a highly resilient virtual **storage area network** (**SAN**) to provide storage for virtual machines. VMware Horizon supports using VSAN, and we will review how to do so in `Chapter 7`, *Using VMware Virtual SAN with Horizon*.

# VMware vCenter Server

VMware vCenter Server is a software service that provides a central administration point for VMware ESXi servers as well as other components of the vSphere suite. vCenter Server performs the actual creation and management of virtual desktops, based on instructions received from the Horizon Connection Server and the Horizon Composer Server.

This book includes some information that applies only to the Windows-based version of VMware vCenter, but rest assured that you are free to use the Linux-based **vCenter Server Appliance (vCSA)** for your VMware Horizon deployment if you wish. The *vCSA* supports up to the Horizon single Pod maximum of 10,000 desktops, so there are no concerns about scalability. The most significant difference you will encounter (aside from the fact that you will not need to create a separate database for vCenter) is that when you use the *vCSA* you will be required to deploy a standalone Horizon Composer server, which is what will be demonstrated in Chapter 3, *Implementing Horizon Composer*.

# Horizon Composer

VMware Horizon Composer is a software service that works alongside the VMware vCenter and Horizon Connection Servers to deploy and manage linked clone desktops. Horizon Composer can be installed directly on the vCenter Server, or on a dedicated server.

Horizon Composer is only required if linked clone desktops will be deployed. Chapter 3, *Implementing Horizon Composer*, provides the information needed to install and configure Horizon Composer.

Horizon Composer is not required when using Instant Clone desktops; it is only required if you are using linked clone desktops. Linked clone and Instant Clone desktops are similar in how they operate when deployed, but the deployment process itself is quite different.

# Horizon Agent

VMware Horizon Agent is a software service that is installed on the systems that will be managed by Horizon. This includes not only a virtual desktop image that will be deployed using Horizon, but any physical desktops or Microsoft RDS Servers as well.

The Horizon agent provides services including, but not limited to, support for connecting the virtual desktop to Horizon's client-attached USB devices, client connection monitoring, Virtual Printing, and single sign-on.

# Horizon Client

VMware Horizon Client is a software application that is used to communicate with a Horizon Connection Server, and initiate connections to desktops and Microsoft Windows RDS servers.

The Horizon Client is available for multiple software platforms, including **Microsoft Windows**, **Apple OSX and IOS**, **Android**, and **Ubuntu Linux**. In addition, there are a number of Thin and Zero clients that come preloaded with Horizon-compatible clients.

# VMware App Volumes

VMware App Volumes is an optional component of VMware Horizon that provides multiple capabilities, particularly in environments where floating assignment desktops are used or changes to a virtual desktop are discarded after every session (also known as **non-persistent desktops**). The deployment and configuration of VMware App Volumes is discussed in detail in `Chapter 9`, *Implementing VMware App Volumes*.

The primary features of VMware App Volumes include:

- The ability for applications to be delivered to Horizon desktops, or Microsoft Windows RDS servers, immediately and dynamically, in a manner that is transparent to the end user. This feature works both with Horizon desktops and Microsoft Windows **RDS servers**, and is called an **App Volumes AppStack**.
- The ability to roam user installed applications across Horizon client sessions, even if a different desktop virtual machine is assigned during the next logon. This feature is designed for use with Horizon desktops only, and is called **Writable Volumes**.

The following diagram shows the logical layering of multiple **AppStack** and a **Writeable Volume** on top of the host operating system. Each of the items is attached to the host virtual machine individually when a user logs in, can be removed individually if changes are required, and will follow a user from one login to the next.

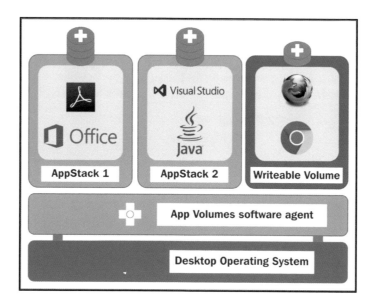

App Volumes AppStacks are packaged as a **Virtual Machine Disk** (**VMDK**) file and attached to one or more virtual machines as needed. The App Volumes agent seamlessly integrates this VMDK into the virtual machines OS; no actual installation is performed. AppVolumes can even capture an application packaged using VMware**ThinApp**, which provides organizations who rely on ThinApp with an additional method for distributing its virtualized application packages.

App Volumes creates a unique Writeable Volume for each user, using a VMDK that is also seamlessly integrated into their current virtual machine. The Writable Volumes is attached to the Horizon desktop when the user logs in, and detached upon logoff.

The combination of VMware App Volumes, and VMware User Environment Manager (discussed next), provides organizations with a way to leverage the efficiencies of floating assignment non-persistent desktops (described in Chapter 10, *Creating Horizon Desktop Pools*), while still providing users a highly personalized desktop experience.

# VMware User Environment Manager

VMware**User Environment Manager** (**UEM**) is an optional component of VMware Horizon that provides the ability to roam end user Windows profile and persona configuration data, including application settings, across different Windows **operating system** (**OS**) versions, or even between physical desktops and virtual desktops or Windows**RDS servers**.

VMware UEM works with all three Microsoft Windows profile types, including mandatory, roaming, or local. *UEM* is not a replacement for any of these profile types as it does not roam user data across sessions or devices, only the profile and persona configuration. User data should be saved using techniques such as roaming profiles, or even folder redirection.

Highlights of the benefits of UEM include:

- A consistent and personalized end user experience, regardless of where a user logs in or which Windows OS they are using.
- Implementation of various settings that previously required AD **group policies**, such as Windows user profile redirection, and some Horizon agent settings.
- Customization of user settings, such as printers, based on log on location.
- Elimination of the need to perform user profile migrations when moving to a newer version of Windows that has a new profile type (such as from Windows 8.1 to Windows 10).
- Robust design that scales to support over a hundred thousand end users.
- Simple design that requires no scripting knowledge, can be implemented rapidly, and requires minimal infrastructure to begin using.

Chapter 8, *Implementing VMware User Environment Manager*, provides information about how to implement and administer UEM.

# VMware ThinApp

VMware ThinApp is an application virtualization platform that integrates with Horizon to provide users with rapid access to new or upgraded applications without having to perform any changes to the virtual desktops. Applications that have been packaged with ThinApp are delivered as a single executable file that runs in complete isolation to both of the other ThinApp packaged applications, as well as applications that are installed on the desktop itself.

ThinApp provides Horizon customers with a number of powerful capabilities. The following list details two popular scenarios where ThinApp can benefit an organization:

- Eliminate application conflicts that can occur when specific programs are installed together within the desktop image
- Virtualize legacy applications to ensure that they will continue to function regardless of the underlying Windows OS

This book does not have a dedicated chapter concerning VMware ThinApp; consult the VMware ThinApp documentation page for details about how it is used (`https://www.vmw are.com/support/pubs/thinapp_pubs.html`).

> In `Chapter 9`, *Implementing VMware App Volumes*, I will provide an overview of how you can use ThinApp virtualization within an AppStack.

# VMware Horizon licensing

VMware Horizon offers four different license levels: **Standard**, **Linux**, **Advanced**, and **Enterprise**. Additionally, the Advanced and Enterprise licenses may be purchased as **named user** (**NU**) or **concurrent connection user** (**CCU**) as needed. Named user licenses are recommended when your staff needs dedicated access to Horizon; concurrent connection user licenses are recommended when access to Horizon will be shared among many users, but only a portion of them will be connected at any one time.

The license levels are differentiated by several factors as outlined in the following section. The licenses themselves are sold in 10 and 100 packs.

- All VMware Horizon license levels include VMware Horizon, vCenter, and vSphere Desktop Edition.
  - **vSphere Desktop Edition** is similar to vSphere Enterprise Plus in terms of functionality, but allows an unlimited number of CPU sockets for the desktop ESXi servers.
- **VMware ThinApp** is included with all versions except the Linux edition
- Standard and Linux offer similar features, the only difference is the desktop OS they are licensed for.
  - Horizon Enterprise edition supports both Windows and Linux desktop OSs under the same license.

- Advanced and Enterprise includes licenses for VMware Mirage, Fusion Pro, Identity Manager Standard Edition, application publishing using Windows RDS servers, and **VMware Virtual SAN Advanced**.
- Enterprise includes licenses for Horizon Instant Clones, **VMware App Volumes**, User Environment Manager, vRealize Operations for Horizon, and the vRealize Orchestrator Plugin for **VMware Horizon**.

Visit the VMware Horizon website (`http://www.vmware.com/products/horizon-view`) for the most recent information concerning licensing options and their costs.

It is important to note that many of the components, particularly those included with either the Advanced or Enterprise licenses, can be licensed separately. When determining which licenses to buy it may be that you don't need all of the features, for all of your users, and that buying a smaller stand-alone license for those users makes sense from a cost perspective. Consult with VMware or your VMware vendor to determine the optimal licensing strategy for your organization.

When listing the different components included with each VMware Horizon license level you may have noticed that not all of them will be discussed in this book. The primary focus of this book is on VMware Horizon View itself, and those components of VMware Horizon are most commonly used to extend its capabilities and potential use cases. For information about those components consult the following VMware resources:

- VMware Fusion Pro (`https://www.vmware.com/products/fusion-pro`)
- VMware Horizon Air (`https://www.vmware.com/cloud-services/desktop/horizon-air-desktop`)

- VMware Horizon FLEX (`https://www.vmware.com/products/horizon-fle x`)
- VMware Identity Manager Standard Edition (`https://www.vmware.com/prod ucts/identity-manager`)
- VMware Mirage (`https://www.vmware.com/products/horizon-mirage`)
- VMware ThinApp (`https://www.vmware.com/products/thinapp`)
- VMware vRealize Orchestrator Plugin for VMware Horizon (`https://pubs.vm ware.com/horizon-61-view/topic/com.vmware.ICbase/PDF/using-hori zon-vro-plugin-12-guide.pdf`)

This link is for the previous version of the plugin; a new version with support for Horizon 7 should be available by the time this book reaches publication.

- VMware vRealize Operations for Horizon (`http://www.vmware.com/product s/vrealize-operations-horizon`)

# VMware Horizon core infrastructure requirements

There are a number of requirements to consider even before the infrastructure needs of the virtual desktops themselves are considered. These include, but are not limited to:

- Operating system requirements for both vSphere and Horizon components
- Database requirements for vCenter Server, Horizon Composer, and Horizon Connection Server
- Required Microsoft infrastructure services and components

The online VMware Compatibility Guide (`http://www.vmware.com/res ources/compatibility/search.php`) and Product Interoperability Matrix (`http://partnerweb.vmware.com/comp_guide2/sim/intero p_matrix.php`) maintain an up-to-date listing of supported operating systems, hardware platforms, and product compatibility for all VMware products.

# Microsoft infrastructure requirements

VMware Horizon requires Microsoft Active Directory to support the virtual desktop infrastructure. VMware Horizon supports all AD domain functional levels starting with Windows 2003 and up to Windows 2012 R2.

Horizon also requires **Domain Name System (DNS)** servers that can resolve requests for the standard Microsoft Active Directory **Service Record (SRV)** and **Resource Record (RR)** DNS entries. Microsoft domain-integrated DNS servers typically store these DNS entries by default. Incomplete or inaccurate DNS entries can lead to issues with tasks, such as virtual desktop deployment and user authentication.

**Dynamic Host Configuration Protocol (DHCP)** servers are required in the Horizon environment to provide **Internet Protocol (IP)** addresses to the virtual desktops. In situations where the virtual desktops cannot self-register the IP addresses they have been assigned, the DHCP server should be configured to register the entries with a DNS server that is accessible by the Horizon Connection Server.

# Operating system requirements

The following table shows which 64-bit, non-Core Microsoft Windows Server OSs are supported for the each of the different software packages that comprise a Horizon infrastructure. App Volumes host OS requirements will be outlined separately in Chapter 9, *Implementing VMware App Volumes*.

| Operating System | vCenter Server 6.0 U1 (Windows-based) | Horizon Connection Server, Security Server, and Composer |
|---|---|---|
| Windows Server 2008 SP2 | Supported | Not supported |
| Windows 2008 R2 (No SP) | Supported | Not supported |
| Windows Server 2008 R2 SP1 | Supported | Supported |
| Windows Server 2012 | Supported | Not supported |
| Windows Server 2012 R2 | Supported | Supported |

While VMware vCenter and the different Horizon servers support a number of different Windows OSs, it is recommended to use the newest supported version to ensure that the servers will not be impacted by any changes in OS support by Microsoft. Additionally, you never know when vSphere or Horizon itself will end support for older OSs, which would impact your ability to perform in-place upgrades.

As Horizon Composer supports only Windows Server 2008 R2 SP1 or 2012 R2, any Horizon installation that plans on deploying linked clone desktops, and installing Composer directly on the vCenter Server, will need to choose that specific version of Windows. Refer to the VMware document **View Installation** (http://www.vmware.com/support/pubs/view_pubs.html) for updated information about which Windows OSs are supported.

# Database requirements

The following list shows which database types are supported for the core components of a Horizon infrastructure, which includes the Horizon Connection Server, Horizon Composer, and vCenter Server. Unless otherwise noted, both 32-bit and 64-bit versions of the specified database platform are supported. Database platforms that support some, but not all, of the components will not be listed. App Volumes database requirements will be outlined separately in Chapter 9, *Implementing VMware App Volumes*.

- Microsoft SQL Server 2014 (Standard and Enterprise, through SP1)
- Microsoft SQL Server 2012 (Express, Standard, and Enterprise; SP2)
- Microsoft SQL Server 2008 R2 (Express, Standard, Enterprise, and Datacenter; SP2, SP3)
- Oracle 12c (Release 1, up to 12.1.0.2)

For VMware Horizon, visit the product installation guide (http://www.vmware.com/support/pubs/view_pubs.html) for updated information on which databases are supported. For VMware vCenter, refer to the Product Interoperability Matrix (http://www.vmware.com/resources/compatibility/sim/interop_matrix.php) for updated information, or to quickly verify if the databases listed in the Horizon documentation are also supported by vCenter.

# vCenter Server requirements

VMware Horizon supports multiple versions of vSphere. The purchase of Horizon licenses entitles users to use the latest supported version of both vSphere and vCenter Servers, although support is maintained for some older versions due to restrictions that some organizations may be under.

The following versions of vSphere are supported by VMware Horizon:

- vSphere 6.0 (Update 1 or later is required to support the latest Horizon features; Update 2 is required to support VSAN 6.2)
- vSphere 5.5 (Update 3b or later recommended; SSLv3 must be re-enabled as described in VMware KB article 2139396) (https://kb.vmware.com/selfserv ice/microsites/search.do?language=en_US&cmd=displayKC&externalI d=2139396)
- vSphere 5.1 (Update 2 with Express Patch 5 or later recommended)
- vSphere 5.0 (Update 3 or later)

Consult the VMware Product Interoperability Matrix for an updated list of the supported versions of vSphere and vCenter Servers. Supporting earlier versions of vSphere and vCenter Servers is important for customers who are already running earlier versions of either software platform, and cannot, or will not, upgrade for some reason. Even with this support, it is recommended to use dedicated ESXi servers and vCenter Servers for your Horizon environment to ensure that all the latest Horizon features are supported.

There are multiple Horizon features that are supported only if certain other prerequisites are met. Some examples of these vSphere version dependent features are:

- vSphere 6 is required to use VMware VSAN, or Windows 10 as a desktop OS
- Prior to vSphere 6, the vCenter Server Appliance could not support the maximum number of desktops that can be deployed in a single Horizon Pod
- Some virtual desktop graphics acceleration technologies such as NVDIA GRID Tesla processor-based server cards (http://www.nvidia.com/object/grid-t echnology.html) require vSphere 6

A complete list of Horizon features that require specific versions of vSphere or vCenter Server may be found in VMware document **View Installation** (http://www.vmware.com/ support/pubs/view_pubs.html) or the **View Release Notes** (http://pubs.vmware.co m/Release_Notes/en/horizon-7-view/horizon-70-view-release-notes.html) that accompany each release of the Horizon platform.

# Horizon Agent supported operating systems

The VMware Horizon Agent supports multiple versions of the Microsoft Windows desktop operating system and Microsoft Windows (RDS) Server. The following table outlines which Windows OSs are currently supported.

| Windows OS Version | Product Edition | Service Pack | Notes |
| --- | --- | --- | --- |
| Windows 10 (32-bit or 64-bit) | Enterprise | None | Instant Clones supported |
| Windows 8.1 (32-bit or 64-bit) | Enterprise or Professional | Latest update | Instant Clones not supported |
| Windows 8 (32-bit or 64-bit) | Enterprise or Professional | None | Instant Clones not supported |
| Windows 7 (32-bit or 64-bit) | Enterprise or Professional | SP1 | Instant Clones supported |
| Windows 2012 R2 (64-bit) | Standard or Datacenter | Latest update | When used as RDS host |
| Windows 2012 R2 (64-bit) | Datacenter | Latest update | When used as desktop |
| Windows 2012 (64-bit) | Standard or Datacenter | None | Can be used as RDS host only |
| Windows 2008 R2 (64-bit) | Standard, Enterprise, or Datacenter | SP1 | When used as RDS host |
| Windows 2008 R2 (64-bit) | Datacenter | SP1 | When used as desktop |

To obtain current information about which desktop operating systems and Microsoft RDS servers are supported, please refer to the online VMware Product Interoperability Matrix.

# VMware Horizon design overview

The primary focus of this book is to show you how to deploy and configure VMware Horizon. Ultimately, the deployment is only one part of a successful Horizon implementation. Determining the infrastructure requirements of your virtual desktops is critical to ensuring that all your hard work, implementing Horizon, won't ultimately be a disappointment because you failed to consider what your desktops actually need.

Some organizations that are virtualizing older desktops, that lack flash drives, may feel that meeting their users' needs will be easy because expectations are low to begin with. Of course, some tend to forget that these same users are probably using flash-based devices at home, so even if the work computing experience is poor, these users do have some expectation of what it is like when they get a *new computer*, which is what their new Horizon desktop will appear to be. So, even if your Horizon infrastructure is capable of providing performance similar to the computers the users have today, that does not mean it will provide an experience that the users will find acceptable.

The goal of this section is to provide some information that you need to consider before you buy your Horizon licenses. Buying those licenses is the easy part, assembling the infrastructure they will be built on is not. Unfortunately, I can't put into words everything you need to know to build an infrastructure that guarantees a good performance for your users, which is why I suggest a detailed analysis of the network and storage infrastructure that you intend to use with your Horizon infrastructure. This analysis, combined with an understanding of the resources your Horizon infrastructure will require, is integral to delivering a superior end user experience.

# Measuring Virtual Desktop resource requirements

One of the most important aspects of any Horizon design is ensuring that an infrastructure has adequate compute, storage, and network resources to host the required number of virtual desktops. Were it not for troublesome things such as budgets, we could simply purchase an excess of all three of those resources and rest easy at night. In general, our goal is to build an infrastructure that is robust enough to support our average user workload, with some capacity in reserve for growth or maintenance purposes.

Determining the resource requirements of a Horizon environment is a complicated task, and one that could, by itself, fill a book. While it is possible to collect desktop performance data using free tools such as Windows Performance Monitor, gathering all of the data you need would be difficult, and interpreting it even more so. The goal in this section is to introduce you to some tools that were created specifically to help in designing and testing virtual desktop infrastructures, so that you understand exactly what is required to ensure a successful implementation.

The following products can assist in determining your resource requirements and ensuring that your vSphere infrastructure has sufficient capacity and the performance capabilities needed to ensure the desktops perform as expected.

- **Lakeside Software SysTrack** (`http://lakesidesoftware.com/vdi-assessm ent-design-planning.aspx`) performs an extensive analysis of your existing desktop workloads, including characterizing those that would be difficult to virtualize, and helps determine infrastructure needs and optimal placement.
- **Liquidware Labs Stratusphere FIT** (`http://www.liquidwarelabs.com/prod ucts/stratusphere-fit`) can assist you in determining virtual desktop resource needs, and performs tasks similar to *Lakeside Software SysTrack*
- **Login VSI** (`http://www.loginvsi.com/`) has created tools that can be used to test the performance of your Horizon infrastructure. Login VSI is used to run a simulated user workload in as many desktops as you want to test the performance of all layers of your virtual desktop infrastructure.

It is important to note that these software packages are typically used as part of a virtual desktop assessment project led by an outside vendor. If your user base has varying requirements, products such as SysTrack and Statusphere FIT may be the only way to find out exactly what infrastructure resources you need to ensure a successful VMware Horizon deployment.

# The need for vSphere reserve capacity

In the event that you choose to determine your own vSphere infrastructure requirements, it is very important to keep in mind the concept of vSphere reserve capacity. I realize that you may choose to do maintenance after hours, so reserve capacity may not be a priority, but what about unplanned downtime, or periods where you can't do maintenance after hours? Many users simply cannot work if they do not have access to their computer, and now that you have virtualized that computer it is your job to ensure it is available whenever it is needed.

Maintaining reserve ESXi server capacity is critical to ensuring that we can accommodate all of our desktops in the event of an ESXi server failure or host maintenance operation. Consider a vSphere cluster with eight ESXi servers hosting 128 desktops each (1024 total desktops):

- Desktop requirements:

> Desktop requirements will vary from one environment to the next; these figures are just an example.

- - Each single vCPU desktop requires 10 percent of one ESXi server CPU core
  - Each desktop requires 2,048 MB of memory
- Eight ESXi servers, each running 12.5 percent of the total number of virtual desktops:
  - *1024 desktops / 8 ESXi servers = 128 desktops per host*
- To continue to run all of the desktops in the event one of the ESXi servers was to become unavailable; we would need to be able to accommodate 18.29 desktops on each of the remaining seven hosts.
  - *128 desktops / 7 remaining vSphere hosts = 18.29 desktops per each ESXi server*
- To continue to run all desktops without any degradation in the quality of service; each server needs to have an excess of capacity that is sufficient to host 18 to 19 desktops. This is:
  - *19 desktops * 10% of a CPU core = 1.9 available CPU cores required*
  - *19 desktops * 2,048 MB of memory = 38,912 MB or 38 GB of available memory required*
  - *19 desktops * 121.21 MB of memory for virtual machine overhead = 2,303 MB or 2.3 GB of additional available memory required*
  - *19 desktops * 0.75 MB network bandwidth = 14.25 MB of available network bandwidth required*
  - *19 desktops * 0.23 MB storage network bandwidth = 4.37 MB of available storage network bandwidth required*

These calculations assume that we want to protect the ability to provide resources for 100 percent of our desktops at all times, which is a very conservative yet valid approach to building a Horizon infrastructure.

The final configuration of the ESXi servers should take into account not only what percentage of desktops are actually in use at a given time, but also the cost of purchasing the additional capacity needed to support ESXi server failures or other events that require downtime.

 Always take into consideration the growth of your Horizon environment. Purchasing equipment that has limited ability to scale may save money today, but could cost you dearly when you need to expand. If a piece of equipment you plan to buy for your Horizon infrastructure just barely meets your needs, look into the next larger model or even a competing product, if necessary.

# Providing sufficient Horizon Client bandwidth

In the era of affordable 10 Gigabit Ethernet (GbE) for servers and 1 GbE for desktops I realize that bandwidth within a single site is typically not a concern. The following information is something to keep in mind for clients who are connecting to their Horizon desktop remotely, either from over the Internet or over a WAN from another company site. Ensuring that sufficient bandwidth is available is just another part of making sure your Horizon clients have an acceptable experience when connecting to the Horizon infrastructure.

The VMware document **View Architecture Planning** (http://www.vmware.com/support /pubs/view_pubs.html) provides some information about how to determine Horizon Client bandwidth requirements. The following table is built upon information obtained from that document as well as other VMware documentation:

| User type | Workload characteristics | Bandwidth in Kilobits per second (Kbps) |
|---|---|---|
| Task worker | 2D display and single monitor. Web and limited Office applications. | 100-150 Kbps |
| Knowledge Worker (2D) | 2D display and single monitor. Office Applications. | 150-200 Kbps |
| Knowledge Worker (3D) | 3D display (Windows Aero) and multiple monitors. Office Applications. | 400-600 Kbps |

| Knowledge Worker (3D) – High User | 3D display (Windows Aero) and multiple monitors. Office Applications. Frequent display changes. | 500 Kbps – 1 Megabits per second (Mbps) |
|---|---|---|
| Power User | 3D display (Windows Aero) and multiple monitors. 480P video and images frequent screen changes. | 2 Mbps |

Bandwidth utilization is heavily dependent on a number of factors, many of which can be controlled with the Horizon PCoIP GPO settings or even Windows OS settings. Actual bandwidth utilization will vary based on usage and PCoIP settings.

Refer to the VMware document **Setting Up Application Pools in View** (h ttps://www.vmware.com/support/pubs/view_pubs.html) for information about the AD group policy templates included with VMware Horizon.

The PCoIP protocol was invented by a company called Teradici. For additional information about how the protocol works, visit the Teradici PCoIP technology page (http://www.teradici.com/pcoip-technolo gy.php).

Even with a careful analysis of user desktop usage patterns, it is important to remember that there will be spikes in usage from time to time. A Knowledge or Task Worker who has a need to use an application with a large amount of screen changes, such as viewing images in succession or watching a video, may cause a brief bandwidth spike of between 500 Kbps and 1 Mbps or more. Preparing for these spikes in bandwidth utilization is important in order to preserve the quality of service for all of the Horizon Client connections.

Refer to Chapter 13, *Creating a Master Horizon Desktop Image*, for information about optimal settings for a Windows desktop, an important topic for those new to virtualizing desktops. Chapter 15, *Using Horizon PowerCLI*, provides useful information for individuals who prefer to use scripts to automate as many tasks as possible, or simply to try and integrate Horizon with existing infrastructure management platforms.

# The importance of a VMware Horizon pilot

Up until now, this chapter has been about introducing us to a variety of different concepts that form the basis of architecting our Horizon infrastructure. If we learn anything from this chapter, it is that our goal is to obtain the resources we need to provide an acceptable end user computing experience.

Classifying our end users and measuring their resource requirements is a valuable exercise that will help us understand what will be required to transition our end user computing resources from the desktop to the datacenter. That being said, no amount of planning can possibly replace a properly run pilot that validates not only the configuration of our master Virtual Desktop image, but also the performance of the Horizon infrastructure and the quality of the experience from an end user perspective.

Our Horizon pilot should involve the same types of users as our user analysis did, but not necessarily the same users within each group. The following list includes a number of goals that our Horizon pilot should attempt to achieve:

- Include multiple users from each user classification: Task Worker, Knowledge Worker, and Power User
- Include fully remote users as well as WAN-connected users at other company sites
- Perform additional performance analysis at all layers of the Horizon infrastructure including:
  - Storage
  - Network
  - ESXi server
  - Guest operating
- Measure the impact of common Horizon scenarios, such as:
  - User logon storms: Large numbers of users logging on within a short time frame.
  - Steady state user load: Measure Horizon infrastructure performance during a period of steady desktop usage by a significant number of users.
  - Antivirus platform performance: Measure the impact of common antivirus platform tasks, such as on demand scans and pattern file updates.
  - Horizon refresh or recompose: Measure the impact of these common Horizon linked clone desktop maintenance operations, described in detail in `Chapter 12`, *Performing Horizon Desktop Pool Maintenance.*
  - A fully populated ESXi server: Measure host performance with higher than normal workloads, such as simulating an outage or another period of higher than usual utilization.

# Performance is the key

Performance deficiencies at any layer of the Horizon infrastructure can lead to a poor end user experience, usually in the form of longer than anticipated application response times. This is why it is critical to involve a large cross-section of our users in the pilot process, and to seek their opinion throughout the program.

The performance data that we collect during the pilot program can be used to measure the average of the actual resource utilization, which can then be compared to the estimated average resource utilization from the initial physical desktop analysis. Ideally, the numbers would be rather close to one another, but if they are not we will want to work to identify the cause. Now that we can measure performance at all layers of the Horizon infrastructure, it should be easy to determine where the higher than expected utilization originates from. Some potential issues to look for include:

- The earlier analysis of the users did not include a sufficient number or a wide enough cross-section of users.
- The Virtual Desktop master image was not properly optimized. Refer to `Chapter 13`, *Creating a Master Horizon Desktop Image*, for details on how to optimize the master desktop image.
- A component of the Horizon infrastructure was improperly configured. This problem can affect any number of components of the infrastructure.
- The pilot program is occurring during a period of higher than normal user workload, for example a recurring event unique to the organization such as financial reporting.

In summary, the Horizon pilot is your best time to learn about how it will perform within your environment, both from a performance perspective and in terms of user acceptance. Use the pilot program to identity any potential barriers to a successful rollout, and make any changes that are needed in order to minimize the risk of failure as the project moves forward.

# Summary

In this chapter, we have been introduced to the different components that comprise a VMware Horizon infrastructure, including the licensing and core infrastructure requirements. Later chapters will discuss how to install and configure each of these components.

We have also been introduced to the basics of what level of research is required even before the first virtual desktop is deployed, including assessing our existing physical desktops, determining bandwidth requirements for remote users, and adjusting our design to accommodate ESXi server maintenance or failure.

We concluded this chapter by learning the basics of running a Horizon pilot, which is critical as it will either validate or invalidate all of the research that we did in the early phases of our design.

In the next chapter, we will begin the installation of our VMware Horizon infrastructure, beginning with the Horizon Connection Server.

# 2
# Implementing Horizon Connection Server

The VMware Horizon Connection Server is a key component of the VMware Horizon infrastructure. In addition to acting as a connection broker between Horizon clients and desktops or Microsoft Windows RDS Servers, it also hosts the Horizon Administrator console.

This chapter will discuss multiple topics surrounding the design, deployment, configuration, backup, and recovery of a Horizon Connection Server. We will also discuss how to install additional Horizon Connection Servers, which are known as **replicas**.

In this chapter we will learn:

- An overview of a Horizon Connection Server
- The virtual machine and operating system requirements of a Horizon Connection Server
- The connection limits of a Horizon Connection Server
- How to determine the number of Horizon Connection Servers required
- Infrastructure and vCenter installation prerequisites
- How to install the first Horizon Connection Server in a Pod
- The initial configuration of a Horizon Connection Server
- The configuration of the **Instant Clone Engine Domain Administrator** account
- How to install additional Horizon Replica Connection Servers in a Pod

- The Horizon Connection Server upgrade process
- How to back up components of the Horizon Connection Server and which components to back up
- How to restore a Horizon Connection Server from backups or in response to a server failure

# Overview of VMware Horizon Connection Server

In Chapter 1, *VMware Horizon Infrastructure Overview*, we discussed some of the roles of the Horizon Connection Server. These roles include:

- Managing connections between Horizon clients and Horizon-managed resources including Horizon desktops and Microsoft RDS servers
- Authenticating user connection requests and providing access to assigned resources
- Hosting the Horizon Administrator console for the VMware Horizon infrastructure
- Working in tandem with VMware vCenter and Horizon Composer to manage, deploy, and maintain virtual desktops

The following diagram shows the placement of the **Horizon Connection Server** in a simple Horizon environment. For now, only the **Horizon Connection Server** is displayed; later chapters will add respective Horizon Servers to this diagram.

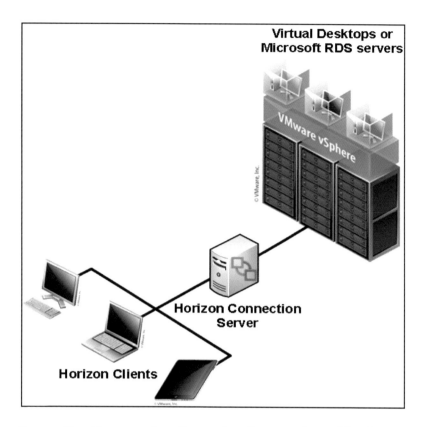

The **Horizon Connection Server** authenticates the clients and provides them with access to the appropriate resources. Depending on the configuration of the **Horizon Connection Server**, the clients may connect directly to the remote resource, or the connection may be tunneled through the **Horizon Connection Server**. The behavior of a Horizon client connection will be discussed further in this chapter, again in Chapter 4, *Implementing Horizon Security Server*, when discussing the Horizon Security Server, and once more in Chapter 5, *Implementing VMware Horizon Access Point*, when discussing the Horizon Access Point.

The Horizon Connection Server also hosts the Horizon Administrator console, the central management point for Horizon resources. The following screenshot shows the dashboard presented to a Horizon administrator upon login:

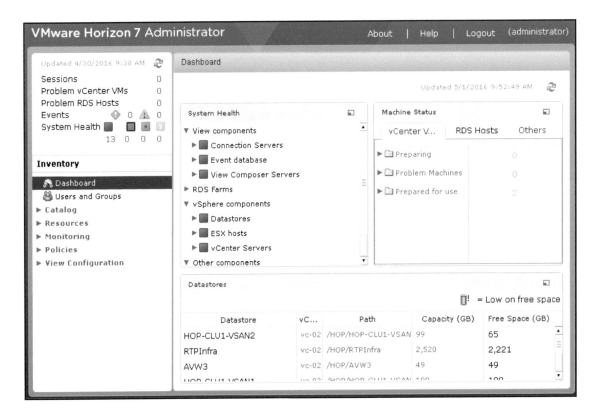

While virtual desktops appear in VMware vCenter in the same format as a typical virtual machine, it is important that all changes to those virtual desktops are done only through the Horizon Administrator console. Horizon maintains configuration information about the virtual desktops within a **Microsoft Active Directory Lightweight Directory Services** (**MS LDS**) database installed on each Horizon Connection Server, and any changes made to those desktops within the vCenter console may lead to problems that prevent the desktop from being managed by Horizon or available for client connections.

# Horizon Connection Server requirements

Like many other software services, Horizon Connection Server requires a minimum server configuration to ensure adequate performance. To properly support Horizon Connection Server, the VMware vCenter Server must also be assigned adequate resources and configured appropriately, based on the projected size of the Horizon infrastructure.

## Hardware requirements

The Horizon Connection Server software has specific requirements with regard to the hardware specifications and host operating system. In addition, all Horizon Connection Servers, regardless of the type, should be installed on a dedicated virtual or physical server.

The first Horizon Connection Server you install will be referred to as a Horizon Standard Connection Server during the installation process. To meet scalability and high availability needs, up to six additional Horizon Connection Servers can be installed per deployment; each of these is referred to as a Horizon Replica Connection Server during the installation process. The limits of a Horizon Connection Server are discussed later in this section.

The following table outlines both the minimum and recommended hardware specifications of a Horizon Connection Server. The same specifications apply to both Horizon Replica Servers and Horizon Security Servers.

| Hardware component | Minimum requirement | Recommended |
|---|---|---|
| Processor | Pentium IV 2.0GHz processor or higher | 4 CPUs |
| Memory | 4GB RAM or higher | A minimum of 10GB RAM for deployments of 50 or more desktops |
| Networking | 100Mbps NIC | 1GBps NICs |
| Hard disk capacity | 40 GB | 40 GB |

Like most other software platforms, the recommended guidelines should be followed to ensure that the Horizon Connection Server performs optimally.

# Software requirements

Each of the three different Horizon Connection Server types, which include Standard, Replica, and Security, support Windows Server 2008 R2 SP1 64-bit or 2012 R2 64-bit as the host operating system. Standard, Enterprise, and Datacenter editions of Windows Server 2008 R2 are supported, as well as Standard and Datacenter editions of Windows Server 2012 R2.

# Limits of a Horizon Connection Server

The limits of a Horizon Connection Server are defined by the maximum number of simultaneous client connections it can support. In previous versions of Horizon, the maximum number of connections varied depending on the connection type; in *Horizon 7* the maximum number of connections is 2,000 per Connection Server regardless of what resource or connection method the Horizon client is using.

Each single Horizon installation supports a maximum of seven Horizon Connection Servers in a 5+2 configuration known as a Pod, supporting a maximum of 10,000 desktops. The term Pod implies that the Horizon environment is managed as one entity, based on the limitations of the Connection Server. This means that five of the servers are considered active, and two are held in reserve as spares. The spare Horizon Connection Servers maintain an up-to-date copy of the **Horizon AD LDS** database so that they can serve clients immediately in the event they are needed.

 Not every Horizon environment will require seven Horizon Connection Servers but at the very least they should have two. Even if the number of desktops to be deployed is less than the concurrent connection limit of 2,000 clients per Connection Server, having two Connection Servers ensures that sufficient capacity exists in the event of a server outage or maintenance event. Always build in extra capacity to accommodate events that can impact availability.

In environments where more than 10,000 virtual desktops are required, you will be required to deploy a second Standard Connection Server, which creates another Horizon Pod. This will create a unique Horizon AD LDS database, rather than a replica of the one in your first Horizon installation, enabling support for additional Horizon Connection Servers and an additional 10,000 desktops. Using the Horizon Cloud Pod feature described in Chapter 6, *Implementing a Horizon Cloud Pod*, you can link up to Pods together, and create a global entitlement that grants simultaneous access to Horizon pools in each.

A single-Pod design is suitable for smaller single-site Horizon environments as it is the easiest to manage. If you plan to install Horizon Connection Servers in multiple sites, you are required to create a unique Pod in each site as VMware does not support a single Pod that spans multiple sites due to the amount of communication traffic generated by Connection Server replication.

> In Chapter 6, *Implementing a Horizon Cloud Pod*, we will create a Cloud Pod, which is a collection of up to four Horizon Pods located at a maximum of two distinct sites. While the Pods are still administered individually, using the Cloud Pod feature we can entitle users to Horizon resources located in multiple Pods from a single interface, and regardless of which Pod a user logs into they will be transparently connected to the appropriate Pod where their Horizon resources are located.

# Load balancing Connection Servers

VMware Horizon provides no native method to load-balance client requests to Horizon Connection Servers. It is recommended that you implement some sort of load-balancing method to help balance the client connections across all the Horizon Connection Servers in your infrastructure. While methods such Round Robin DNS and Microsoft Windows **Network Load Balancing** (NLB) could be used to provide basic load-balancing capabilities, a physical or virtual load-balancing appliance is the preferred method due to the advanced features and capabilities these platforms typically offer. The next section provides an overview of the capabilities of dedicated load-balancing solutions.

## Load-balancing appliances

Dedicated load-balancing appliances are available both in physical and virtual formats. The difference between the physical and virtual versions will differ from one vendor to another, so it is important to understand the impact of choosing one over the other.

Dedicated load balancers often have the capability to balance client connections based on a number of different factors. The following load-balancing metrics are not from any specific vendor, but are simply examples of the metrics that various solutions use:

- Server load
- Recent server response times
- Server up/down status
- Number of active connections

- Geographic location
- How much traffic has been assigned to a given host

In addition to any advanced features, dedicated load-balancing appliances do not require additional resources on the servers they are balancing traffic for, which is one additional advantage they have over using Microsoft NLB.

# vCenter Server requirements

You should use a dedicated VMware vCenter Server for VMware Horizon wherever possible, particularly if you are using Horizon Composer to deploy linked-clone desktops. For larger Horizon deployments, this will ensure that your vCenter Server is configured based on the exact requirements of your Horizon infrastructure, ensuring optimal performance and providing maximum flexibility when future upgrades or updates are required.

While Horizon and vCenter supports up to 10,000 desktops per vCenter Server instance, for performance reasons VMware recommends no more than 2,000 desktops per vCenter Server.

Using a dedicated vCenter Server for the Horizon provides a number of benefits over using an existing vCenter Server. These benefits include:

- A new Horizon deployment that plans to use an existing vCenter Server may require a version of vCenter that is currently not in use, necessitating an upgrade that may not be possible based on environmental or licensing constraints.
- If a Horizon upgrade or patch requires an accompanying vCenter Server upgrade or patch, this operation will not affect the existing vCenter server.
- The existing vCenter Server may not be properly sized to handle the planned number of virtual desktops, and may require changes to CPU, memory, the operating system version, or vCenter Server settings.
- For organizations that plan to deploy linked-clone desktops using Horizon Composer, the vCenter Server will be placed under a significant load during various Composer Operations. Isolating these operations to a dedicated vCenter Server ensures that this load does not affect the management of other, non-Horizon related, ESXi servers.

The installation and configuration of VMware vCenter can proceed as outlined in the VMware **vSphere Installation and Setup Guide** (http://www.vmware.com/support/pubs/vsphere-esxi-vcenter-server-pubs.html).

# Horizon installation prerequisites

The installation and configuration process for the first Horizon Connection Server, referred to as a Horizon Standard Connection Server during installation, requires some amount of preparation. This section will outline what is required prior to beginning the installation.

## Infrastructure and other prerequisites

There are a number of prerequisites that should be addressed prior to installing the first VMware Horizon Connection Server. The previous chapter discussed the infrastructure requirements. These included:

- Windows 2003 or later Active Directory
- An Active Directory user account or security group that will be granted full Horizon administrator access
- A Static IP address for the Horizon Connection Server
- Local administrator access on the host server
- A Horizon license key
- A Horizon event log database

In addition to the items described in Chapter 1, *VMware Horizon Infrastructure Overview*, the following items should be prepared in advance for the installation.

# Create a vCenter role and grant permissions

VMware Horizon requires access to the vCenter Server in order to perform tasks related to the creation or management of virtual desktops. To facilitate this access, we first need to create an AD user account that the Horizon Connection Server will use to access the vCenter Server; in this chapter we will use an account named `svc-horizon`. To make it easier to update the Horizon Connection Server AD account in the future, we will create a vCenter role that includes all the required privileges. Once created, the role can be quickly applied to AD user accounts. Perform the following steps to create the role in vCenter:

1. In **vSphere Web Client**, navigate to **Home** | **Administration** | **Roles**, click the green **+** sign indicated by the red arrow, and then enter a role name such as `Horizon Connection Server` as shown in the following screenshot:

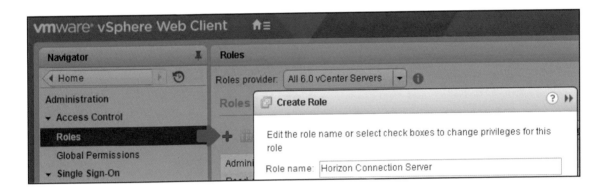

2. From within the Create Role window, expand each privilege group listed in the following table and check the required privilege items. All listed privileges must be checked in order for the Horizon Connection Server to function properly. Click on **OK** when you have finished creating the role.

| vCenter privilege group | Privilege subsection | Privilege |
|---|---|---|
| Datastore | | Allocate space |
| Folder | | • Create Folder <br> • Delete Folder |
| Global | | Act as vCenter Server |
| Host | Configuration | Advanced settings |
| Profile Driven Storage | | All |
| Resource | | Assign virtual machine to resource pool |
| Virtual Machine | Configuration | • Add or remote device <br> • Advanced <br> • Modify device settings |
| | Interaction | • Perform wipe or shrink operations <br> • Power Off <br> • Power On <br> • Reset <br> • Suspend |
| | Inventory | • Create new <br> • Create from existing <br> • Remove |
| | Provisioning | • Customize <br> • Deploy template <br> • Read customization specifications |

3. In the vSphere Web Client, click the following in order, **Home | Hosts and Clusters**, the vCenter Server at the top level of the inventory, the **Manage** tab, the **Permissions** section, and finally the green + sign indicated by the red arrow. This will open the **Add Permission** window used in the next step.

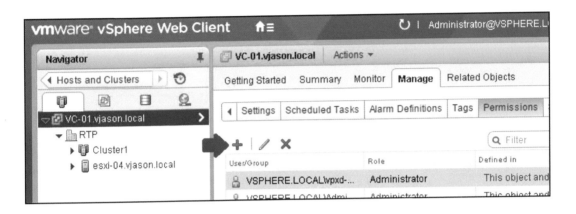

4. In the **Add Permission** window, click on the **Add...** button to open the **Select Users/Groups** window.

5. In the **Domain:** drop-down menu, select the **AD** domain that contains the Horizon administrator user or security group. In our example, the domain is named **VJASON**.

6. In the **Users and Groups** list, select the **Horizon Connection Server** service account. For our sample environment, we have searched for and selected an account named svc-horizon. Once selected, click on the **Add** button as shown in the following screenshot. Click on **OK** to close the **Select Users/Groups** window.

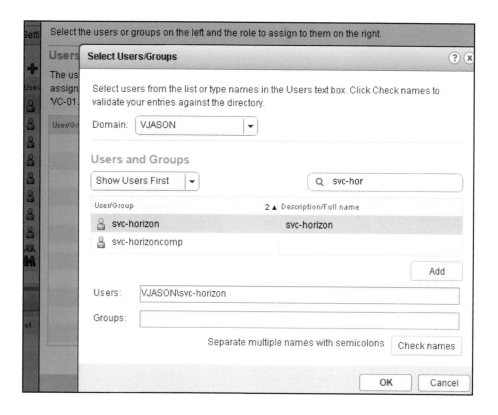

7. In the **Add Permission** window then **Assigned Role** drop-down menu, select the **Horizon Connection Server** role we created in step 2 as shown in the following screenshot, and then click **OK** close the window and complete the action.

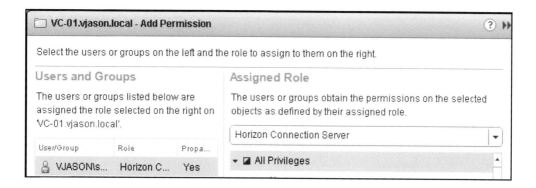

The Horizon Pod now has sufficient permissions on the vCenter Server it will use to deploy and manage desktops and Windows RDS servers.

# Horizon event database

VMware recommends using an external Horizon Connection Server event database in order to record retain detailed, Pod-wide information about any events that occur. Without an event database, only minimal information is recorded within the log files on each individual Horizon Connection Server. It is recommended that you create a database, both to retain historical data about Horizon events, as well as to support any troubleshooting that may need to be done. Only one database is required for each Horizon Pod, and it is possible to share a database among Horizon Pods by using unique database headers for each as shown later on in this chapter.

Chapter 1, *VMware Horizon Infrastructure Overview*, outlines different database types that can be used to record Horizon Connection Server events. In addition to using a supported database platform, the following database configurations must be done:

- For SQL Server:
    - Horizon requires an account on the database server with SQL Server authentication
    - The Horizon database user account must have permission to read from, write to, and create tables and views
- For Oracle:
    - Horizon requires an Oracle database user account
    - The Oracle database user account must have permission to read from, write to, and create tables, views, triggers, and sequences

The database schema will be installed when the database is configured within the Horizon Administrator console.

# Deploying the first Horizon Connection Server

Deploying the first Horizon Connection Server is broken down into two stages; the installation of the Connection Server software and the final setup using the Horizon Administrator console.

# Installing the first Horizon Connection Server

The Horizon Connection Server software is delivered as a single executable (EXE) file, named in a format similar to `VMware-viewconnectionserver-x86_64-x.x.x-yyyyyy.exe`. This installer is used for all three Horizon Connection Server types, which include Standard, Replica, and Security. The following steps outline the installation process:

1. Double-click on the **Horizon Connection Server** installer EXE file to launch the installer.
2. In the **Welcome to the installer for VMware Horizon 7 Connection Server** window, click on **Next>**.
3. Review the **License Agreement** section, select the **I accept the terms in the license agreement** radio button, and click on **Next>**.
4. Select the installation directory and click on **Next>**.
5. Highlight the Horizon Connection Server instance type. Since this is the first Horizon Connection Server in the environment, we will choose **Horizon 7 Standard Server** as shown in the following screenshot, and then click on **Next>**.

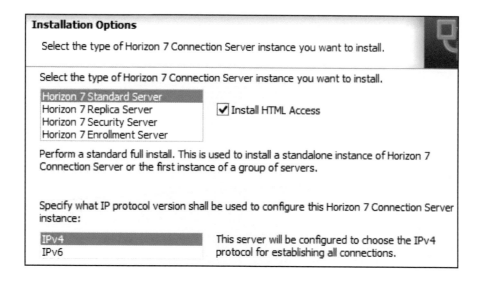

6. Enter a data recovery password and an optional password reminder and click on **Next>**. Record this password, as it will be required for any future restores of this Horizon Connection Server configuration. We will review how to standardize this password across all Horizon Connection Servers in this Pod later on in this chapter.

7. Select the **Configure Windows Firewall automatically** option and click on **Next >**.

Windows Firewall must be enabled and properly configured to ensure that communications between Horizon Security Servers and the Connection Server can be encrypted.

8. Select the **Authorize a specific domain user or domain group** radio button, enter either a single AD account or AD security group that is designated as the Horizon Administrator, and click on **Next>**. As shown in the following screenshot, we will use the AD security group titled **Horizon_Admins** in the domain VJASON in the format `domain-name\group-name`.

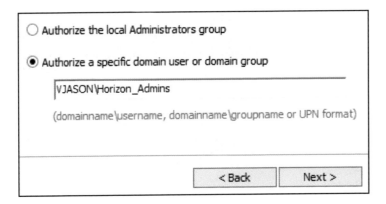

9. Configure the drop-down menus for the **User Experience Improvement Program**, or uncheck the **Participate anonymously in the user experience improvement program** checkbox, and click on **Next >**.

10. Review the final installation screen to ensure that the installation directory is correct. If changes are required, click on the **< Back** button to reach the necessary configuration screen and make the required changes. Assuming that the settings are correct, click on **Install** to begin the automated installation process

11. Click on **Finish** when prompted at the completion of the installation process.

The installation process will install all the components required for a Horizon Standard Connection Server, including the Connection Server software and the AD LDS database used to store configuration information. The final configuration steps will be completed in the Horizon Administrator console, and will be detailed in the next section.

# Configuring the first Horizon Connection Server

Once the installation of the first Horizon Connection Server has completed, we need to log in to the Horizon Administrator Console. The console URL will be in the format `https://Connection Server FQDN/admin`. You must use lowercase letters when typing admin.

By default, the installation process creates a self-signed SSL certificate to encrypt connections to the Horizon Connection Server. While the server will function with this default self-signed certificate installed, it is recommended you replace the default certificate with one from a trusted internal or commercial certificate authority. Until the default certificate is replaced, Horizon clients will be notified about the untrusted certificate each time they connect. In addition, the Horizon Administrator console will display an informational error. `Chapter 14`, *Managing Horizon SSL Certificates*, will provide the process used to replace the default SSL certificates for all Horizon components.

Complete the following steps to configure the first Horizon Connection Server:

1. Log in to the Horizon Administrator console using an AD account that was granted administrative permissions during the installation process. The following screenshot shows the login page for our sample Horizon Connection Server, which was accessed at the URL `https://viewcs01.vjason.local/admin`.

2. Upon successful login to the first Horizon Connection Server that was installed, the dashboard will open to the **Product Licensing and Usage** window in the **View Configuration** page as shown in the following screenshot. Click on the **Edit License** button to open the **Edit License** window.

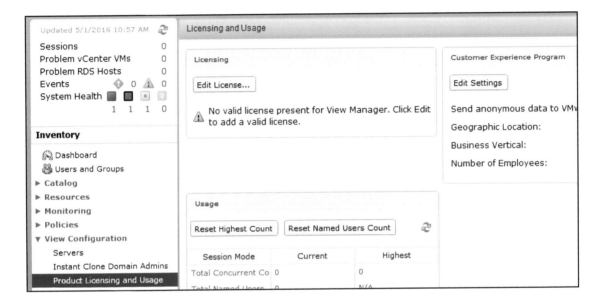

3. Enter the 25-character license key, including the dashes, and click on **OK** to complete the license entry.

4. Open the **Event Configuration** window in the **View Configuration** page within the console. Click on **Edit...** in the **Event Configuration** page to open the **Edit Event Database** window.

5. Fill in the information for the Horizon event database configuration including **Database server**, **Database type**, **Port**, **Database name**, **User name**, **Password**, and optionally the **Table prefix**. The **Table prefix** field is used to identify this Horizon installation within the database itself, and would be used when sharing the database among multiple Horizon Pods. The following screenshot shows the database configuration for our sample server. Click on **OK** once all the information has been provided, and Horizon will complete the database configuration assuming the necessary privileges have been granted as outlined earlier in this chapter.

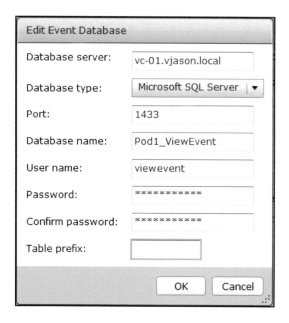

The console **Event Configuration** page also allows us to customize how events are displayed in the Horizon Administrator console. The VMware Horizon documentation (`https://www.vmware.com/support/pubs/view_pubs.html`) provides detailed information about these settings, which can be changed at any time.

6. Navigate to **View Configuration | Servers** to bring up the **vCenter Servers** tab of the **Servers** window. Click on **Add...** to open the **Add vCenter Server** window.

7. In the **Add vCenter Server | vCenter Server Information** window, fill in the information required to link the vCenter Server that we will be using for desktops to our Horizon Connection Server. The information required includes the vCenter Server address in a **fully qualified domain name (FQDN)** format, the Horizon vCenter AD user name that we created earlier in this chapter in the format `domain-name\user-name`, and the password for the account. Click on **Next>** when the required information has been provided. The following screenshot shows the completed screen for our sample server:

The **vCenter Server Information** window also allows us to specify advanced options for increasing the number of concurrent vCenter tasks our Horizon Connection Server can initiate. The VMware Horizon documentation (`https://www.vmware.com/support/pubs/view_pubs .html`) provides detailed information about these settings, which can be changed at any time.

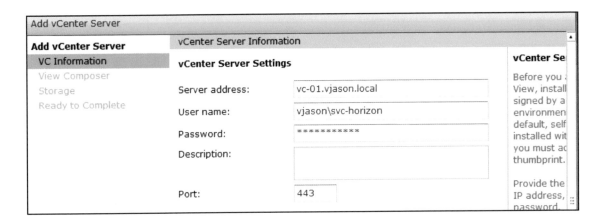

8. Horizon Connection Server will attempt to verify the SSL certificate of the vCenter Server as part of the linking process. If the vCenter Server is still using the default self-signed certificate, a window will open and announce that the identity of the specified vCenter Server cannot be verified. If this happens, click on **View Certificate...** to open the **Certificate Information** window, verify that the certificate information is correct, and click on **Accept** to move to the next window, **View Composer**.

9. Chapter 3, *Implementing Horizon Composer*, will outline how to deploy VMware Horizon Composer. Since Composer is not yet installed, select the **Do not use View Composer** radio button and click on **Next>** to open the **Storage** window. Horizon Composer can be enabled within the Horizon Administrator console at any time after it has been installed.

10. The **Add vCenter Server | Storage** window is used to enable two different Horizon storage-related features. Click the **Reclaim VM disk space** check box, then the **Enable View Storage Accelerator** check box, set the **Default host cache size:** value to 2048, the maximum allowed, and then click **Next >**.

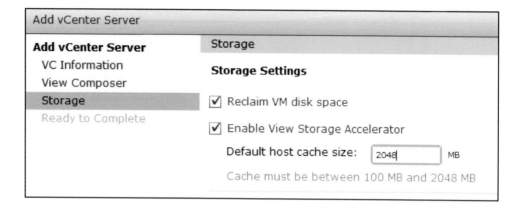

Reclaim VM disk space periodically scans the Horizon desktop VMDK files for blocks that are no longer in use, and releases them to the storage array for reuse. This feature is particularly useful when using a storage platform that relies on **deduplication** to reduce array physical capacity requirements. However, running a reclaim operation can place significant stress on a storage array and should not be enabled without consulting the storage vendor beforehand. Horizon Storage Accelerator caches critical Horizon desktop data in RAM on the ESXi server, which can significantly reduce the amount of read IO that needs to be serviced by the storage array. Consult the VMware Horizon documentation (https://www.vmwa re.com/support/pubs/view_pubs.html) for detailed information about both of these features.

11. The **Ready to Complete** window will provide a summary of the options chosen in the previous steps. Review the summary and click on **Finish** to complete the process and link the vCenter Server to the Horizon Connection Server.

12. The vCenter Server will now be displayed in the **View Configuration** | **Servers** | **vCenter Servers** window, as shown in the following screenshot:

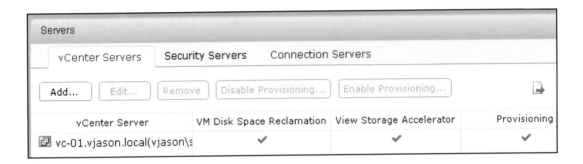

13. Repeat steps *6* through *11* as needed to link additional vCenter Servers.

At this point, the basic configuration of the Horizon Connection Server has been completed; if we had a virtual desktop image, we could deploy full clone virtual desktops. However, before moving forward to the next step it is advisable to set up a second Horizon Connection Server; this one will be a replica of our first one. The *Deploying a Horizon Replica Connection Server*, will outline how to install a Horizon Replica Connection Server.

# Configuring the Horizon Instant Clone Engine

While Horizon does not require a Composer Server to deploy and manage Instant Clone desktops, we are required to provide an AD account that it will use to create and manage the Instant Clone desktop AD computer objects. In this section we will create the AD account, grant it the permissions required in AD, and provide the account details in the Horizon Administrator console.

# Configuring the Instant Clone Engine AD user account

Horizon requires an AD account with specific permissions in order to manage the desktop AD computer objects for Instant Clone desktops. Refer to the *Delegate permissions for Horizon Composer in Active Directory* section of `Chapter 3`, *Implementing Horizon Composer*, for the procedure used to delegate these permissions, although refer to the following list of updates to that procedure as the permissions required and AD account used are different. It is assumed that prior to performing this procedure you have already created the AD user account you intend to use (`svc-horizonic` in this example).

- In step 5 of the preceding section—in the **Select Users**, **Computers**, or **Groups** window, type the name of the Horizon Composer service account (`svc-horizonic`), click **OK** to return to the **Delegation of Control Wizard – Users or Groups** window, and then click **Next >**.

Note that we are using a dedicated AD account for Instant Clone operations. I recommend using dedicated accounts for Horizon, Horizon Composer, and Horizon Instant Clone (AD operations) for security reasons and to make it easier to troubleshoot any issues that may occur.

- In step 8 of the preceding section—in the **Delegation of Control Wizard | Permissions** window, click the **General**, **Property-specific**, **Read**, **Read All Properties**, **Write All Properties**, and **Reset password** check boxes, and then click **Next >**.

# Update the Instant Clone Engine Domain Administrator setting

The following steps outline the procedure used to specify the AD user account we created as our Instant Clone Engine Domain Administrator:

1. Log on to the Horizon Administrator console using an AD account that has administrative permissions within Horizon.
2. Open the **View Configuration | Instant Clone Domain Admins** window within the console.

3. Click on the **Add...** button in the **Instant Clones Engine Domain Administrators** window to open the **Add Domain Admin** window.

4. Provide the **User Name:** (`svc-horizonic`) and **Password:** as shown in the following screenshot and then click **OK** to return to the previous window:

5. Verify that the account was added successfully as shown in the following screenshot:

Horizon is now able to deploy Instant Clone desktops using the procedure described in `Chapter 10`, *Creating Horizon Desktop Pools*. Note that if the permissions for this account were not granted correctly, we will likely not notice until we attempt to create an Instant Clone desktop pool.

# Deploying a Horizon Replica Connection Server

The installation process for a Horizon Replica Connection Server is straightforward as the configuration information is copied from the Horizon Standard Connection Server that was installed in the previous section. This section will explain how the installation process differs with regard to options that are chosen during installation.

## Installing a Horizon Replica Connection Server

The steps required to install a Horizon Replica Connection Server are largely the same as those for a Standard Connection Server; only a few steps differ. The following list outlines where the installation process differs, using the numbered steps provided within the *Deploy the first Horizon Connection Server* section as a reference:

- In step *5*: **Installation Options** | Choose **Horizon 7 Replica Server** as the instance type and click on **Next>**.
- New Step: **Source Server** then provide the FQDN for the Horizon Standard Connection Server deployed in the previous section and click on **Next>**. For our sample server, the FQDN is `viewcs03.vjason.local`. Refer to the following screenshot as an example:

A group of Horizon 7 Connection Server instances that share the same configuration data is called a Horizon 7 Connection Server group. Setup will replicate configuration data from an existing server instance.

Enter the server name of an existing Horizon 7 Connection Server instance to make this server part of that group.

Example server: view.internal.vmware.com.

Server:     viewcs03.vjason.local       (hostname or IP address)

This installation step is unique to the Horizon Replica Connection Server installation.

- Steps *6*, *8*, and *9* are not required.

During the installation process, the Horizon Replica Connection Server will install all the same components as a Standard Connection Server but the AD LDS database will be a replica of the Standard Connection Server AD LDS database. The AD LDS database holds the configuration data for the Horizon environment, so no additional configuration is needed beyond the installation itself.

Once the installation has successfully completed, the Horizon Replica Connection Server will be displayed in the **View Configuration** | **Servers** | **Connection Servers** window in the Horizon Administrator console as shown in the following screenshot:

At this point, the Horizon Connection Server would be available to broker connections to whatever resources have been configured within the Horizon Administrator console.

Once installed, a Horizon Replica Connection Server is a full peer of all other Horizon Standard Connection Servers and Horizon Replica Connection Servers within the installation. Unlike some software platforms, which have a master-slave or split role architecture, all Horizon Standard Connection Servers and Horizon Replica Connection Servers share the same responsibilities and capabilities.

As previously mentioned, Horizon lacks any native load-balancing capabilities. As a result, unless a load-balancing solution of some sort is deployed, clients will need to manually choose which of the two Horizon Connection Servers they want to connect to. Since this is likely to lead to an unbalanced distribution of client resources, it is recommended that you consider one of the previously mentioned options for load-balancing the Horizon client connections.

# Upgrading an existing Horizon Connection Server

Upgrading an existing Horizon Connection Server is a straightforward process that typically requires no more than a few minutes to complete, not counting the time required to plan the operation. Regardless, it is important to block access to the Connection Server while the upgrade is being performed to ensure no Horizon clients attempt to connect to it, or at the very least to perform the upgrade during a period of time in which the Connection Server is not expected to be used.

If you are using a load balancer to distribute traffic among multiple Horizon Connection Servers, the easiest way to block access to the Connection Server is to remove it from the load-balancing group. This prevents connections from being sent to it, while at the same time being transparent to the end users.

Do not disable the Connection Server network cards during the upgrade to ensure that any needed AD LDS replication will occur.

# Upgrading prerequisites

Each release of VMware Horizon includes release notes that summarize the differences between the new release and the previous release. New releases are just as likely to include bug fixes as they are new or deprecated features, so it is important to read these notes prior to performing any upgrade.

The release notes are available on the VMware Horizon documentation homepage (`https://www.vmware.com/support/pubs/view_pubs.html`).

The following are items to look for when reviewing Horizon release notes prior to an upgrade:

- Are features I use being removed?
    - One example of this is that Horizon 6 supported Windows XP and Windows Vista if an extended support agreement was purchased, but Horizon 7 does not offer this option.

- Are any other components of my Horizon infrastructure required to be upgraded first?
    - One example of this occurred with Horizon 6.2.1, which removed support for certain older cipher suites used by older Horizon client software. In this case, the Horizon client software should be upgraded first to ensure those clients don't experience any errors or other interruption in service.

- Am I required to update the rest of the Horizon components immediately, or are they backward compatible and therefore can wait until another time?
    - Examples of this include Horizon Composer, the Horizon Agent, and so on.

These are just a sample of the things we need to look for prior to performing an upgrade.

# Backing up the existing Horizon configuration

By default each Horizon Connection Server backs up the AD LDS database nightly to a local folder; this backup is key to restoring the configuration of the Pod-wide Horizon AD LDS instance were there problems with the upgrade. Chapter 3, *Implementing Horizon Composer*, talks about backing up the Composer database, which should also be performed prior to an upgrade. The following list summarizes the backups we should make or verify prior to performing an upgrade:

- **Horizon AD LDS database**: Performed by default, but can be done on demand as described later on in this chapter. Each Horizon Connection Server hosts a copy of this backup.
- **Horizon event database**: Backed up using native backup procedures for the hosting database platform.
- **Horizon vCenter databases**: These databases would typically not be impacted by a Horizon upgrade, but as mentioned later in this chapter they are critical to any larger Horizon disaster recovery operations.

# Horizon upgrade process

A Horizon Connection Server upgrade is performed using the same installer used to perform new Horizon Connection Server installations. The following steps outline how an upgrade is performed; they should be repeated on each Horizon Connection Server in the Pod until all have been successfully upgraded.

1. Double-click on the Horizon Connection Server installer EXE file to launch the installer.
2. In the **Welcome to the Installation Wizard for VMware Horizon 7 Connection Server** window, click on **Next >**.
3. Review the VMware End User License Agreement section, select the **I accept the terms in the license agreement** radio button, and click on **Next >**.
4. Verify the installation directory (you will not be able to change it) and click on **Install**.
5. Once the upgrade process has been completed, click **Finish** to close the installer window.
6. In the Horizon Administrator console, navigate to **View Configuration | Servers | Connection Servers** window and verify that the Connection Server displays the new version number as indicated by the red arrow in the following screenshot.

Once the functionality and compatibility of the upgraded Connection Server has been verified, the remaining Connection Servers in the Pod can be upgraded using the same procedure.

In the event that vSphere VM snapshots are used to restore a VMware Horizon Connection Server to a previous state, the Connection Server will stop replicating its AD LDS database to other Connection Servers. In the event you wish to retain the configuration contained within the AD LDS database on the server where the snapshot was reverted, all other Connection Servers within the same Horizon Pod will need their Connection Server software and AD LDS database uninstalled and reinstalled from scratch. Refer to the **View Upgrades** guide (`http://www.vmware.com/support/pubs/view_pubs.html`) for additional information about what is required if a Horizon Connection Server is reverted to an earlier snapshot.

# Backing up a Horizon Connection Server

The information required to restore a Horizon Connection Server is stored in two different databases:

- Horizon Connection Server AD LDS database
- vCenter Server database

Horizon Composer, described in `Chapter 3`, *Implementing Horizon Composer*, also uses a database that contains critical Horizon configuration information. Horizon installations that utilize Horizon Composer will also need to back up the Composer database as part of their backup and recovery plan.

# Backing up the vCenter Server database

The vCenter Server database should be backed up using whatever method is available within your environment. This includes options such as:

- Native backups based on the capabilities of the database platform, such as Microsoft SQL Server backup or Oracle Recovery Manager (**RMAN**) backup
- Third-party database backup solutions

There are no specific requirements with regard to database backup methodologies, so long as you can recover the database to a previous state; either to the same database server or an alternative. Consult with your database server or backup software documentation if additional information about performing database backups is required.

Consult the **VMware vSphere Installation and Setup Guide** (https://www.vmware.com/support/pubs/vsphere-esxi-vcenter-server-6-pubs.html) for additional information about how to back up the components of a vSphere installation.

# Backing up the Horizon AD LDS database

The VMware Horizon Connection Server AD LDS database contains key Horizon configuration information and should be backed up on a regular basis. By default, a Horizon Standard Connection Server or Replica Connection Server will perform a nightly backup of the AD LDS database at midnight (12:00 AM).

A limited number of changes to the Horizon Connection Server backup policy can be made within the Horizon Administrator console. These changes include:

- Backup frequency
- Number of backups to retain
- Data recovery password

These options can be configured using the following steps in the Horizon Administrator console:

1. Navigate to **View Configuration** | **Servers** | **Connection Servers**.
2. Highlight the targeted Horizon Connection Server and click on **Edit...** to open the **Edit Connection Server Settings** window.
3. Click on the **Backup** tab and make any desired changes; refer to the following screenshot for an example. Note that setting the data recovery password on this page will update it for all Connection Servers in the Pod.

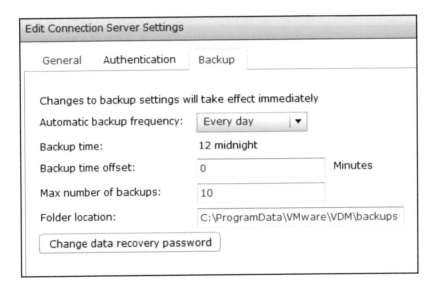

# Horizon Connection Server recovery

The process to restore a Horizon Connection Server varies based on the scenario that necessitated the restore.

If you are restoring all of your Horizon Connection Servers from scratch, the Horizon Composer database will need to be restored as part of the recovery process as its contents are tied to those of the Horizon AD LDS database. Refer to the *Restoring the Horizon Composer database* section in `Chapter 3`, *Implementing Horizon Composer,* for additional information about restoring the Composer database.

In situations where it is required to restore multiple Horizon-related databases at once, you should use backups that were taken as closely together as possible when performing the restore. Ideally, backup plans for all Horizon components should coincide as closely as possible to ensure that the data shared between them is consistent. The further apart the backups are taken, the less likely it is that the contents will match when a restore is required. This could lead to issues that require the assistance of VMware Support as items within one or more of the databases may need to be removed or edited.

# Restoring a single Horizon Connection Server

Horizon configuration settings are stored in the local AD LDS database on each Connection Server. If the Horizon Connection Server software becomes corrupt, you can simply uninstall and reinstall it without having to perform any additional configuration.

If a Horizon Connection Server cannot be accessed due to a hardware or software failure, and you need to replace it, you must remove it from the AD LDS replication set first. The following steps should be executed from an existing Horizon Connection Server. In this example, we will remove the server named `VIEWCS02` from the AD LDS replication set using the `vdmadmin.exe` utility:

1. Navigate to the `Program Files\VMware\VMware View\Server\tools\bin` directory.
2. Execute the following command:

   ```
   vdmadmin.exe -S -r -s VIEWCS02
   ```

The failed Horizon Connection server VIEWCS02 has now been removed from the AD LDS replica set and can now be replaced.

 To learn about all the options available for the `vdmadmin.exe` command, run `vdmadmin.exe /?`.

To restore or replace the server, simply reinstall the Horizon Connection Server on a replacement server and follow the procedure outlined in the *Deploy a Horizon Replica Connection Server* section of this chapter. The software will be installed and the server will be joined to the existing Horizon Pod.

# Removing a Horizon Connection Server

To remove a functioning Horizon Connection Server from your environment, perform the following steps:

1. Open the **Windows Programs and Features** control panel on the target Connection Server.
2. Uninstall the **VMware Horizon 7 Connection Server** software.
3. Uninstall the **AD LDS Instance VMwareVDMDS** software.
4. Reboot the server to complete the removal of the Connection Server software.

When performed on a functioning Horizon Connection Server this procedure automatically removes the server from the Pod-wide AD LDS instance, which means that the procedure described in the previous section to forcibly remove the non-functional server from AD LDS is not required.

# Restoring the vCenter database

The vCenter database is restored using the same tools used to perform the backup. Consult with the database server or backup software documentation for information about how to perform the restore operation.

Consult the **VMware vSphere Installation and Setup Guide** (`http://www.vmware.com/s upport/pubs/vsphere-esxi-vcenter-server-pubs.html`) for additional information about how to restore the components of a vSphere installation.

# Restoring the Horizon Connection Server AD LDS database

The Horizon Connection Server AD LDS database can be restored using the `vdmimport` utility, located in the VMware Connection Server installation drive in the `Program Files\VMware\VMware View\Server\tools\bin` directory. The utility is a command-line tool and is executed from a Windows command prompt. The utility requires administrative access to the Horizon infrastructure, so the AD user account used to run it must have administrative rights within the target Horizon Pod. If the AD account does not have sufficient rights, errors will be displayed during the restore operation.

To learn about all the options available for the `vdmadmin.exe` command, run `vdmimport.exe /?`.

The AD LDS database is not usually restored unless all the Horizon Connection Servers are lost or the AD LDS database is found to be corrupt. If you are having problems with just a single Horizon Connection Server, you should refer to the *Restoring a single View Connection Server* section in this chapter for instructions on how to restore or remove just that server.

The restore operation requires two commands:

1. Decrypt the AD LDS database backup titled `backup.LDF` to a file titled `decrypted.LDF`, and replace the password with the data recovery password specified during the installation of the first Horizon Connection Server or the global data recovery password set using the Horizon Administrator console.

   ```
   vdmimport -d -p password -f backup.LDF > decrypted.LDF
   ```

2. Restore the decrypted backup.

   ```
   vdmimport -f decrypted.LDF
   ```

Once the restore is complete, the remaining Horizon Connection Servers will replicate the restored data into their local AD LDS databases.

# Summary

In this chapter, we have been introduced to the key component of a VMware Horizon installation: the Connection Server. We have learnt what is required to deploy a Connection Server, what the limits of a Connection Server are, how to perform the installation and initial configuration, and how to install additional Replica Connection Servers.

We have also discussed how to back up to the Horizon Connection Server configuration, including the vCenter databases.

We concluded this chapter by discussing how to restore the Horizon Connection Server configuration, and how that process varies based on the recovery scenario.

In the next chapter we will implement Horizon Composer; the component of a Horizon installation that enables the deployment of linked-clone virtual desktops.

# 3
# Implementing Horizon Composer

VMware Horizon Composer is a feature of Horizon that enables the rapid provisioning of linked clone virtual desktops. A pool of linked clone desktops shares the same master image and writes any changes to a dedicated virtual hard disk, also known as a **delta disk**. This drastically reduces the amount of per-virtual desktop storage required compared to full clone virtual desktops, as each of those requires its own copy of the master image. In addition, linked clone desktops can be provisioned much more quickly than full clone desktops, which is beneficial in and of itself and also enables new ways of managing desktops throughout their lifecycle.

This chapter will discuss benefits, installation, configuration, backup, and recovery of the Horizon Composer component of VMware Horizon.

In this chapter, we will learn:

- An overview of the capabilities and benefits of Horizon Composer
- The hardware requirements of Horizon Composer
- Horizon Composer pre-installation tasks and other requirements
- How to deploy Horizon Composer
- How to configure Horizon Composer
- How to back up components of Horizon Composer and what components to backup
- How to restore Horizon Composer from backups

Horizon Composer requires Microsoft **Key Management Services (KMS)** in order to activate linked clone desktops. **Multiple Active Key (MAK)** licenses are not natively supported by Horizon Composer, and if used, the frequent need to reactivate Windows will quickly exhaust the key activation limit. If KMS is not available, VMware KB article 1026556 (`http ://kb.vmware.com/selfservice/microsites/search.do?languag e=en_US&cmd=displayKC&externalId=1026556`) provides details about a registry key that can be set in the master virtual desktop image to skip the Windows activation process during the customization of the linked clone desktop.

# Overview of VMware Horizon Composer

Horizon Composer is used to provision linked clone virtual desktops, which are a type of virtual machine that shares a common virtual desktop master image, sometimes referred to as a golden image. Horizon and vSphere support up to 4,000 desktops for each single replica of the virtual desktop master image, which enables significant storage savings over traditional full clone virtual desktops.

The concept behind a linked clone desktop is demonstrated in the following diagram, which shows the relationship between the master **Replica Disk Read Only** and the **Linked Clone Disk**.

This diagram is to illustrate the concept of a linked clone, the actual architecture of a linked clone virtual machine is explained next.

When a pool of linked clone desktops is provisioned, a replica of the virtual desktop master image is copied to storage accessible by the Horizon ESXi servers. This replica will be used as a read-only copy of the virtual desktop master image; all writes are redirected to unique disks that are attached to each linked clone. Linked-clones are provisioned using thin virtual disks, the configuration of which varies depending on the desktop pool settings.

Beginning with Horizon 6.2, Composer gained the ability to create linked clone Windows RDS servers. Much of the information or language contained in this chapter will refer primarily to linked clone desktops, but understand that Composer is also required if you wish to use linked clone Windows RDS servers, and both use the concept of a shared replica.

The following diagram shows the configuration of two linked clone virtual desktops that share the same virtual desktop master image.

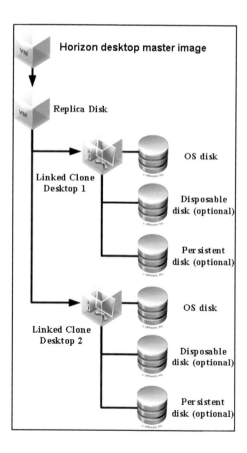

In this diagram, each **Linked Clone Desktop** is configured with optional disposable disks and persistent disks. Chapter 10, *Creating Horizon Desktop Pools*, explains the different options that affect the configuration of these and other linked clone disks.

When the linked clone desktops are powered on for the first time, they will begin redirecting any writes to the linked clone disks and will also create a **virtual swap (vswp)** file of a size equal to the amount of unreserved **virtual RAM (vRAM)** allocated to the virtual machine.

> Controlling the growth of a linked clone desktop requires an understanding of multiple topics, all of which will be described within this book. The following chapters contain valuable information that can help you control the storage utilization of linked clone desktops:
>
> - Chapter 8, *Implementing VMware User Environment Manager*
> - Chapter 10, *Creating Horizon Desktop Pools*
> - Chapter 12, *Performing Horizon Desktop Pool Maintenance*
> - Chapter 13, *Creating a Master Horizon Desktop Image*

Horizon Composer works at the direction of the Horizon Connection Server to provision and manage linked clone desktops. Horizon Composer uses the vSphere **application program interface (API)** to initiate whatever tasks are required based on the operation that is being performed. To achieve this, Horizon Composer requires specific permissions within vCenter Server, as well as permissions within Microsoft Active Directory, both of which will be described later in this chapter.

Horizon Clients do not come into contact with Horizon Composer; its role as an orchestration tool is to perform actions based on the configuration of the Horizon desktop pool. As such, Horizon Composer is depicted in the following architectural diagram as a stand-alone component that works directly with the vSphere and Horizon infrastructure.

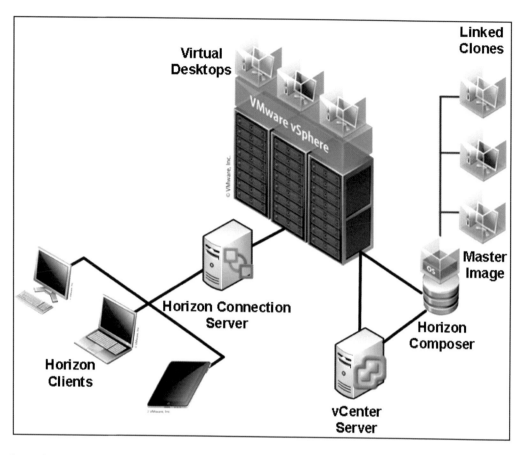

The benefits of Horizon Composer do not start and end with gains in storage efficiency. The following features are just some of the ways with which you can leverage Horizon Composer to change how you manage desktop maintenance.

# Refreshing linked clone desktops

The changes made to a linked clone desktop can be discarded on demand or upon user logoff. This operation is called a **refresh**, as it refreshes the desktop back to the exact configuration that it was in when it was first provisioned. User persistent data disks, if used, are not impacted by this action.

Horizon also supports deleting the desktop as an additional option. After the desktop has been deleted, a new desktop is provisioned to replace it.

By refreshing desktops you maintain tight control over their storage utilization as all writes to the dedicated linked clone virtual disk are discarded. In addition, when all changes are discarded, the desktop is returned to the same state it was in when it was provisioned, which enables tight control over the end-user computing experience.

The refresh process is described in detail in Chapter 12, *Performing Horizon Desktop Pool Maintenance*.

Refer to Chapter 8, *Implementing VMware User Environment Manager*, and Chapter 10, *Creating Horizon Desktop Pools*, for more information about how to preserve user persona data during recompose or refresh operations.

# Recomposing linked clone desktops

A virtual desktop recompose operation is used when you need to update the master desktop replica image. One of the key methods of maintaining the storage efficiencies of linked clone desktops is to control the amount of data that is written to the linked clone disks, which if left unchecked will grow in size during the course of regular use. Traditional per-desktop administrative tasks such as installing applications and applying patches can quickly increase linked clone storage utilization, as the writes would be made to the linked clone disk of each desktop that was the target of the action. In addition, these operations would need to be repeated on each desktop, which can require significant management overhead.

A recompose operation replaces the linked clone replica disk with an updated version that uses the same operating system. Recomposing to a completely different operating system is not supported. During the recompose process, all virtual desktops will be provisioned again and linked to the new replica disk. If the desktop was configured with a persistent disk for storing user profile data—an option for dedicated assignment desktop pools—that disk would be retained and attached to the recomposed desktop.

Technically speaking, a recompose operation requires a refresh operation. Either of these operations will temporarily reduce the amount of vSphere datastore capacity your persistent Horizon desktops are using.

The recompose process is described in detail in `Chapter 12`, *Performing Horizon Desktop Pool Maintenance.*

When a desktop is recomposed, it will maintain the same computer name but will obtain a new DHCP lease. Your DHCP server must have a large enough pool of addresses available to handle these requests. In addition, it is recommended you use a short address lease period so that the now unused leases are quickly removed and the associated addresses are made available for use.

# Horizon Composer requirements

Horizon Composer requires a minimum server configuration to ensure adequate performance and to properly support linked clone provisioning and maintenance operations. In this section we will focus on the hardware requirements, the supported OSs were already listed in `Chapter 1`, *VMware Horizon Infrastructure Overview.*

## Hardware requirements

The Horizon Composer software has specific requirements with regard to the hardware specifications and host operating system. Horizon Composer may be installed on a dedicated virtual or physical server, or on an existing vCenter virtual or physical server. The vCenter Server Linux-based virtual appliance also supports Horizon Composer but requires that it be installed on a dedicated server.

The following table outlines both the minimum and recommended hardware specifications of a dedicated Horizon Composer server. Additionally, the server hosting Horizon Composer must have a static IP address.

| Hardware component | Minimum requirement | Recommended |
|---|---|---|
| Processor | 1.4 GHz x64 and 2 CPUs | 2 GHz x 64 or faster and 4 CPUs |
| Memory | 4GB RAM or higher | 8GB RAM or more for deployments of 50 or more desktops |
| Networking | One or more 100Mpbs NICs | 1Gbps NIC |
| Hard disk capacity | 40 GB | 60 GB |

If Horizon Composer is installed on the same host server as vCenter Server, the only requirement is that vCenter meets the established requirements for the number of virtual desktops and ESXi servers that it will manage. The VMware **vSphere Installation and Setup Guide** (`https://www.vmware.com/support/pubs/vsphere-esxi-vcenter-server-6-pubs.html`) provides detailed information about the hardware requirements of vCenter Server; in particular, how those requirements change as the number of virtual machines or ESXi servers changes.

Due to the critical importance of vCenter Server and Horizon Composer within the Horizon environment, it is recommended that you use a dedicated server for each Horizon Composer rather than installing them on the same server. Separating the two components ensures that the maximum performance will be obtained with regard to linked clone provisioning and maintenance operations. In addition, separating the two components ensures that maintenance operations that involve either Horizon Composer or vCenter Server do not affect the availability of either component, be it owing to downtime or other issues that may occur.

Like most other software platforms, the recommended guidelines should be followed to ensure that the Horizon Composer performs optimally.

# Limits of Horizon Composer

A single Horizon Composer instance can support only one vCenter Server. A single vCenter Server can support up to 10,000 desktops, which is the maximum number of desktops supported in a single Horizon Pod. As a result, while Horizon can support multiple vCenter Servers, each with its own dedicated Horizon Composer instance, only one of each is actually required to manage up to the maximum number of desktops supported in a single Horizon Pod.

If you still wish to have multiple vCenter Servers in your Horizon environment, you will need multiple instances of Horizon Composer as a single instance can service only one vCenter Server. Each additional instance of Horizon Composer will also require its own database, as the databases cannot be shared between Horizon Composer instances.

# Horizon Composer installation prerequisites

There are a number of prerequisites that should be addressed prior to installing Horizon Composer:

- At least one configured Horizon Connection Server with a license key installed
- An Active Directory user account or security group that will be granted the necessary permissions within Microsoft Active Directory and the vCenter Server
- A dedicated host server for Horizon Composer or an existing Windows-based vCenter Server; whichever is selected must be running supported host OS
- A Static IP address for the dedicated Horizon Composer host server (required only if you are using a dedicated server)
- Local administrator access on the host server
- A supported Horizon Composer database as referenced in Chapter 1, *VMware Horizon Infrastructure Overview*
- A 64-bit ODBC connection to the Horizon Composer database configured on the Composer host server

In addition to the items described in Chapter 1, *VMware Horizon Infrastructure Overview*, the following items should be prepared in advance of the installation.

# Horizon Composer service account

Horizon Composer requires access to the vCenter Server in order to perform tasks related to the creation and management of virtual desktops. To facilitate this access, you can either grant additional permissions to the Horizon Connection Server vCenter user account created in Chapter 2, *Implementing Horizon Connection Server*, or create a dedicated AD user account that Horizon Composer will use to access the vCenter Server and Active Directory.

In Chapter 2, *Implementing Horizon Connection Server*, we granted the vSphere permissions required just for the Horizon Connection Server itself. In the examples provided in this chapter we will use the same SvC-Horizon account for Horizon Composer, although you can create a dedicated account if you desire. Just remember to grant whichever account you use with Composer local administrator access on the Composer host server, as well as the needed privileges in AD as outlined in this chapter.

If you install Horizon Composer directly on the vCenter Server, you have no option but to use the Horizon Connection Server vCenter AD account for Horizon Composer. If this is the case, you will need to grant that account or security group the additional vCenter and AD permissions outlined in this section.

This section assumes that you will use a dedicated AD account and a stand-alone instance of Horizon Composer.

# Horizon Composer vCenter permissions

The following table outlines only those vCenter permissions required for Horizon Composer. Using the procedure outlined in Chapter 2, *Implementing Horizon Connection Server*, we can create a vCenter role just for the Composer service account, or we could modify the existing role we created to add the permissions is outlined in the following table:

| vCenter privilege group | Privilege subsection | Privilege |
| --- | --- | --- |
| Datastore | | <ul><li>Allocate space</li><li>Browse datastore</li><li>Low level file operations</li></ul> |
| Global | | <ul><li>Act as vCenter Server</li><li>Disable methods</li><li>Enable methods</li><li>System tag</li></ul> |
| Network | | All |
| Profile Driven Storage | | All |
| Resource | | <ul><li>Assign virtual machine to resource pool</li><li>Migrate powered off virtual machine</li></ul> |
| Virtual Machine | Configuration | All |
| | Inventory | All |
| | Provisioning | <ul><li>Allow disk access</li><li>Clone virtual machine</li></ul> |
| | Snapshot management | All |

The decision on whether or not to use separate AD accounts for the Horizon Connection Servers and Horizon Composer is up to you. In some cases organizational security policies will require it in order to minimize the permissions any one account has within your down, which makes the decision an easy one.

For the purpose of this chapter we will create the following:

- AD service account named: `svc-horizoncomp`
- vSphere role with the above listed permissions named: `Horizon Composer`

## Create a Horizon Composer vCenter role and grant permissions

The following steps outline how to create a vCenter role for Horizon Composer and grant the permissions. If examples are needed, refer to the screenshots for this process found in `Chapter 2`, *Implementing Horizon Connection Server*. The process of creating a vCenter role is the same in this case; all that is changed is the role name, vCenter permissions granted, and target AD account.

1. In vSphere Web Client, navigate to **Home** | **Administration** | **Roles**, click the green **+** sign, and then enter a role name such as `Horizon Composer`.
2. From within the **Create Role** window, expand each privilege group listed in the table provided previously in this section and check the required privilege items. All listed privileges must be checked in order for Horizon Composer to function properly. Click on **OK** when finished with creating the role.
3. In the vSphere Web Client, click the following in order, **Home** | **Hosts and Clusters**, the vCenter Server at the top level of the inventory, the **Manage** tab, the **Permissions** section, and finally the green **+** sign. This will open the **Add Permission** window used in the next step.
4. In the **Add Permission** window, click on the **Add...** button to open the **Select Users/Groups** window.
5. In the **Domain:** drop-down menu, select the **AD domain** that contains the Horizon Composer user. In our example, the domain is named **VJASON**.
6. In the **Users and Groups** list, select the **Horizon Composer** service account. For our sample environment, we will search for and select the account named `svc-horizoncomp`. Once selected, click on the **Add** button. Click on **OK** to close the **Select Users/Groups** window.
7. In the **Add Permission** window | **Assigned Role** drop-down menu, select the **Horizon Composer** role we created in step 2, and then click **OK** to close the window and complete the action.

Horizon Composer now has sufficient permissions on the vCenter Server to deploy and manage linked clone virtual desktops and Windows RDS servers.

# Horizon Composer Active Directory permissions

The Horizon Composer AD account requires permission to manage the AD Computer objects for the virtual desktops that it creates. As there is some risk associated with granting accounts direct access to AD in order to create and delete computer objects, it is important to minimize the access granted to the Horizon Composer account.

To minimize risk, the following guidelines are recommended:

- Create an AD **organizational unit (OU)** that will be used only to store linked clone virtual machines created using Horizon Composer
- Grant the Horizon Composer AD account the minimum permissions required in order to manage the AD computer accounts contained within the OU

To grant the necessary permissions, you need at a minimum full control over the OU which will contain the Horizon linked clone AD computer accounts. This gives you the ability to not only delegate the required permissions for Horizon Composer, but also to create additional child OUs to enable additional control over the various Horizon pools that you provision.

> Separating the AD computer accounts of desktop pools into separate OUs enable us to customize the group policies for each.

# Delegate permissions for Horizon Composer in Active Directory

The following steps outline the process used to delegate the minimum permissions required for Horizon Composer. In our example, we will be granting to the AD account svc-horizoncomp the necessary permissions for the **Horizon | Computers** OU.

1. From the Windows Start menu, select **Administrative Tools | Active Directory Users and Computers**.

2. Right-click on the parent OU that will contain the virtual desktops created using Horizon Composer and select **Delegate Control...** as shown in the following screenshot to open the **Delegation of Control Wizard**. In our example, the OU is named **Computers**.

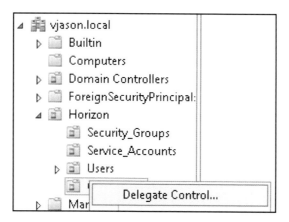

3. In the **Delegation of Control Wizard** window, click **Next >**.

4. In the **Delegation of Control Wizard | Users or Groups** window, click **Add...**to open the **Select Users, Computers, or Groups** window as shown in the following figure.

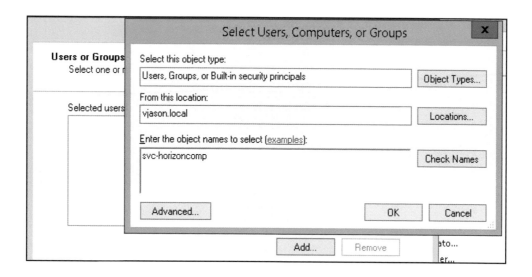

5. In the **Select Users, Computers, or Groups** window, type the name of the Horizon Composer service account (svc-horizoncomp), click **OK** to return to the **Delegation of Control Wizard– Users or Groups** window, and then click **Next >**.

6. In the **Delegation of Control Wizard | Tasks to Delegate** window, click the **Create a custom task to delegate** radio button and then click **Next >**.

7. In the **Delegation of Control Wizard | Active Directory Object Type** window, click the **Only the following objects in the folder** radio button, then click the **Computer objects**, **Create selected objects in this folder**, and **Delete selected objects in this folder** check boxes as shown in the following screenshot, and then click **Next >**.

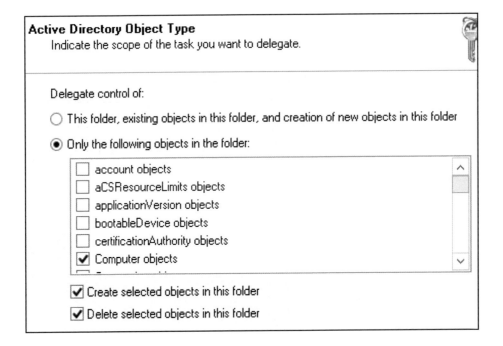

8. In the **Delegation of Control Wizard | Permissions** window, click the **General**, **Property-specific**, **Read**, **Read All Properties**, **Write All Properties**, and **Change password** check boxes as shown in the following screenshot, and then click **Next >**.

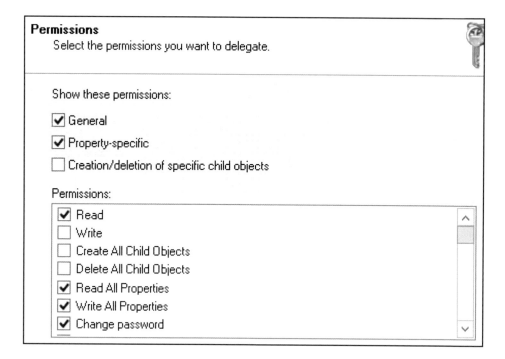

9. In the **Delegation of Control Wizard | Completing the Delegation of Control Wizard** window, review the changes, making any changes if needed, and then click **Finish**.

The Horizon Composer service account now has the permissions needed to manage AD computer objects in the selected OU and any child OUs within it.

# Horizon Composer database

Horizon Composer requires an external database in order to store information about vCenter Server connections, AD connections, and linked clone desktops and Windows RDS servers as well as their associated virtual hard disks.

Chapter 1, *VMware Horizon Infrastructure Overview*, outlines the different database types that are supported by Horizon Composer. In addition to using a supported database platform, the following database configuration item must be performed for both Microsoft SQL Server and Oracle databases:

- Create a 64-bit **Database Source Name** (**DSN**) connection for the Horizon Composer database on the Composer host server. This process is outlined in the Microsoft How-to guide titled **Using the ODBC Data Source Administrator** (http://windows.microsoft.com/en-us/windows/using-odbc-data-source-administrator)

When using Horizon Composer with SQL Server databases the following general requirements must be met:

- **Local SQL instance**: Windows NT authentication is supported; database owner permissions are required if not already present
- **Remote SQL instance**: Requires an SQL Server user account, SQL Server authentication, and the account must have database owner permissions

When using Horizon Composer with Oracle databases the following general requirements must be met:

- The database should be created with the general purpose or transaction processing template using the Database Configuration Assistant
- An Oracle database user account is required with a minimum of the following permissions:
    - Connect
    - Resource
    - Create view
    - Create sequence
    - Create table
    - Create materialized view
    - Execute on dbms_lock
    - Execute on dbms_job
    - Unlimited tablespace

The database schema (for both Oracle and SQL Server) will be installed during the installation of Horizon Composer.

# Deploying Horizon Composer

The deployment of Horizon Composer is broken down into two stages: the installation of the Horizon Composer software, and the final setup using the Horizon Administrator console.

# Installing Horizon Composer

The Horizon Composer software is delivered as a single executable (EXE) file, named in a format similar to VMware-viewcomposer-x.x.x-yyyyyy.exe. The following steps outline the installation process:

If you plan to use a custom SSL certificate for Horizon Composer, install that certificate prior to installing Composer. If you install the certificate now, you can select it during the installation process. Refer to Chapter 14, *Managing Horizon SSL Certificates*, for instructions on how to obtain and deploy a new SSL certificate for Horizon Composer.

1. If it has not already been done, grant the Horizon Composer service account (svc-horizoncomp) local administrator access on the Horizon Composer host server.
2. Double-click on the Horizon Composer installer EXE file to launch the installer.
3. In the **Welcome to the Installation Wizard for VMware Horizon 7 Composer** window, click on **Next >**.
4. Review the **License Agreement**. Then select the **I accept the terms in the license agreement** radio button and click on **Next >**.
5. Select the installation directory and click on **Next >**.

6. Provide the name of the Horizon Composer **Data Source Name** (**DSN**), database user, and the password. The following screenshot shows the required information for our sample environment. Click on **Next >** to move on to the next step.

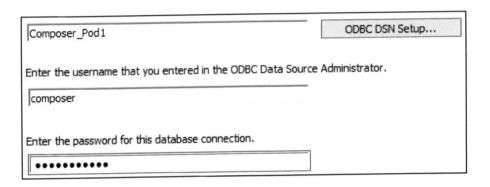

7. If no SSL certificates were previously installed, select **Next >** to accept the default port settings as shown in the following screenshot. If a SSL certificate was preinstalled, select the **Use an existing SSL certificate** radio button and highlight the desired certificate from the list provided. Click on **Next >** to move on to the next step.

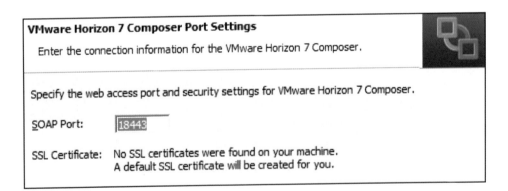

8. Click on **Install** to initiate the installation process and reboot the Composer server as requested when the installation is complete.

Horizon Composer is now ready to be configured, which is done using the Horizon Administrator console.

# Configuring Horizon Composer

To link Horizon Composer to the Horizon Pod, you need to log in to the Horizon Administrator console. The console URL will be in the format `https://Connection Server FQDN/admin`. The following steps outline the configuration process:

1. Log in to the Horizon Administrator console using an AD account that has administrative permissions within Horizon.
2. Navigate to **View Configuration** | **Servers** within the console.
3. Select the **vCenter Servers** tab in the **Servers** window, highlight the vCenter Server you wish to enable for Horizon Composer, and click on **Edit** to open the **Edit vCenter Server** window. In the following screenshot, we edit the **vc-01.vjason.local** vCenter Server. Note the appearance of the green and yellow vCenter icon to the left of the vCenter Server name; that icon will change once Horizon Composer is enabled.

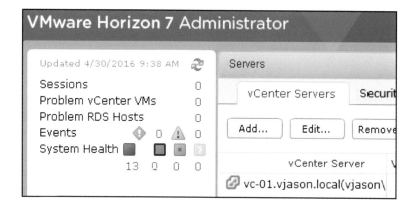

Any errors that occur during the remaining steps are likely related to insufficient permissions for the Horizon Composer service account to either AD or vCenter. If errors occur, review the *Horizon Composer service account* section and verify that the necessary permissions have been granted.

4.  If Horizon Composer was installed on the vCenter Server, select the **View Composer co-installed with vCenter Server** radio button and proceed to the next step. If using a dedicated server to host Horizon Composer, check the **Standalone View Composer Server** radio button and complete the following tasks:

    1.  Populate the **Server address** field with the FQDN of the dedicated Horizon Composer host server.

    2.  Provide **User name** and **Password** for the dedicated Horizon Composer AD account. Use the format `domain-name\user-name` for the username.

    3.  Since we used the default port when installing Horizon Composer, we do not need to change the **Port** value.

5.  Click on **Verify Server Information** shown in the following screenshot to verify Horizon Composer access to the AD domain.

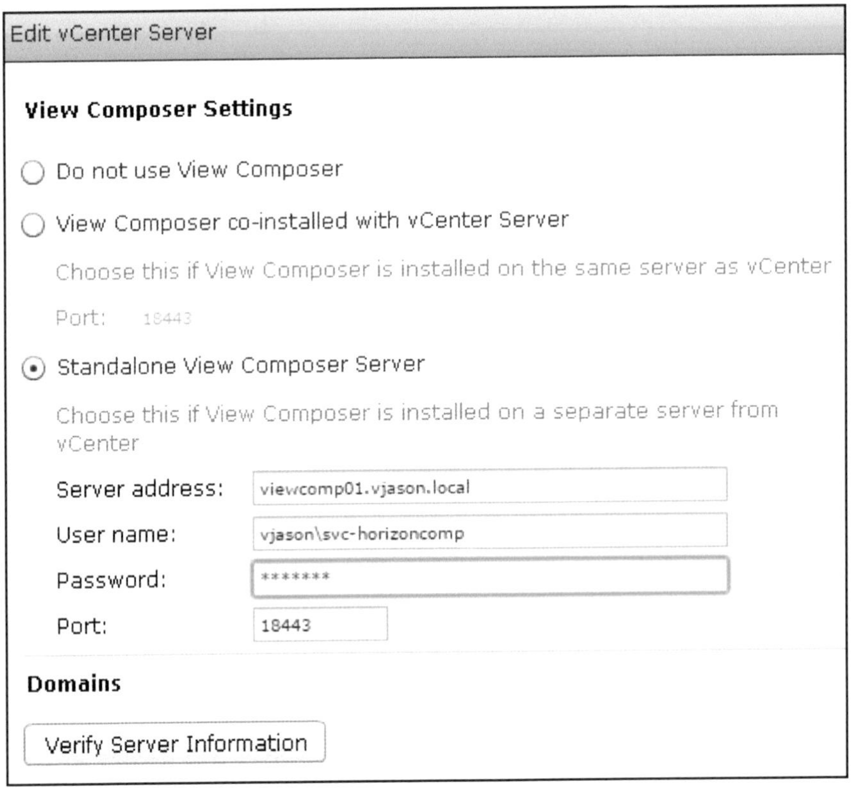

Edit vCenter Server

**View Composer Settings**

○ Do not use View Composer

○ View Composer co-installed with vCenter Server

   Choose this if View Composer is installed on the same server as vCenter

   Port:   18443

◉ Standalone View Composer Server

   Choose this if View Composer is installed on a separate server from vCenter

| | |
|---|---|
| Server address: | viewcomp01.vjason.local |
| User name: | vjason\svc-horizoncomp |
| Password: | ******* |
| Port: | 18443 |

**Domains**

Verify Server Information

6. If the Horizon Composer server was installed with the default, untrusted SSL certificate the **Invalid Certificate Detected** window will be displayed. Click the **View Certificate...** button to open the **Certificate Information** window.

7. In the **Certificate Information** window, review the certificate and click **Accept** to return to the **Edit vCenter Server** window.

8. In the **Edit vCenter Server** window under **Domains**, click **Add...** to open the **Edit Domain** window as shown in the following screenshot:

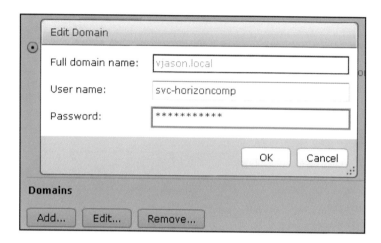

9. Provide the **User name** and **Password** for the Horizon Composer service account and click **OK** to return to the **Edit vCenter Server** window.

10. Confirm that the **Standalone View Composer Server** and **Domains** fields have been populated as shown in the following screenshot:

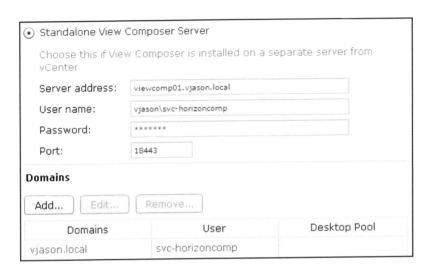

11. Click **OK**, and then **OK** again in the parent **Edit vCenter Server** window to complete the Horizon Composer configuration.

12. Review the vCenter icon to the left of the vCenter Server name in the **View Configuration | Servers** page within the console; as Horizon Composer is now enabled, that icon will be displayed within a yellow square as shown in the following screenshot:

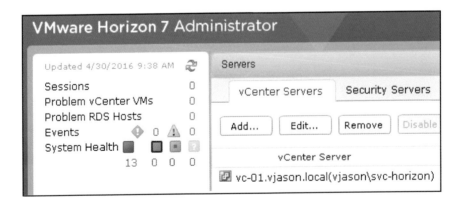

Horizon Composer is now linked to the Horizon Pod, and available to provision linked clone desktops or Windows RDS servers.

# Backing up Horizon Composer

The information required to restore Horizon Composer is stored in two different locations:

- Horizon Composer database
- Horizon Composer SSL certificates or RSA key container

The Horizon Composer database should be backed up as part of a larger backup plan that includes the vCenter database, the Horizon Connection Server AD LDS database, and the Horizon Event database. By default, each Horizon Connection Server backs up both the AD LDS database and the Composer database to a folder on the Connection Server.

# Backing up the Horizon Composer database

The Horizon Connection Server backs up the Horizon Composer database as part of its own native backup process. This is the preferred method of backing up the Horizon Composer database as it will be backed up at the same time as the Horizon Connection Server ADAM database. As these databases contain related information, it is critical that they are backed up at the same time.

The default location for the Horizon Connection Server database backups is on any Horizon Connection Server in the `C:\ProgramData\VMware\VDM\backups` folder. The Horizon Composer database backups will have an SVI extension and include the name of the Horizon Composer host server in the filename. In our example, the most recent Horizon Composer database backup file is named `Backup-2015-1223101427-viewcomp01_vjason_local.SVI`. `Viewcomp01` and is the name of the dedicated Horizon Composer host server in our sample environment.

The Horizon Composer database may also be backed up using native database backup tools. This includes options such as:

- Native backups based on the capabilities of the database platform, such as Microsoft SQL Server backup or Oracle RMAN backup
- Third-party database backup solutions

Remember that, while native database backups will work, they may not be usable for restore purposes if they were not performed at the same time as the Horizon Connection Server AD LDS database backup. It is recommended you use the backups performed by the Horizon Connection Server, if you need to restore the Horizon Composer database.

Refer to your database server or backup software documentation if additional information about performing database backups is required.

# Backing up the Horizon Composer SSL certificates

The process used to back up the default Horizon Composer SSL certificate requires Microsoft .NET Framework to be installed on the Horizon Composer host server.

The following steps explain how to back up the SSL certificates:

1. From the command prompt on the Horizon Composer host server, navigate to the c:\Windows\Microsoft.NET\Framework\v4.0.xxxxx directory.
2. Execute the following command to export the Horizon Composer RSA key container to a local file named keys.xml:

```
aspnet_regiis -px "SviKeyContainer" "keys.xml" -pri
```

The following screenshot shows the expected output if the command was successful:

```
c:\Windows\Microsoft.NET\Framework\v4.0.30319>aspnet_regiis.exe -px "SviKeyConta
iner" "keys.xml" -pri
Microsoft (R) ASP.NET RegIIS version 4.0.30319.34209
Administration utility to install and uninstall ASP.NET on the local machine.
Copyright (C) Microsoft Corporation.  All rights reserved.
Exporting RSA Keys to file...
Succeeded!
```

The keys.xml file should be backed up to an alternative location to be used in the event that the Horizon Composer software needs to be installed on a new server.

Chapter 14, *Managing Horizon SSL Certificates*, outlines the process by which you can obtain new certificates for all Horizon components. During this process, you obtain a copy of the SSL certificate that can be used when restoring a Horizon Connection server from backups. If you choose to use a custom SSL certificate, you do not need to use the `aspnet_regiis` command to export the Horizon Composer RSA key container. During the creation of your custom SSL certificate, you should have been given a copy of it with the private key intact, which is what is required to perform a restore.

# Horizon Composer recovery

The same process is used to recover or move Horizon Composer to a new host server. To retain the current settings, all that needs to be restored is the Horizon Composer database and the RSA key container or custom SSL certificate.

# Restoring the Horizon Composer database

The Horizon Composer database should be restored using the native Horizon command line tool `sviconfig.exe`. This tool is located within the install directory of Horizon Composer, which is at the following location on our sample server: `D:\Program Files (x86)\VMware\VMware View Composer`.

You will need the following information to restore the database:

- The name of your **Database Source Name** (**DSN**) connection on the Horizon Connection Server. On our sample server, the name is: `Composer_Pod1`
- Horizon Composer database username. On our sample server, the name is: `composer`
- * Horizon Composer database password. On our sample server, the password is: `Password123`
- The backup file path location of the `Backup-2015-1223101427-viewcomp01_vjason_local.SVI.Viewcomp01` file referenced in the *Backing up the Horizon Composer database* section of this chapter. On our sample server, the file is located in `C:\Temp`.

 The Horizon Composer database and Horizon Connection Server AD LDS databases contain related data. If one is being restored, the other should also be restored, using the restore data from the same backup set. Failure to adhere to this rule can lead to database inconsistencies that will require the assistance of VMware Support in order to fix them.

The following steps outline the process used to restore the database, using the information from our sample server:

1. Stop the VMware Horizon Composer service.
2. From the command prompt, navigate to the Horizon Composer installation directory.
3. Execute the following command to restore the Horizon Composer database backup. A screenshot which shows the command input is provided after the command:

```
sviconfig -operation=restoredata -dsnname=Composer_Pod1 -
username=composer -password=Password123 -
backupfilepath="C:\Temp\ Backup-2015-1223101427-
viewcomp01_vjason_local.SVI. Viewcomp01"
```

```
c:\Program Files (x86)\VMware\VMware View Composer>sviconfig -operation=restored
ata -dsnname=Composer_Pod1 -username=composer -password=Password123 -backupfilep
ath="C:\Temp\Backup-20151223101427-viewcomp01_vjason_local.SVI"
```

4. The restore process should output several lines of status information. The last few lines of the output are shown in the following screenshot, the last of which indicates that the restore was successful.

```
Object type AdConfigEntryDo found in the backup
Object type VcConfigEntryDo found in the backup
Object type AuthorizedUserDo found in the backup
Object type SequenceNumDo found in the backup
Object type VmNameDo found in the backup
Object type GuestComputerNameDo found in the backup
Object type ReplicaDo found in the backup
Object type DeploymentGroupDo found in the backup
Object type SimCloneDo found in the backup
Restoring data finished successfully.

c:\Program Files (x86)\VMware\VMware View Composer>
```

5. Start the Horizon Composer service.

Horizon Composer is now operating with the restored database.

# Restoring the Horizon Composer SSL certificates

The process to restore Horizon Composer SSL certificates varies depending on the scenario. The following sections explain the procedure you should use based on whether or not you plan to re-use an existing SSL certificate. Both of these procedures assume that you have already restored your Horizon Composer database and configured an ODBC connection to that database on your Horizon Composer host server.

## Restoring Horizon Composer with a new default SSL certificate

Prior to installing the Horizon Composer software, restore the RSA key container that was backed up in the section *Backing up the Horizon Composer SSL certificates*. The following steps outline the full restore process:

1. Copy the `keys.xml` backup file to a location on the new Horizon Composer host server. In our example, the file has been placed within the folder from which we will be executing the restore command.

2. From the command prompt on the new Horizon Composer host server, navigate to the `c:\Windows\Microsoft.NET\Framework\v4.0xxxxx directory`.

3. Execute the following command to import the Horizon Composer RSA key container. A screenshot which shows the expected output if the command was successful is provided after the command.

```
aspnet_regiis -pi "SviKeyContainer" "keys.xml" -exp
```

4. Reinstall Horizon Composer using the steps provided in the section *Installing Horizon Composer*. Since this is a new server, Horizon Composer will note that no SSL certificates are available and will create a new one.

Horizon Composer is now ready to be linked to the Horizon Connection server using the steps provided in the section *Configuring Horizon Composer*. If only Composer was restored, and the link between the Connection Servers and Composer is already present, you will need to re-verify the SSL certificate as described starting with step 5 of *Configuring Horizon Composer*.

# Restoring Horizon Composer with a custom SSL certificate

The process used to restore a Horizon Connection server with a custom SSL certificate is straightforward as all the steps are handled within either the Microsoft Certificates MMC Snap-in or during the installation of Horizon Composer. The following steps outline the full restore process:

 Since we are re-using the same SSL certificate, it is important to remember that the new Horizon Composer host server needs to have the same computer name as the old one.

1. Install the custom SSL certificate on the new Horizon Connection server using the procedure outlined in `Chapter 15`, *Managing Horizon SSL Certificates*.
2. Reinstall Horizon Composer using the steps provided in the section *Installing Horizon Composer*. Since the SSL certificate has already been installed, select the option **Use an existing SSL certificate**, and select the designated certificate.
3. Complete the installation and reboot the Horizon Composer host server.

Horizon Composer is now ready to be linked to the Horizon Connection server using the steps provided in the section *Configuring Horizon Composer*. If only Composer was restored, and the link between the Connection Servers and Composer is already present, you may need to re-verify the SSL certificate as described starting with step 5 of *Configuring Horizon Composer*. If the certificate was in fact already trusted by the Connection Server this step is typically not required.

# Summary

In this chapter, you have been introduced to an important and powerful component of the Horizon installation: VMware Horizon Composer. You have learnt what is required to deploy Horizon Composer, what the limits of Composer are, and how to perform its installation and configuration.

We also discussed how to back up the Horizon Composer configuration, which includes the RSA key container and Horizon Composer database.

We concluded this chapter by discussing how to restore the Horizon Composer database and RSA key container or SSL certificate, and how that process varies based on the recovery scenario.

In the next chapter, we will implement Horizon Security Server, the component of a Horizon installation that enables secure access to Horizon resources from over the Internet.

# 4
# Implementing Horizon Security Server

VMware Horizon Security Server is a core feature of the Horizon platform that enables secure remote access to applications and desktops, without the need to use a **virtual private network(VPN)** connection or provide direct access from the Internet to the Horizon Connection Server. The Horizon Security Server is a specialized installation of the Horizon Connection Server that serves as the connection point between remote Horizon Clients and desktops or applications hosted on a private network.

This chapter will discuss the installation, configuration, backup, and recovery of the Horizon Security Server.

By the end of this chapter, we will learn:

- An overview of the Horizon Security Server
- The connection limits of a Horizon Security Server
- Horizon Security Server network protocol and port usage
- Horizon Security Server prerequisites
- How to enable the Horizon PCoIP Secure Gateway setting
- How to install a Horizon Security Server
- How to update the Horizon Security Server and Connection Server settings
- How and what components of the Horizon Security Server to backup
- How to restore or upgrade a Horizon Security Server

# Horizon Security Server overview

The Horizon Security Server is a type of Horizon Connection Server that is designed to add an additional layer of security between remote Horizon Clients and Horizon resources that are located on a private network. Rather than provide remote Horizon clients with direct access to the Horizon Connection Server, organizations can deploy a Horizon Security Server within a DMZ or other secure network to provide secure remote access to Horizon-managed resources. Some of the functions and features of the Horizon Security Server include:

- Provides remote Horizon Clients with their own dedicated Horizon connection broker, ensuring an optimal user experience
- Brokers connections between remote Horizon Clients and internal Horizon-managed resources
- Authenticates user connection requests
- Supports **RSA SecurID** and **RADIUS** for enabling optional two-factor user authentication
- Can be placed in a DMZ to further isolate the Security Server from the private network
- Does not need to be a member of an Active Directory domain

The following diagram shows the placement of a Horizon Security Server in a simple Horizon environment. The Horizon Security Server brokers access to a number of different components of the private Horizon infrastructure, each of which is shown in the diagram:

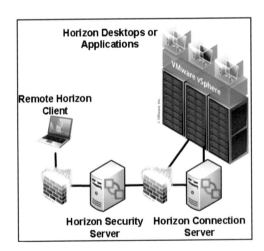

The **Horizon Security Server** authenticates the clients by contacting the **Horizon Connection Server**, and then provides them with access to the entitled resources including **Horizon Desktops or Applications**.

 Horizon Access Point is a hardened, Linux-based virtual appliance that provides similar capabilities to a Horizon Security Server. Chapter 5, *Implementing VMware Horizon Access Point,* provides details about the installation and configuration of this newer Horizon component, which is an alternative to the Horizon Security Server.

# Horizon Security Server limits

A Horizon Security Server has the same connection limitations as a Horizon Connection Server, which means it can support up to 2,000 simultaneous Horizon client connections. Despite this limit, it is important to remember that multiple Security Servers should be deployed to ensure both capacity and availability requirements are met.

Each Horizon Security Server is a stand-alone instance; therefore, there is no specific guidance with regard to how many can be deployed. A Horizon Security Server can only be paired with one Horizon Connection Server while a Connection Server can be paired with multiple Security Servers.

# Horizon Security Server additional considerations

The following are additional considerations that should be kept in mind when deploying a Horizon Security Server:

- If you require Windows IPsec encryption to be applied to the network traffic between the Horizon Security Server and the Horizon Connection Server, the Windows firewall service must be enabled for both hosts in order for Horizon to create the required Windows IPsec policies. The firewall service is enabled by default; if it was disabled, visit the Microsoft TechNet article **Windows Firewall with Advanced Security Overview** (https://technet.microsoft.com/en-us/library/hh831365.aspx) for information about how to manage the feature. It is recommended to enable the firewall service prior to the installation of any Horizon software component, as the installer will then automatically configure the appropriate settings.

- Like Horizon Connection Servers, Horizon Security Servers have no native load-balancing functionality. It is recommended that you implement some sort of load-balancing functionality to help balance the client connections across all the Horizon Security Servers in your infrastructure. Refer to the *Load-Balancing Connection Servers* section in `Chapter 2`, *Implementing Horizon Connection Server*, for information about load-balancing options.
- When installed, the Horizon Security Server is configured with a self-signed SSL certificate that will not be trusted by Horizon clients. It is recommended that you replace the self-signed certificate with one issued from an internal or commercial certificate authority that the Horizon clients will trust. `Chapter 14`, *Managing Horizon SSL Certificates* will provide the process used to replace the default SSL certificates for all Horizon components.
- Options such as tunneling connections and two-factor authentication are set on a per-Connection Server basis. If either of these options is going to be used, and you do not want to subject internal Horizon clients to the additional security measures, you are required to deploy additional Connection Servers with these settings enabled to be used solely with the Horizon Security Servers.

# High availability overview

When deploying Horizon Security Servers it is important to understand how that impacts our high availability requirements. This section will provide an overview of what a highly available Horizon infrastructure that must service both internal and external clients might look like.

The following diagram illustrates a Horizon infrastructure that meets the following four requirements:

- Internal Horizon clients use load-balanced connections to Connection Servers
- Remote Horizon clients use load-balanced connections to Security Servers
- Security Servers installed in a DMZ
- Two-factor authentication or connection tunneling policies that apply only to remote Horizon clients

The diagram does not show the connections to the Horizon desktops or applications; it is only meant to illustrate the placement of load-balancing appliances, and show how true high-availability might be achieved in an environment that includes multiple Horizon Security Servers. In addition, it shows that additional Connection Servers are being used for internal clients, as these connections do not require the same security settings as the remote clients do.

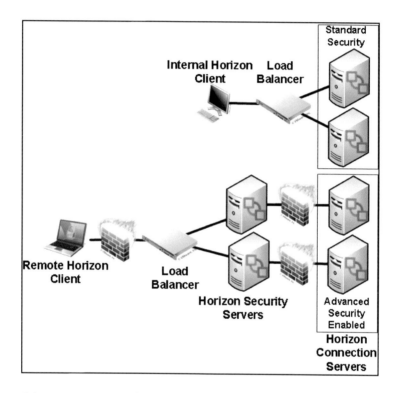

This Horizon architecture ensures that Horizon clients will be able to connect or reconnect if either of these two scenarios were to occur:

- Failure of any one of the four Connection Servers shown in the diagram
- Failure of any one of the Security Servers

As a single Horizon Security Server cannot be paired with more than one Connection Server, there is no need to place a load-balancer between the Security Servers and the Connection Servers. Load-balancing the Security Servers ensures that the Horizon client connection will be maintained regardless of which server fails, be it a Security Server or the Connection Server that it is paired to.

# Security Server network requirements

The following diagram illustrates how the primary protocols used by the Horizon Security Server work with other components of the Horizon infrastructure. The diagram shows the following components of a Horizon infrastructure:

- Communication between the **Horizon Security Server** and the **Horizon Desktop or Application**
- Communication between the **Horizon Security Server** and the **Horizon Connection Server**

The arrows indicate the direction in which each protocol travels, assuming that the default settings are used.

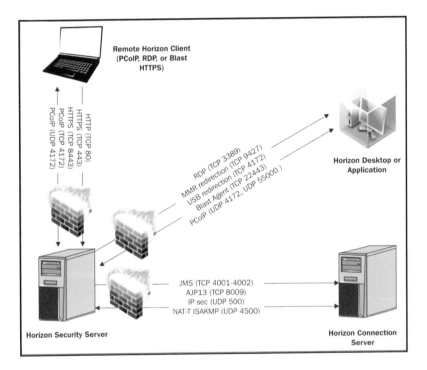

This list of ports used by the core components is outlined in the following table. Additionally, consult the **Firewall Rules for DMS-Based Security Servers** in the VMware document **View Architecture Planning** (http://pubs.vmware.com/horizon-62-view/ topic/com.vmware.horizon-view.planning.doc/GUID-B8D3225D-0CB2-42D3-B2B8 -EB7DED0F3B5E.html) for additional information concerning the function of each component, and when the associated port is actually required to be opened in the firewall.

| Protocol or Service | Port | Notes |
|---|---|---|
| AJP13 (Apache Tomcat Connector) | TCP 8009 | Not used if IPsec is enabled and the DMZ backend firewall uses one-way or two-way NAT. |
| Blast Agent | TCP 22443 | Used to connect to the Blast (HTML Access) Agent on the desktop. |
| HTTP/HTTPS | TCP 80/443/8443 | Port TCP 8443 is only used for HTML Access (web) clients. |
| JMS (Java Messaging Service) | TCP 4001-4002 | If upgrading existing Horizon Security Servers, port TCP 4002 might not be open as it was not previously required. |
| MMR (Multimedia redirection) | TCP 9427 | Used alongside RDP; uses client rather than server resources to render DirectShow-based media and codecs. |
| NAT-T ISAKMP | UDP 4500 | Used to negotiate IPsec security; if the DMZ backend firewall uses one-way or two-way NAT, and IPsec is enabled, UDP port 4500 must be allowed in each direction between the Security Server and the Horizon Connection Server. |
| PCoIP | TCP/UDP 4172, UDP 55000 | |
| RDP | TCP 3389 | |
| IPsec | UDP 500 | |
| USB Redirection for PCoIP and RDP | TCP 32111 | TCP 32111 is used to support USB redirection to Horizon clients. |

# Installing and configuring Horizon Security Server

The installation and configuration process for the Horizon Security Server requires some amount of preparation. This section will outline what is required prior to beginning the installation.

## Installation prerequisites

There are a number of prerequisites that should be addressed prior to installing a Horizon Security Server:

- At least one configured Horizon Connection Server with a license key must be installed
- A dedicated Windows 2012 R2 server is needed to host the Horizon Security Server role
- You must have two network adapters and a static IP address for each on the Security Server host (one adapter will be public facing, the other private facing)
- The Security Server host should be able to resolve the FQDN of the Connection Server it will pair with, either using DNS or the local hosts file
- You must have a valid Horizon Connection Server pairing password is needed
- Firewall access is required between the Horizon Security Server and the necessary Horizon components on the private network
- Firewall access between the Internet and the Horizon Security Server
- A resolvable public URL that will be used for accessing the Horizon Security Server
- You must have local administrator access on the host server

In addition to the items described in Chapter 1, *VMware Horizon Infrastructure Overview*, the following items should be prepared in advance of the installation.

# Security Server pairing password

The Horizon Security Server is paired to a Horizon Connection Server using a password that is specified in the Horizon Administrator console. This password is entered during the installation of the Security Server, and enables secure communication between it and the Connection Server on the private network. The following steps outline how to generate the password:

1. Log on to the Horizon Administrator console using an AD account that has administrative permissions within Horizon.
2. Navigate to the **View Configuration** | **Servers** page within the console.
3. Select the **Connection Servers** tab in the **Servers** window.
4. Highlight the Connection Server that you wish to pair with the Security Server, click on the **More Commands** button, and select **Specify Security Server Pairing Password….** In the following screenshot, we have highlighted the **VIEWCS02** Connection Server:

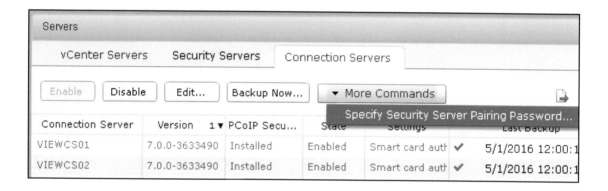

5. In the **Specify Security Server Pairing Password** window, specify a password and the amount of time it will be valid for. Click on **OK** when finished. The following screenshot shows the **Pairing password:**, **Confirm password:**, and **Password timeout:** fields:

With the password specified, the installation of the Security Server can now proceed. In the event that the installation cannot be completed prior to the password expiring, simply generate a new password.

# Deploying a Horizon Security Server

Deploying a Horizon Security Server is broken down into two stages: the installation of the Horizon Security Server software, and the final setup using the Horizon Administrator console.

# Enable PCoIP Secure Gateway

By default, once a Horizon client has authenticated a Horizon Connection Server, it allows a direct connection to their target desktop or server hosting applications. The Connection Server is responsible only for brokering the connection, not maintaining it. While this is the optimal configuration for clients located on the private network where the desktops are located, it is not recommended for clients using public Internet connections as they do not have direct access to their desktops.

In order for external Horizon clients to gain access, the Horizon Connection Server must be configured with the appropriate PCoIP Secure Gateway settings. External clients are required to tunnel their connections through the Security Server, which, as we know, is designed to be the public Internet-facing component of VMware Horizon. The option that controls this behavior is known as the **PCoIP Secure Gateway**, and it is not updated when you pair a Horizon Security Server with the Connection Server.

The PCoIP Secure Gateway configuration must be changed prior to placing a Security Server into production. The following steps outline how to enable the setting on the Connection Server we will use with our Security Servers. This setting may also be updated after the Security Servers have been installed.

1. Log on to the Horizon Administrator console using an AD account that has administrative permissions within Horizon.
2. Navigate to the **View Configuration** | **Servers** page within the console.
3. Select the **Connection Servers** tab in the **Servers** window.
4. Highlight the Connection Server that we intend to pair with the Security Server, and click on the **Edit...** button shown in the following screenshot to open the **Edit Connection Server Settings** window.

5. In the **Edit Connection Server Settings** window, check the **Use PCoIP Secure Gateway for PCoIP connections to machine** check box as shown in the following screenshot, and then click **OK**.

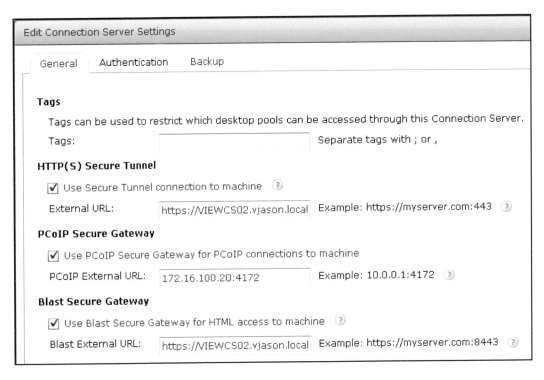

The PCoIP Secure Gateway feature is now enabled, and any attempt to connect to Horizon desktops or applications will be tunneled through the Security Server or even through the

Connection Server if the connection is made from within the private network.

A similar settings screen is available for each Horizon Security Server in the **View Configuration** | **Servers – Security Servers** tab in the Horizon Administrator console. That page is shown in the section of this chapter titled *Security Server options*.

# Installing a Horizon Security Server

The Horizon Security Server software is delivered as a single executable (EXE) file, named in a format similar to `VMware-viewconnectionserver-x86_64-x.x.xyyyyyy.exe`. The following steps outline the installation process:

1. Double-click the Horizon Connection Server installer EXE file to launch the installer.

2. In the **Welcome to the Installation Wizard for VMware Horizon 7 Connection Server** window, click on **Next >**.

3. Review the **License Agreement**, select the **I accept the terms in the license agreement** radio button, and click on **Next >**.

4. Select the installation directory and click on **Next >**.

5. Select **Horizon 6 Security Server** as shown in the following screenshot, and then click on **Next >**.

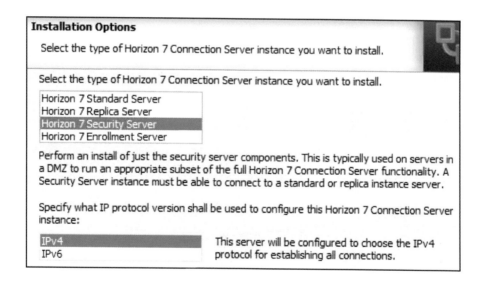

6. Enter the name of the Horizon Connection Server that the Horizon Security Server should be paired with in the **Server:** field and click on **Next >**.

---

**Paired Horizon 7 Connection Server**

Select a Horizon 7 Connection Server that this instance will talk to.

A Horizon 7 Security Server is paired with an existing instance of a Horizon 7 Connection Server. Enter the server name of any existing Horizon 7 Connection Server instance.

Example server: view.internal.vmware.com.

Server:

| viewcs02.vjason.local |                              (hostname or IP address)

---

7. In the **Password:** field, enter the Security Server Pairing Password that was specified earlier and click on **Next >**.

---

**Paired Horizon 7 Connection Server Password**

Enter a password to pair with the Horizon 7 Connection Server.

A password is required to pair this Security Server with a Connection Server.

First specify the Pairing Password for the Connection Server in Horizon 7 Administrator.

This password is set in Horizon 7 Administrator in "Horizon 7 Configuration" > "Servers". Select the specified Connection Server and go to "More Commands" > "Specify Security Server Pairing Password".

Password:      ••••

---

8. Enter each of the publicly resolvable URLs as requested in the **External URL:**, **PCoIP External URL:**, and **Blast External URL:** fields. Click on **Next >** when complete.

---

**Horizon 7 Security Server Configuration**

Specify Security Server settings.

---

Enter the External URLs for this Security Server.

The External URLs specified are used by Horizon Clients to establish connections to this Security Server for the secure tunnel, PCoIP and Blast protocols respectively. The URL names and IP addresses must not be load balanced.

Note that the hostnames must be resolvable by the Horizon Client and the PCoIP External URL must contain an IP address.

External URL:  `https://VIEWSE01.vjason.local:443`

PCoIP External URL:  `172.16.100.21:4172`

Blast External URL:  `https://VIEWSE01.vjason.local:8443`

---

The PCoIP External URL must be entered as an IP address that remote clients will use to access the Horizon Security Server. The other values shown may be changed later if required.

9. Select either the **Configure Windows Firewall automatically** or **Do not configure Windows Firewall** radio button and click on **Next >**. If the option **Do not configure Windows Firewall** was selected, configure the firewall manually using the settings provided earlier in the chapter.

10. Review the final installation screen to ensure that the installation directory is correct. If changes are needed, click on the **< Back** button to reach the necessary configuration screen and make the required changes. Assuming that the settings are correct, click on **Install** to begin the automated installation process.

11. Click on **Finish** when prompted at the completion of the installation process.

12. The installation process will install all the components required for the Horizon Security Server. The same process can be used to install additional Horizon Security Servers, although a new Security Server pairing password would need to be generated as each is only valid for one use.

13. Navigate to the Security Server web page and verify that it is displayed as shown in the following screenshot. The page can be accessed using the URL `https://SecurityServerFQDN`; since we have not yet replaced the default self-signed SSL certificate, our web browser will likely display an error.

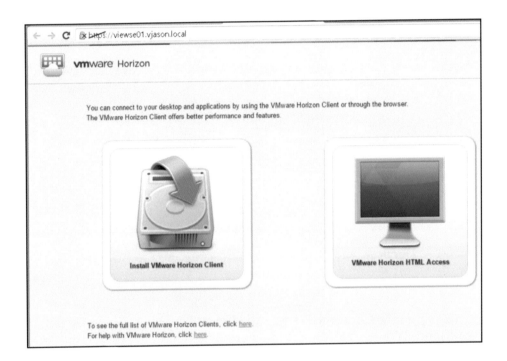

 The procedure used to replace the Security Server self-signed SSL certificates is described in `Chapter 14`, *Managing Horizon SSL Certificates*.

14. Navigate to the **View Configuration** | **Servers** page within the Horizon Administrator console.

15. Select the **Security Servers** tab in the **Servers** window and verify that the security server is listed as shown in the following screenshot.

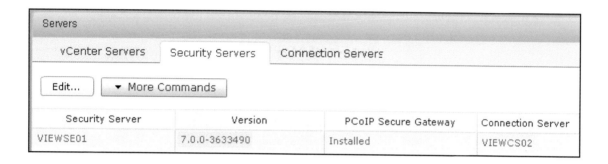

| Servers | | | |
| --- | --- | --- | --- |
| vCenter Servers | Security Servers | Connection Servers | |
| Edit...  ▾ More Commands | | | |
| Security Server | Version | PCoIP Secure Gateway | Connection Server |
| VIEWSE01 | 7.0.0-3633490 | Installed | VIEWCS02 |

16. Repeat this process as needed to install additional Security Servers; you will also need to generate a new Security Server pairing password as well.

The final configuration steps will be completed in the Horizon Administrator console, and will be detailed in the next section.

When the installation process has been completed, be sure to read the VMware Horizon Read Me file. By default this file will be opened when you click **Finish** after the installation process. The Read Me file typically contains important information that you should know prior to placing your new or upgraded servers into production, and may save you wasted troubleshooting time later.

# Updating the Horizon Security Server settings

Once paired to a Horizon Connection Server, the Security Server settings can be changed using the Horizon Administrator console. The following sections illustrate where within the console you update the Security Server Settings.

# Horizon Security Server options

The following steps outline how to verify or update the Security Server options.

1. Log on to the Horizon Administrator console using an AD account that has administrative permissions within Horizon.
2. Open the **View Configuration** | **Servers** page within the console.
3. Select the **Security Servers** tab in the **Servers** window.

4. Highlight the Security Server you wish to update, and click on **Edit** to open the **Edit Security Server** window as shown in the following screenshot:

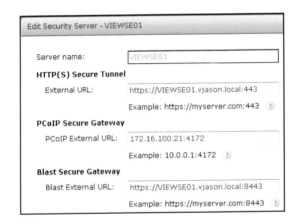

In the event that either the external URL or IP address of the Security Server is changed, it should be changed in this page to ensure that Horizon will function properly.

# Horizon Security Server backup

A Horizon Security Server contains no information about the configuration of the Horizon installation, and therefore has no backup requirements. Assuming that the self-signed SSL certificate was replaced with one from a trusted internal or commercial certificate authority, it is important to maintain a backup of that certificate that includes the private key.

As the Horizon Security Server is a publicly accessible server, you may wish to back up the log files on a regular basis. These files are located in the same folder on every type of Horizon Connection Server: `%ALLUSERSPROFILE%\Application Data\VMware\VDM\logs`.

# Horizon Security Server recovery or upgrade

The process used to recover a Horizon Security Server is almost identical to that used to perform an upgrade. The only difference is that when performing an upgrade the target server is typically in a usable state, and when doing a recovery a new server may be required. This section will provide one set of instructions that will cover both an upgrade or a recovery of a Horizon Security Server.

The simplest way to restore a Horizon Security Server is to simply reinstall the software using the steps provided earlier in this chapter, and re-pair the Security Server with the Horizon Connection Server.

The following steps outline how to restore a Horizon Security Server in a scenario where the previous one is unavailable, or how to upgrade an existing Security Server: (Steps which are specific to a recovery will be identified as such).

1. Generate a new Security Server pairing password using the process outlined earlier in this chapter.
2. Configure a new Security Server host using the same server name and IP address (only required for a recovery).
3. Log on to the Horizon Administrator console using an AD account that has administrative permissions within Horizon.
4. Open the **View Configuration** | **Servers** page within the console.
5. Select the **Security Servers** tab in the Servers window.
6. Verify which Security Server needs updating by reviewing the **Version** column. In the following screenshot, we can see that **VIEWSE02** is running an older version of the View Security Server software (highlighted in red) and needs updating (only required for an upgrade).

7. Highlight the Security Server you wish to remove or upgrade, click on the **More Commands** option, and then the **Prepare for Upgrade or Reinstallation...** button as shown in the following screenshot:

8. Click on **OK** in the **Warning** window shown in the following screenshot to remove the Connection Server IPsec rules in preparation for the upgrade or reinstallation:

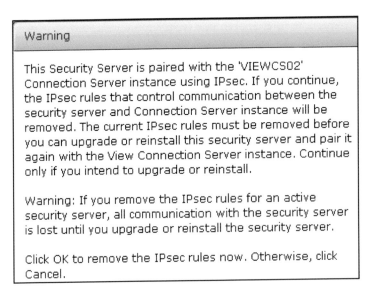

This process permanently dissociates the Security Server from the Horizon Connection Server. Once selected, the only way to restore the connection is to reinstall the Horizon Security Server software.

9. Install the Security Server software using the process outlined earlier in this chapter in the section titled *Install a Horizon Security Server*. If performing an upgrade, the name of the Connection Server to pair with as shown in step 6 of that section should already be supplied.
10. Verify the Security Server settings in the Horizon Administrator console and test remote Horizon client connections.

# Summary

In this chapter, we have been introduced to the VMware Horizon Security Server, a feature of Horizon that provides organizations with the ability to provide secure remote access to Horizon desktops or applications. We have learnt what is required to deploy and configure a Horizon Security Server, what the limits of a Security Server are, and where the Security Server fits in within the Horizon infrastructure.

We also discussed which components of the Security Server need to be backed up, and which are custom SSL certificates, as well as the Security Server logs.

We concluded this chapter by discussing how to restore or upgrade a Horizon Security Server. In the next chapter, we will discuss Horizon Access Point, which provides similar capabilities as a Horizon Security Server but is provided as a hardened, Linux-based virtual appliance.

# 5
# Implementing VMware Horizon Access Point

VMware Horizon Access Point is a core feature of the Horizon platform that enables secure remote access to applications and desktops, without the need to use a **virtual private network (VPN)** connection or provide direct access from the Internet to the Horizon Connection Server. The Horizon Access Point is delivered as a hardened, Linux-based virtual appliance that serves as the connection point between external Horizon Clients and desktops or applications hosted on a private network.

This chapter will discuss the installation and configuration of the Horizon Access Point.

By the end of this chapter, we will have learned:

- An overview of Horizon Access Point
- The connection limits of an Access Point
- Access Point network protocol and port usage
- Access Point installation prerequisites
- How to configure Horizon Connection Servers to use with Access Point
- How to deploy an Access Point
- How to troubleshoot an Access Point
- Updating the configuration of an Access Point

# Horizon Access Point overview

The Horizon Access Point is a type of Horizon Connection Server that is designed to add an additional layer of security between remote Horizon Clients and Horizon resources that are located on a private network. Rather than providing remote clients with direct access to the Connection Server, organizations can deploy an Access Point within a DMZ or other secure network to provide secure remote access to Horizon-managed resources. Some of the functions and features of the Horizon Access Point include:

- Providing remote Horizon clients with their own dedicated connection broker, ensuring an optimal user experience
- Brokering connections between remote Horizon clients and internal Horizon-managed resources
- Authenticating user connection requests
- Supporting **RSA SecurID**, **RADIUS**, **Smart Cards**, and **Security Assertion Markup Language (SAML)** based authentication for enabling optional two-factor user authentication
- Ability to be placed in a DMZ to further isolate the Access Point from the private network

Horizon Access Points perform the same tasks as Security Servers, but provide additional benefits such as being delivered as a virtual appliance, and they can work with more than one Connection Server at a time.

The following diagram shows the placement of a **Horizon Access Point** in a simple Horizon environment. The **Horizon Access Point** brokers access to a number of different components of the private Horizon infrastructure, each of which is shown in the diagram:

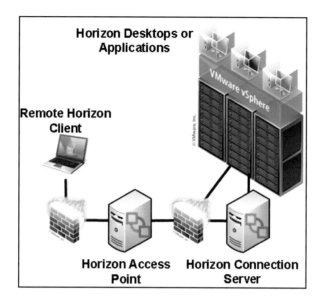

The Horizon Access Point authenticates the clients by contacting the Horizon Connection Server, and then provides them with access to the entitled resources including Horizon desktops or applications.

At some point in the future, VMware has indicated that they are likely to phase out or at least deprecate Horizon Security Server (http://blogs.v mware.com/euc/2015/09/vmware-horizon-access-point-secure-remote-access-end-user-computing.html). Access Point is not a new product; it was initially created for use with **Horizon Air**, which is a version of Horizon used to provide **Desktop as a Service** (**DaaS**). It is still used with Horizon Air, and has now been updated to work with Horizon. The relationship between Access Point and Security Server today is similar to that of **User Environment Manager** and **Horizon Persona Management**: Both are still available, but VMware are only focusing their resources on continuing to develop one of them (User Environment Manager and Access Point in this case).

# Horizon Access Point limits

A Horizon Access Point has the same connection limitations as Horizon Connection and Security Servers, which means it can support up to 2,000 simultaneous Horizon client connections. Despite this limit, it is important to remember that multiple Access Point appliances should be deployed to ensure both capacity and availability requirements are met.

Each Horizon Access Point is a stand-alone instance; therefore, there is no specific guidance with regard to how many can be deployed. However, unlike a Horizon Security Server, a Horizon Access Point can be used with multiple Connection Servers at once, although those Connection Servers must be placed behind a load balancer.

# Horizon Access Point additional considerations

The following are additional considerations that should be kept in mind when deploying a Horizon Access Point:

- Like Horizon Connection and Security Servers, Horizon Access Points have no native load-balancing functionality. It is recommended to implement some sort of load-balancing functionality to help balance the client connections across all the Horizon Access Points in your infrastructure. Refer to the Load-Balancing Connection Servers section in `Chapter 2`, *Implementing Horizon Connection Server*, for information about load-balancing options.
- As stated previously, a load balancer is also needed when you wish to use an Access Point to connect to more than one Connection Server.
- When installed using the vSphere client **Deploy OVF Template** option, the Horizon Access Point is configured with a self-signed SSL certificate that will not be trusted by Horizon clients. It is recommended to replace the self-signed certificate with one issued from an internal or commercial certificate authority that the Horizon clients will trust; in this chapter we will do so during the deployment of the Access Point using the command line-based VMware **OVF Tool**.

- `Chapter 14`, *Managing Horizon SSL Certificates*, details the procedures used to replace the default SSL certificates for Horizon servers or other components that have already been deployed.
- Similarly to Horizon Security Servers, Access Points require that the Connection Servers, client connection options are changed to a configuration not suitable for internal clients. Owing to this, dedicated Connection Servers are recommended when deploying Access Points.

# High availability overview

When deploying Horizon Access Points, it is important to understand how this impacts our high availability requirements. This section will provide an overview of what a highly available Horizon infrastructure that must service both internal and external clients might look like.

The following diagram illustrates a Horizon infrastructure that meets the following requirements:

- Internal Horizon clients use load-balanced connections to Connection Servers
- Remote Horizon clients use load-balanced connections to Access Points
- Access Points use load-balanced connections to Connection Servers
- Access Points must be installed in a DMZ
- There must be dedicated Connection Servers for use with Access Point appliances; these are configured with the settings outlined in this chapter

The following diagram does not show the connections to the Horizon desktops or applications; it is only meant to illustrate the placement of load-balancing appliances, and show how true high availability might be achieved in an environment that includes multiple **Horizon Access Points**. In addition, it shows that additional Connection Servers are being used for internal clients, as these servers do not require the same client connection settings as the ones used with Access Points do.

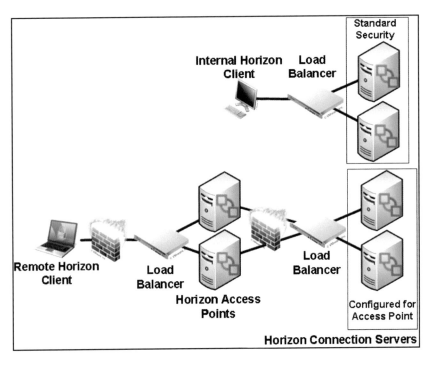

This Horizon architecture ensures that Horizon clients will be able to connect or reconnect if either of these two scenarios were to occur:

- Failure of any one of the four Connection Servers shown in the diagram
- Failure of any one of the Access Points

Load-balancing the Access Points ensures that the Horizon client connection will be maintained regardless of which server fails, be it an Access Point or the Connection Server that it is paired to.

> While not specifically mentioned, it is assumed that your load-balancers are also redundant to ensure that the failure of any one of them will not impact Horizon client connections.

# Horizon Access Point network requirements

The following diagram illustrates how the primary protocols used by the Horizon Access Point work with other components of the Horizon infrastructure. The diagram shows the following components of a Horizon infrastructure:

- Communication between the Horizon Access Point and the Horizon desktops or applications
- Communication between the Horizon Access Point and the Connection Servers

The arrows indicate the direction in which each protocol travels, assuming that the default settings are used.

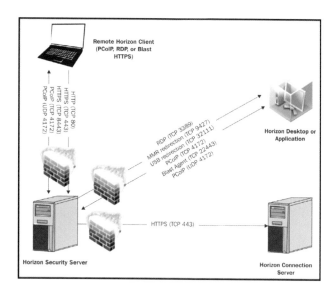

This list of ports used by the core components are outlined in the following table. Additionally, consult the *Firewall Rules for DMZ-Based Access Point Appliances* section in the VMware document **Deploying and Configuring Access Point** (`https://www.vmware.com/support/pubs/view_pubs.html`) for additional information concerning the function of each component, and when the associated port is actually required to be opened in the firewall.

| Protocol or Service | Port | Notes |
|---|---|---|
| Blast Agent | TCP 22443 | Used to connect to the Blast (HTML Access) Agent on the desktop |
| HTTP/HTTPS | TCP 80/443/8443 | Port TCP 8443 is only used for HTML Access (web) clients |
| MMR (Multimedia redirection) | TCP 9427 | Used alongside RDP; uses client rather than server resources to render DirectShow-based media and codecs |
| PCoIP | TCP/UDP 4172 | |
| RDP | TCP 3389 | |
| REST API | TCP 9443 | Not shown; Horizon administrators use this port to connect to and configure an Access Point after it has been deployed |
| Syslog | UDP 514 | Not shown; Access Points can be configured to send Syslog events on this port |
| USB Redirection for PCoIP and RDP | TCP 32111 | TCP 32111 is used to support USB redirection to Horizon clients |

# Preparing the infrastructure for a Horizon Access Point

The installation and configuration process for the Horizon Access Point requires some amount of preparation. This section will outline what is required prior to beginning the installation.

The procedure detailed in `Chapter 14`, *Managing Horizon SSL Certificates*, in the *Converting a certificate from PFX to PEM* format section can be used here to covert a **PFX** format SSL certificate to the **PEM** format required by our Access Point.

# Installation prerequisites

There are a number of prerequisites that should be addressed prior to installing a Horizon Access Point:

- Sufficient vSphere resources for each appliance, which includes 2.5 GB (thin provisioned) or 20 GB (thick provisioned) of disk space, 2 vCPU, 4 GB of RAM, and one, two, or three network interfaces.
- The OVF file should automatically select the recommended values for disk capacity, CPU, and RAM; only the number of network interfaces should be changed.
- Three network interfaces are recommended for security purposes, as this allows us to separate internal facing, external facing, and management network traffic. If two network interfaces are selected, the internal and management traffic share the same interface; if just one is selected, all network traffic shares the same interface.
- At least one configured Horizon Connection Server with a license key installed.
- At least one Horizon pool to use to test the functionality of the Access Point.

Chapter 10, *Creating Horizon Desktop Pools*, and Chapter 11, *Implementing Horizon Application Pools*, discuss how to create pools that can be used to test the function of our Access Points.

- A vSphere **Network Protocol Profile** (also known as an **IP Pool**) must be created for and assigned to the DMZ network where the Access Point will be installed; this process is described in the VMware document *vSphere Networking – Configuring Protocol Profiles for Virtual Machine Networking* section (http://pubs. vmware.com/vsphere-60/index.jsp).

We won't actually use the IP addresses allocated in the Network Protocol Profile / IP Pool, but it is used to obtain other information about the DMZ network such as the subnet mask.

- Three static IP addresses in the DMZ for each Access Point.

While an Access Point can be deployed with just one or two network interfaces, for security reasons and to make network traffic easier to analyze I recommend three (one external facing, one internal facing, and one for administration).

- Firewall access between the Horizon Access Points and the necessary Horizon components on the private network.
- A URL that will be used by external clients for connecting to our Horizon infrastructure.

In Horizon production environments this URL would typically point to a load balancer that is placed in front of two or more Access Points.

- Firewall access between the Internet and the Horizon Access Points (and any load balancer used with them).

Depending on your load-balancer configuration, it may or may not be necessary to provide access from the Internet directly to the Access Points themselves. Consult your load-balancer documentation to understand how client connections are maintained, specifically if it tunnels the connections or hands them off to an available Access Point.

- The SSL certificate **Thumbprint** for each of the Connection Servers that the Access Points will connect to, obtained from the certificate Details tab as shown in the following screenshot:

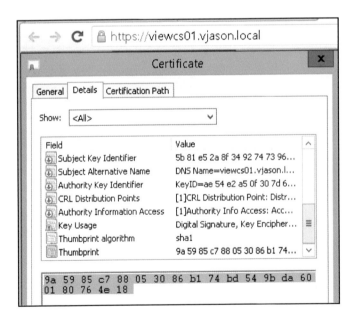

- A SSL certificate chain in PEM format that includes a certificate for the Access Point, as well as any root or intermediate certificate authority certificates involved in creating the certificate.
  - The certificate should include **Subject Alternative Names (SAN)** that include the external FQDN of the Access Points (such as `horizon.vjason.com`).
  - Refer to `Chapter 14`, *Managing Horizon SSL Certificates*, if your certificate is in PFX format, and you need to convert it to the PEM format and export the certificate **private key.**
- The private key for the Access Point SSL certificate.
  - The private key is contained in the `server.key` file referenced in `Chapter 14`, *Managing Horizon SSL Certificates.*
- Obtain the following tools which we will use during the installation process:
  - VMware Access Point Deployment Utility (`https://labs.vmware.com/flings/vmware-access-point-deployment-utility`).
  - VMware OVF Tool (`https://www.vmware.com/support/developer/ovf/`).

These tools are technically optional, but you'll find they make deployment much easier than using the native vSphere Deploy OVF Template feature and completing the configuration using the Access Point REST API.

# Deploying a Horizon Access Point

The procedure used to deploy a Horizon Access Point can be broken down into the following stages:

- Infrastructure preparation as outlined in the previous section of this chapter
- Using the Horizon Administrator console to reconfigure the Connection Server client settings
- Using the VMware OVF Tools to deploy the Access Point appliances

# Configuring the Connection Servers

A Horizon Access Point provides secure gateway and tunneling capabilities for external client connections. In order for external Horizon client connections to connect to their destination desktops and Windows RDS servers on the internal network, it is necessary to disable these features on each of the Connection Servers used with our Access Point appliances.

The following steps outline how to disable the tunneling and gateway features on our Connection Servers:

1. Log on to the Horizon Administrator console using an AD account that has administrative permissions within Horizon.
2. Open the **View Configuration** | **Servers** window within the console.
3. Click on the **Connection Servers** tab in the **Servers** window.
4. Click on the Connection Server that we intend to use with an Access Point, and then click the **Edit...** button shown in the following screenshot to open the **Edit Connection Server Settings** window.

5. In the **Edit Connection Server Settings** window, uncheck the **HTTP(S) Secure Tunnel** and **Blast Secure Gateway** check boxes as shown in the following screenshot, and then click **OK**.

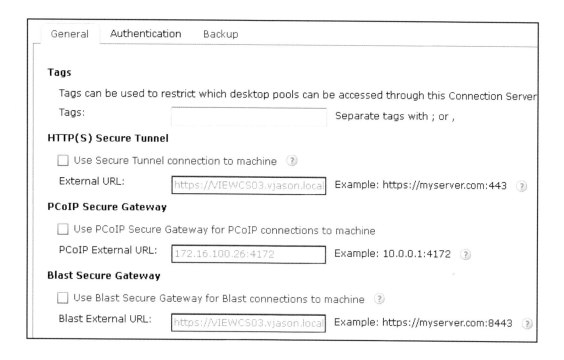

6. Repeat steps 4 and 5 for all other Connection Servers that will be used with Access Points.

Our Horizon Connection Servers are now ready for use with our Access Points. The deployment of the Access Points will be covered in the next section.

# Deploying a Horizon Access Point

The Horizon Access Point software is delivered as a single **open virtual appliance (OVA)** file, named in a format similar to `euc-access-point-x.x.x.x-yyyyyyy_OVF10.ova`. The following steps outline the deployment process:

1. If not already installed, install the VMware OVF Tool on the Windows-based computer you will use to deploy the Horizon Access Point.
2. If not already extracted, extract the **VMware Access Point Deployment Utility** files, then double click on the `Access_Point_GUI.exe` file to launch the program as shown in the following screenshot:

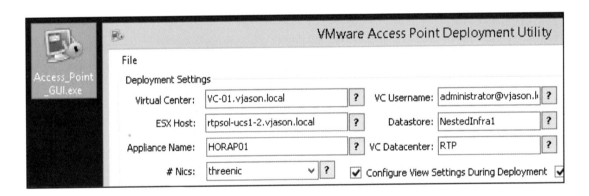

3. Check the **Configure Certificates During Deployment** check box, paste the Access Point SSL certificate chain into the **Certificate Chain:** field and then click **Update Certificates**; repeat this with the certificate private key, pasting it into the **Private Key:** field and then clicking **Update Private Key**. When finished, those fields will look similar to the following screenshot.

4. In the View Thumbprints field, type in `sha1=`, and then paste the first Connection Server SSL certificate thumbprint. If multiple Connection Servers will be used, separate the thumbprints using a comma, but do not repeat the `sha1=`. When finished, it will look similar to the following screenshot.

| View Thumbprints: | sha1=9a 59 85 c7 88 05 30 86 b1 74 bd 54 9b da 60 01 80 76 4e 18,91 01 1c 8f c9 18 4a f0 5c 3a db 64 ae 16 de e0 d9 95 ! |
| --- | --- |

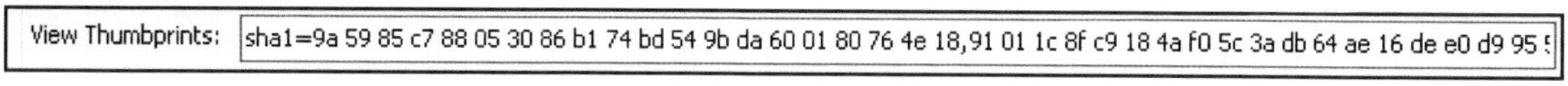

5. Populate the remaining fields as shown in the following screenshot. Note the following:

- By default only one network interface will be deployed; use the **# Nics:** drop down menu to change that to three nic.
- Check the **Configure View Settings During Deployment** check box to unlock the **View Settings** fields.
- **ESX Host:** refers to the host where the appliance will be initially deployed.
- The three **IP** fields (**External**, **Management**, and **Backend**) should be populated with the IPs allocated for the appliance in the DMZ network, and their associated **Network** fields should be populated with the name of the DMZ vSphere virtual machines network.
- **Destination URL:** points to the IP address used on the load balancer we are using to balance traffic for our two destination Connection Servers; the configuration of the load balancer should be verified prior to deploying the Access Point.
- The **PCOIP URL:** field must use an IP address, not a DNS name.

- The remaining **URL** fields should be populated with the URL that will be used by external Horizon clients.

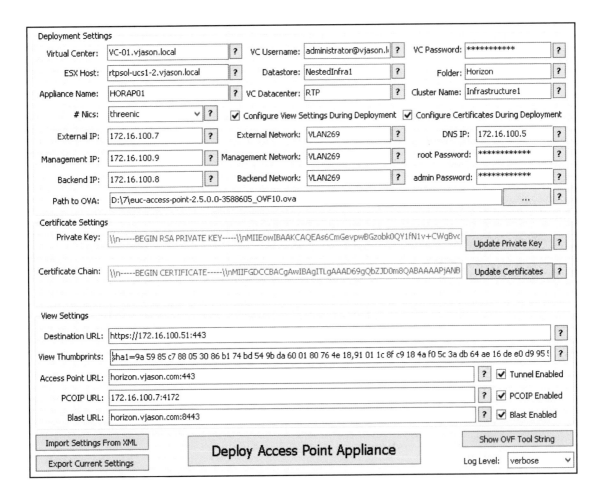

6. Click on the **Log Level:** drop down menu and select verbose; this ensures that we see any errors associated with the Access Point deployment process.
7. Click on the **Export Current Settings** button to open the **Export Deployment Settings** Window. Provide a unique **File name** that indicates which Access Point these settings are for, and then click **Save**.

8. Click the **Deploy Access Point Appliance** button to open the **Deploy Access Point Appliance** window, and then click **Yes** to start the deployment.

9. Monitor the **Deploying Access Point Appliance** window shown in the following screenshot, as well as the vSphere client for any errors during the deployment process; the appliance will automatically power on and complete the configuration when the OVA deployment process finishes. Close the **Deploying Access Point Appliance** window when you have completed reviewing the deployment logs.

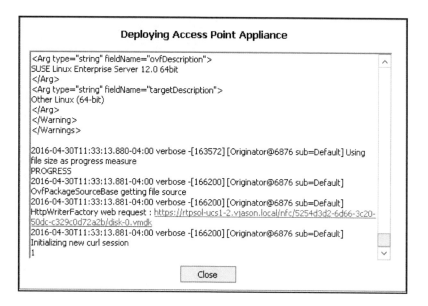

10. Once the Access Point appliance VMware tools status shows as **Running**, use the Horizon Client to connect to it, and then use an account that is entitled to log on and access a Horizon desktop or application pool.

11. Repeat steps *3* through *10* as these are needed to deploy and test additional Access Points. Note that each will need their own unique IP address, Access Point appliance name, and SSL certificate.

The Access Point appliances have now been deployed, and you may implement load-balancing in front of the Access Point appliances themselves if desired. In the next section we will review some of the resources that can be used to troubleshoot the deployment or functionality of an Access Point.

# Troubleshooting a Horizon Access Point deployment

While the actual process of troubleshooting a Horizon Access Point deployment is likely to require research beyond the scope of what we can cover in this chapter, we can review the various options for obtaining the information needed to perform that troubleshooting:

- Review the contents of the **Deploying Access Point Appliance** window described in the previous section
- An Access Point log file bundle used for general troubleshooting may be downloaded from each Access Point using the management IP address and the following
  URL: `https://AccessPointManagementIP:9443/rest/v1/monitor/support-archive`
- For errors during the deployment process itself, such as those where it will not successfully deploy, you may rerun the installation using the command line version of the OVF Tool using the following steps

This is technically the same task that the Access Point deployment utility performs, but I have found it can be useful to use the command line when troubleshooting in the way described as follows:

1. In the VMware Access Point Deployment Utility window, click the **Show OVF Tool String** button to open the **Generated OVF Input String** window shown in the following screenshot. Copy the contents of this window and then click **OK**.

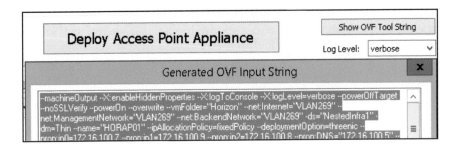

The meaning of each OVF option is outlined on the VMware document **Deploying and Configuring Access Point** (`https://www.vmware.com/s upport/pubs/view_pubs.html`).

2. Open a command prompt on the workstation and change into the directory where the VMware OVF Tool is installed (`C:\Program Files\VMware\VMware OVF Tool` by default).

3. Type in `ovftool.exe`, a space, paste the OVF input string obtained in step *1* as shown in the following screenshot, and hit *Enter* to initiate the Access Point deployment process.

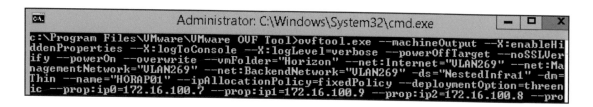

4. Monitor the installation process as needed, reviewing the results identify the source of any errors that prevent the deployment from completing.

It is important to remember that it only takes a few minutes to deploy a new Access Point appliance. If an Access Point stops working suddenly, it may be easier simply to delete it, load your saved Access Point Deployment Utility settings, and redeploy a new appliance.

# Updating the Horizon Access Point configuration

Unlike Horizon Connection Servers, an Access Point does not have an administrative web page. Technically speaking, neither does a Security Server, but you can change some of their settings using the Horizon Administrator console.

The only option for updating the configuration of an Access Point is to submit **JSON** requests to REST API interface, a process discussed in `Chapter 14`, *Managing Horizon SSL Certificates*. In the *Replacing a Horizon Access Point certificate* section of that chapter, you can see how to use a JSON request to replace the existing Access Point SSL certificate with a new one. Using the procedure detailed in that section to establish the connection to the Access Point REST API, you can perform almost any configuration task needed.

The *Using the Access Point REST API* section of the VMware document *Deploying and Configuring Access Point* (`https://www.vmware.com/support/pubs/view_pubs.html`) provides a full list of the configuration settings, and the syntax of the commands needed to update them.

In this chapter we used the **VMware Access Point Deployment Utility** and the **OVF Tool** to configure all of the options needed when deploying the Access Point appliance, so there is no need to perform any additional configuration using the API. The same cannot be said if you use the vSphere **Deploy OVF Template** feature to deploy an Access Point, as you will not be prompted for all of the possible settings, including those which virtually everyone would want, such as using a custom SSL certificate.

So, while you are welcome to use the REST API to make changes, never forget that it may be easier just to use the deployment utility to deploy a new appliance instead. In the future, VMware is likely to incorporate a more detailed Access Point deployment process that eliminates the need to use the deployment utility if not the REST API itself, but until that happens you will need to be familiar with one or the other, and sometimes even both.

# Summary

In this chapter we have been introduced to the VMware Horizon Access Point, a feature of Horizon that uses a hardened, Linux-based appliance to provide Horizon customers with the ability to provide secure, remote access to Horizon desktops or applications.

We have learnt what is required and how to deploy and configure a Horizon Access Point, what the limits of an Access Point are, and where the Access Point fits in within the Horizon infrastructure.

We have also discussed what resources are available to assist in troubleshooting a Horizon Access point, and how to obtain that information. We concluded the chapter by discussing the techniques used to update the configuration of a Horizon Access Point, which at the moment is limited to using the platforms REST API.

In the next chapter, we will discuss how to deploy and configure a Horizon Cloud Pod, a feature of Horizon which enables us to create global Horizon entitlements that span multiple Horizon pods.

# 6

# Implementing a Horizon Cloud Pod

This chapter discusses how to enable, configure, and administer a VMware Horizon **Cloud Pod**. The Cloud Pod feature enables Horizon administrators to deploy multi-site, multi-pod View environments that support cross-Horizon pod user entitlements. Additionally, when deployed in a multi-pod configuration Horizon is capable of supporting up to 50,000 client connections, or five times as many as a single Horizon pod. In this chapter, we will review the concepts behind a VMware Horizon Cloud Pod and cover key areas related to the Horizon Cloud Pod functionality.

In this chapter, we will cover the following topics:

- VMware Horizon Cloud Pod overview
- Cloud Pod port requirements and topology limits
- Configuring a Cloud Pod
- Configuring and associating users and groups to Horizon sites
- Creating Global Entitlements for Horizon desktop and application pools
- Updating Global Entitlements
- Determining the effective Horizon site for a user
- Monitoring connections to Cloud Pod Global Entitlements

# Horizon Cloud Pod overview

A VMware Horizon Cloud Pod consists of an integrated set of Horizon pods, which may or may not be located within the same datacenter, and which clients are entitled to, and can, access as if it were a single pod. Prior to the introduction of the Cloud Pod feature, each pod was entitled and accessed separately, which made it difficult to deploy a multi-site Horizon architecture that appeared as a single pod to Horizon clients.

 Cloud Pods are mostly used with floating assignment desktop pools or application pools. If you use dedicated assignment pools, be aware that once a user has been assigned a desktop, they will always return to that desktop for subsequent client connections. This would negate most of the reasons why we use Cloud Pods, which are meant to provide access to Horizon resources across multiple sites or pods, using methods that are transparent to Horizon clients.

In a traditional VMware Horizon implementation, each pod is managed independently. With the Cloud Pod feature you can join together multiple View pods to form a single Horizon implementation called a **Pod Federation**. While the Horizon pools are still managed at the pod level, Cloud Pod entitlements span all member pods, and Horizon clients can access any entitled pool from any member Connection or Security server.

The terms Cloud Pod and Pod Federation will be used somewhat interchangeably in this chapter. You will also encounter this if you review the VMware document **Administering View Cloud Pod Architecture** (`https://www.vmware.com/support/pubs/view_pubs.html`).

A Cloud Pod can span multiple sites and offers the following benefits (among others) over the previous single-Horizon pod model:

- Centralized management of global entitlements to Horizon pools in up to five distinct sites.
- Cloud Pods can balance the Horizon client load across multiple datacenters using centralized rather than individual login portals.
  - While a Cloud Pod aggregates Horizon pools from multiple Pods into a Cloud Pod, Horizon can automatically route client connections to desktop or application pools located at their home site.

- Clients can be entitled to desktop or application pools in up to 25 Horizon pods across five sites. Rather than selecting which pool to use when logging in to the Horizon client, the user is presented with only one pool, and the assignment of resources is handled automatically based on how the global entitlement is configured.
- Using Horizon Cloud Pods, we can enable native **disaster recovery (DR)** for the Horizon infrastructure.

The following figure is an example of a basic Horizon Cloud Pod architecture:

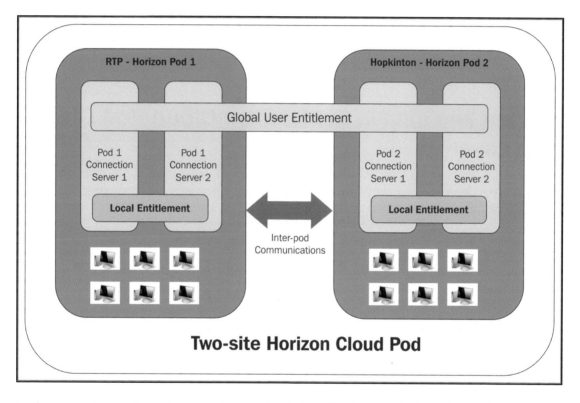

In the example topology, two previously standalone Horizon pods in different data centers are joined together to create a Pod Federation. In a Pod Federation, an end user can connect to a Horizon Connection Server instance in the **Research Triangle Park (RTP)** datacenter and can be assigned a desktop located in a completely different Horizon pod located in the **Hopkinton** datacenter.

When a Horizon client connects, accesses a globally entitled Horizon pool within a Cloud Pod, and connection tunneling is required to maintain that session, the tunnel will be maintained by the Horizon Connection Server, Security Server, or Access Point to which the client originally connected. Using the example provided, this means that a Connection Server, Security Server, or Access Point in Hopkinton could conceivably manage a client session for Horizon pools located in RTP.

By default, Horizon Connection Servers do not tunnel client connections and instead allow direct connections once a Horizon pool is selected. However, some organizations have unique security requirements, and as such enable connection tunneling for internal clients to allow for greater control over how those connections are maintained. Security Servers and Access Points tunnel all Horizon client connections, which are required due to their typical placement within an organizations' DMZ.

# Sharing key data in the Horizon Cloud Pod Global Data Layer

The Horizon Connection Server instances in a Horizon Pod Federation use something called a **Global Data Layer** to share the key data. The data that is shared includes information on the Pod Federation topology, user and group entitlements, Horizon policies, and other information concerning the configuration of the Pod Federation.

In a Horizon Pod Federation, the shared data is replicated between every member in the Horizon Connection Server instance. The entitlement and topology configuration information stored in the Global Data Layer determines where and how desktops are allocated across the Pod Federation.

When the Cloud Pod feature is enabled, or additional pods are added to an existing Pod Federation, the Global Data Layer is configured on each Horizon Connection Server instance.

# Sending messages between Horizon pods

The Horizon Connection Server instances in a Pod Federation communicate using an interpod communications protocol called the **View InterPod API** (**VIPA**).

Horizon Connection Server instances use the VIPA interpod communication channel to launch new desktops or applications, find existing desktops or applications, and share health status data and other information. The VIPA interpod communications channel is configured when the Cloud Pod feature is enabled.

# Cloud Pod port requirements

A Horizon Cloud Pod uses two different network ports to replicate the data and status information. This communication occurs between Horizon Connection Servers located in different sites. The following table details the port numbers and their respective function within the Cloud Pod:

| Port | Service | Description |
|------|---------|-------------|
| 8472 | View Interpod API (VIPA) interpod communication channel | The shared data is replicated to every Horizon Connection Server instance within the Cloud Pod. Each Horizon Connection Server instance in a Cloud Pod runs a second LDAP instance to store this shared data. |
| 22389 | Global data layer LDAP | Horizon Connection Server instances use the VIPA interpod communication channel to launch new desktops, find existing desktops, and share the health status data and other information. |

# Cloud Pod topology limits

The following table details the configuration limits of a Horizon Cloud Pod:

| Component | Limit |
|-----------|-------|
| Client connections (per Cloud Pod) | 50,000 |
| Maximum number of Horizon pods in a Cloud Pod | 25 |
| Maximum number of sites where Cloud Pod member Horizon pods can be located | 5 |
| Maximum number of Horizon Connection Servers supported in a Cloud Pod | 125 |
| Maximum number of desktops per individual Horizon pod | 10,000 |

It is important to note that while a single Horizon pod can contain up to 10,000 desktops, a single Cloud Pod composed of up to ten individual Horizon pods can support no more than 50,000 client connections, even though (if not members of a Cloud Pod) those pods could support up to 100,000 desktops.

A similar restriction exists for Horizon Connection Servers. For example, a single Horizon pod supports up to seven Connection Servers in a five active plus two standby configuration, while a Cloud Pod containing twenty individual Horizon pods supports a maximum of 125 Connection Servers, which is 15 less than is possible based on the limits of each pod.

The configuration maximums of a Horizon Cloud Pod are subject to change as new versions of Horizon are released. Consult the VMware Horizon documentation (`https://www.vmware.com/support/pubs/view_pubs.html`) for current information concerning platform limits.

Admittedly, most readers of this book are not likely to be impacted by the architectural limitations of a Horizon Cloud Pod. Just know that while the feature does expand upon the limits of a single Horizon pod, it doesn't expand them linearly.

# Configuring a Horizon Cloud Pod

A Horizon Cloud Pod is configured using the Horizon View Manager Admin console for each Pod that will be a member. In this section, we will create a Cloud Pod consisting of two Horizon pods.

1. Log on to the Horizon View Manager Admin console of the intended first member of the Cloud Pod using an AD account that has administrative permissions within Horizon.
2. Open the **View Configuration** | **Cloud Pod Architecture** window within the console.
3. Click on the **Initialize the Cloud Pod Architecture** feature link to open the **Initialize** window, as shown in the following screenshot. Click **OK** to proceed, and monitor the status window that will be displayed.

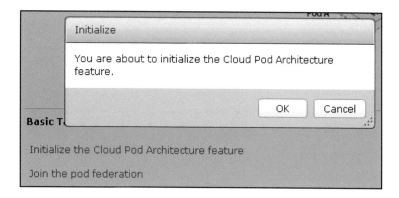

4. When the Cloud Pod feature has finished configuring, click **OK** in the **Reload** window to reload the console and refresh the **View Configuration** | **Cloud Pod Architecture** window, as shown in the following screenshot.

5. Log on to the Horizon View Manager Admin console of the intended second member of the Cloud Pod using an AD account that has administrative permissions within Horizon, and open the **View Configuration** | **Cloud Pod Architecture** window within the console.

6. Click the **Join the Pod Federation** link to open the **Join** window shown in the following screenshot. Provide the details for the Connection Server used in the previous steps, give the user name and password for an account with administrative permissions within Horizon, and then click **OK** to join the Pod Federation. Monitor the status window that will be displayed.

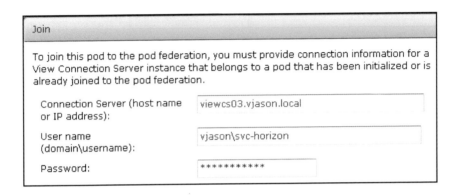

7. When the Cloud Pod feature has finished configuring, click **OK** in the **Reload** window to reload the console and refresh the **View Configuration** | **Cloud Pod Architecture** window, as shown in the following screenshot.

8. Repeat steps 5 through 7 as needed to add additional pods to the Cloud Pod.
9. Once finished, open the Horizon View Manager Admin console **Dashboard** and expand the **Remote Pods** section under **System Health**, as shown in the following screenshot. The status of all other pods in the Cloud Pod will be displayed here to make it easier to quickly identify whether there are issues that require further investigation.

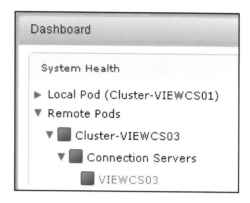

The Horizon Cloud Pod is now configured, although we have not yet defined our Horizon **sites**. Horizon sites allow us to prioritize which Horizon pool a user is directed to, while retaining the ability to use any available resources within the Cloud Pod. The purpose and configuration of Horizon sites is described in the next section.

# Configuring Horizon sites

A Horizon site is used to assign a Horizon pod to a location for the purpose of pinning users to it for Horizon resource prioritization. In many ways it is similar to an Active Directory site, which (among other things) is used to automatically direct users to Active Directory resources in their immediate location.

Sites are most commonly used when your Horizon pods are located in the same physical or geographical location as your user base. For example, if you prefer users in your RTP office to use Horizon pools in that office, rather than the ones in Hopkinton, but in the event of maintenance or downtime in RTP want to retain the ability to use Horizon pools in Hopkinton, you can use a Horizon site.

It is important to note that creating Horizon sites does not by itself alter how users are assigned resources in a Cloud Pod. If and how sites are used is configured within a Horizon **Global Entitlement**, which we will configure in the next section. Additionally, you don't have to use sites with all users. In our example, we are only concerned about users physically located at those two sites, so we will only designate sites for them, and users located at other sites will be connected to Horizon pools at either site.

The example I'm using here is within the US, but feel free to think bigger. Sites are whatever you want them to be: continents, countries, states, cities, and so on. The most common reason for using sites is to not only to prioritize what resources specified clients use first, but also to preserve the capabilities of a Cloud Pod. Take your time, draw your proposed site configuration, and make sure it accomplishes what you are trying to do.

In this section, we will rename the default Horizon site to match one of our locations, create an additional site, and modify our Cloud Pod configuration to assign a Horizon pod to each:

1. Log on to the Horizon View Manager Admin console of any member of the Cloud Pod, using an AD account that has administrative permissions within Horizon.
2. Open the **View Configuration | Sites** window within the console.
3. Under the **Site** column, click on **Default First Site**, and then click the **Edit...** button to open the **Edit Site** window, as shown in the following screenshot. Rename the site as needed (RTP in the example provided), provide an optional description, and click **OK** to return to **Sites** window. Right now, all existing Horizon pods are a member of this site; we will move them as needed after all sites are configured.

4. Click the **Add...** button to open the **Add Site** window. Provide a name for this second site (**Hopkinton** in this case), an optional description, and click **OK** to return to the **Sites** window.

5. Repeat step *4* as needed to add additional sites.

6. Under the Pod column, click on the Horizon pod you wish to associate with the new site you created in step *4* and then click the **Edit...** button to open the **Edit Pod** window, as shown in the following screenshot. Click on the **Site** drop-down menu, then click on the site the Horizon pod should be associated with, and then click **OK** to return to the **Sites** window.

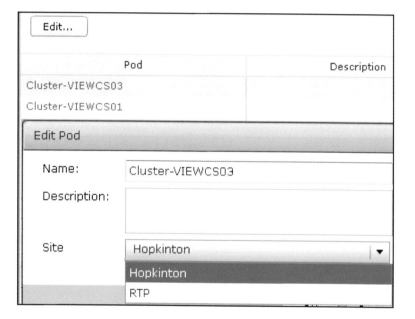

By default, Horizon pods are named for the first Connection Server that was installed, in the format `Cluster-VIEWCSNAME`. The name of the pod is not visible to Horizon clients, and is typically only seen when working with Cloud Pods.

7. Repeat step 6 as needed to associate any additional Horizon pods with their associated sites.

8. Verify when finished that the **Sites** window shows each site required, and that each displays the correct number of associated pods, as shown in the following screenshot. You can click on a site to display which pods are associated with it; in the example provided, the **Hopkinton** site is associated with the **Cluster-VIEWCS03** pod.

The Horizon sites are now configured, although we have not yet assigned users to their associated sites. The process used to assign Horizon sites is described in the next section.

# Associating users with Horizon sites

In the previous section, we created and configured our Horizon sites, but until we associate users with them they have no impact on how client sessions are distributed to the Horizon pools in our Cloud Pod. Our goal is to use Horizon site assignments to ensure that clients use locally hosted resources first, but will still be able to use resources in the other datacenters if the local one is at capacity or otherwise unavailable.

In the example provided we have created AD security groups for the RTP and Hopkinton offices, and populated each with the accounts of the users who work in those offices. The following steps detail how to associate those security groups with their appropriate Horizon site:

1. Log on to the Horizon View Manager Admin console of any member of the Cloud Pod using an AD account that has administrative permissions within Horizon.
2. Click on **Users and Groups** under **Inventory**, and then click on the **Home Site** tab.
3. Click the **Add...** button to open the **Add Home Site** window, as shown in the following screenshot. Use the **Name** field to search for the AD security group you will associate with a site (`Horizon_Homesite_Hop` in the example provided), click the **Find** button, click on the group in the **Name** column, and click **Next** to continue.

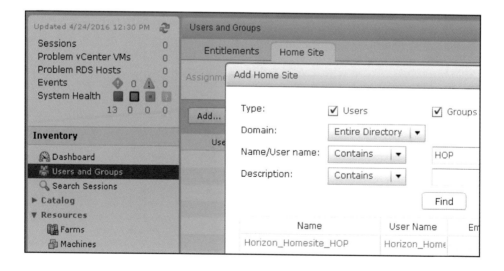

You can also add individual users to a site, but I prefer security groups as most organizations already have existing location-based security groups. By using those groups here, it ensures that users will automatically be added to those groups as needed, although if not, you can still add them individually here.

4. Click on the **Home Site** drop down menu, select the Horizon site to associate the AD group with (**Hopkinton** in the example provided), as shown in the following screenshot, and then click **Finish**.

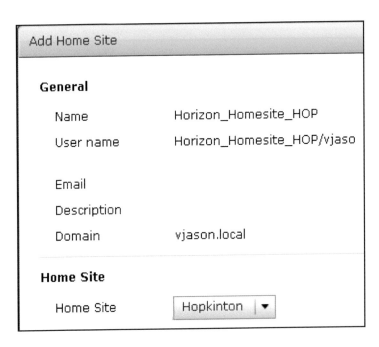

5. Repeat steps 3 and 4 as needed to associate AD security groups with other sites, or additional groups with the same site.

6. From the **Users and Groups** window | **Home Site** tab shown in the following screenshot, verify that all required AD security groups or individual users have been associated with the desired Horizon site.

The AD security groups are now associated with Horizon sites. In the next section, we will create Horizon Global Entitlements, and see what option we must configure in order to ensure that our site assignments are used.

# Creating Cloud Pod Global Entitlements

A Global Entitlement is unique to Horizon Cloud Pods, and is what we create in order to grant access to Horizon pools in two or more standalone pods. The process is somewhat similar to creating a Horizon pool, in that you specific some policy settings, but no actual pool is created as part of the process. You must create your Horizon pools individually in each pod that is a member of the Cloud Pod.

You do not specify the target Horizon pools when creating the Global Entitlement, only after, so it is not explicitly required to create them prior to creating the entitlement itself. For the examples provided in this section, we have already created both a desktop and application pool in each Cloud Pod member, and we will walk though creating and configuring a global entitlement for each.

From an end-user perspective, a Global Entitlement appears as a desktop or application pool within the Horizon client. Owing to this, you should not individually entitle desktop or application pools within the standalone pods to users who will also be added to the Global Entitlement, as it would enable them to see and directly access those individual pools in the Horizon client, when we only want them to use the Global Entitlement. You are only required to entitle users to the Global Entitlement, and Horizon will automatically grant users the required access to the destination pool. This entitlement process is transparent; you will not notice any changes to the list of entitled users to the destination pools of the Cloud Pod members.

# Create and configure a Global Entitlement for a Horizon desktop pool

The following steps detail how to create and configure a Global Entitlement for a Horizon desktop pool. The creation of the pools themselves will not be shown, only those steps required to create and configure the entitlement.

1. Log on to the Horizon View Manager Admin console of any member of the Cloud Pod, using an AD account that has administrative permissions within Horizon.
2. Open the **Catalog | Global Entitlements** window within the console. This window is only available if the Cloud Pod feature has been enabled in the pod.
3. In the **Type** tab, click the **Add...** button to open the **Add Global Entitlement** window, as seen in the following screenshot. We are creating a **Desktop Entitlement** in this section, so accept the default options and click **Next** to continue.

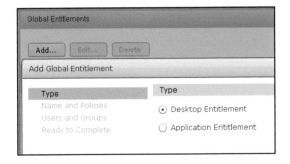

4. In the **Names and Policies** tab, provide a **Name** for the Global Entitlement, select any options as required, and click **Next** to continue. In the example provided, we have selected **Floating** user assignment, specified a **Scope** of **Within site** to ensure that users who do not have an assigned Horizon site access desktops in a pod local to their client connection if possible, selected **Use Home Site** to ensure that users with an assigned site use their local desktop pool if possible, instructed Horizon to **Automatically clean up redundant sessions** so clients do not have to prior to logging in, and clicked the **Allow users to reset their machines** and **HTML Access** checkboxes to enable those options. Review the descriptions of each option on the right side of the window as needed, and note that most can be changed later on if needed.

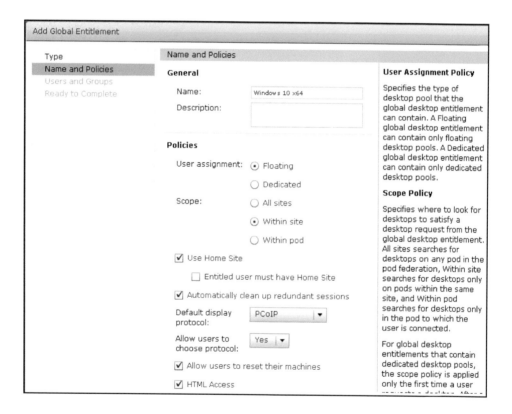

You will only be able to use Horizon pools with the Global Entitlement if you have the same settings as are configured here. For example, a dedicated assignment pool cannot be added to a floating assignment Global Entitlement. If clients experience errors logging in once the Global Entitlement is created, check the Horizon event logs to see if a mismatch in pool and Global Entitlement settings is the reason.

5. In the **Users and Groups** tab, use the **Add...** button to add users or security groups to the Global Entitlement, as shown in the following screenshot, and click **Next** to continue. This process is identical to that used to entitle Horizon pools.

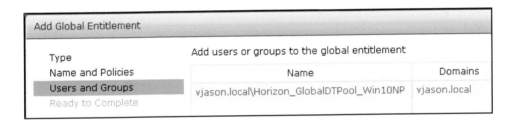

6. In the **Ready to Complete** tab, review the Global Entitlement settings, make any changes if needed using the **Back** button, and then click **Finish** to return to the **Catalog – Global Entitlements** window, as shown in the following screenshot. Note that at this time, we have not yet associated any Horizon pools with the entitlement; additional steps are required for this.

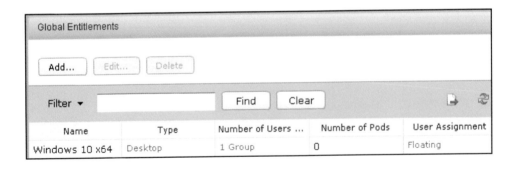

You can also use this screen to delete Global Entitlements; simply click on the one you wish to delete and then click **Delete**.

7. Double-click on the Global Entitlement we just created, click the **Local Pools** tab, and click the **Add...** button to open the **Assign Pools** window as shown in the following screenshot:

 Only those pools which meet the requirements of the Global Entitlement will be shown. If no pools are available that meet the requirement, a popup will appear explaining this restriction.

8. Click on the desktop pool you wish to add to the Global Entitlement and then click **Add** to return to the **Local Pools** tab, as shown in the following screenshot. Note that only those pools in the Horizon pod you are logged in to will be shown.

9. Repeat steps *7* and *8* using the Horizon View Manager Admin console of each member of the Cloud Pod that has pools you wish to grant the Global Entitlement.

The Horizon desktop Global Entitlement has now been created and configured, and entitled users will now be able to log in and access the target resources. The following screenshot shows what a Horizon client will see, which, as indicated earlier, looks no different than a pool hosted in a standalone Horizon pod. The screenshot also shows a Global Entitlement for a Horizon application pool, which we will create in the next section.

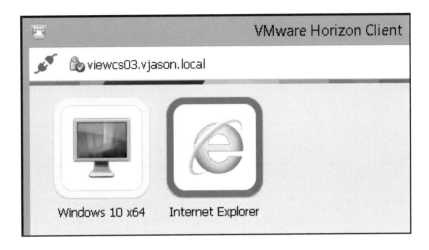

# Create and configure a Global Entitlement for a Horizon application pool

The following steps detail how to create and configure a Global Entitlement for a Horizon application pool. The creation of the pools themselves will not be shown, only those steps required to create and configure the entitlement. All but one step of this differs from the procedure used to create a Global Entitlement for a desktop pool, so fewer screenshots will be shown:

1. Log on to the Horizon View Manager Admin console of any member of the Cloud Pod, using an AD account that has administrative permissions within Horizon.
2. Open the **Catalog – Global Entitlements** window within the console.
3. In the **Type** tab, click the **Add…** button to open the **Add Global Entitlement** window. Click the **Application Entitlement** radio check box, and click **Next** to continue.

4. In the **Names and Policies** tab, provide a **Name** for the Global Entitlement, select any options as required, and click **Next** to continue. In this example, where applicable, we used the same settings as the desktop Global Entitlement created in the previous section. Review the descriptions of each option on the right side of the window as needed.

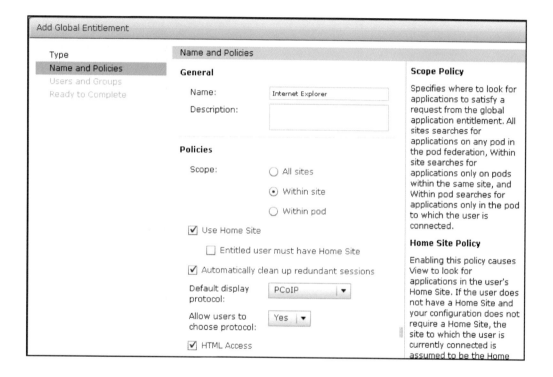

5. In the **Users and Groups** tab, use the **Add...** button to add users or security groups to the Global Entitlement, and click **Next** to continue.
6. In the **Ready to Complete** tab, review the Global Entitlement settings, make any changes needed using the **Back** button, and then click **Finish** to return to the **Catalog – Global Entitlements** window.

7. Double-click on the Global Entitlement we just created, click the **Local Pools** tab, and click the **Add...** button to open the **Assign Pools** window, as shown in the following screenshot:

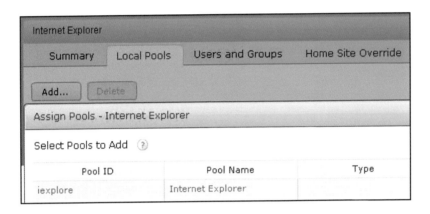

8. Click on the application pool you wish to add to the Global Entitlement and then click **Add** to return to the **Local Pools** tab.
9. Repeat steps *7* and *8* using the Horizon View Manager Admin console of each member of the Cloud Pod that has pools you wish to the Global Entitlement.

The Horizon application Global Entitlement has now been created and configured, and entitled users will now be able to log in and access the target resources.

# Removing a Horizon pod from a Cloud Pod

The following steps outline how to remove a Horizon pod from a Pod Federation, and disable the Cloud Pod Architecture feature. You do not need to delete the individual pods' desktop or application pools as part of this, but you will need to remove them from any Global Entitlements they are part of.

1. Log on to the Horizon View Manager Admin console of the Horizon pod you wish to remove from the Cloud Pod.
2. Remove any desktop or application pools managed by this pod from the Global Entitlements; this is accomplished using the screen displayed in step *6* of the *Create and configure a Global Entitlement* sections of this chapter; simply click on the pool to remove and click **Delete** (this does not delete the pool itself, it simply removes it from the Global Entitlement).

3. Open the **View Configuration | Cloud Pod Architecture** window within the console.

4. In the **Pod Federation** pane, click **Unjoin...**, click **OK** when prompted, and click **OK** again when promoted to reload the Horizon View Manager Admin console.

> This step is only performed if there are currently two or more members of the Cloud Pod.

5. In the **Pod Federation** pane, click **Uninitialize...**, click **OK** when prompted, and click **OK** again when prompted to reload the Horizon View Manager Admin console.

> To complete, remove the Cloud Pod, and repeat steps 1 through 5 on all Pods in the Cloud Pod until only one pod remains. For the final pod in the Cloud Pod, omit step 4 but perform all remaining steps.

The pod is now operating as a stand-alone Horizon pod, and the Cloud Pod feature and associated components have been disabled or removed as needed. The remaining members of the Cloud Pod will continue to function as before, even if only one pod remains in the Pod Federation.

# Updating the settings of a Global Entitlement

Global Entitlements can be edited once created, much like desktop and application pools. Like desktop and application pools, some settings, such as the user assignment method cannot be changed without deleting and recreating the object in question.

The following Global Entitlement settings may be edited after deployment:

- General settings, as seen in step 4 of the sections where we created a Global Entitlement (excluding those which cannot be changed)
- Local pools which are members of the Global Entitlement, although remember that these changes must be made from the pod where the pool is hosted

- Users and groups who are entitled to use the pool
- **Home Site Overrides**, which allow us to set explicit overrides to any home site assignments:
    - The uses for a Home Site Override vary, but one example would be an employee who lives in one area, but for performance reasons prefers using applications or desktops in another.
    - You create a Home Site Override by identifying a user or group, and by then selecting a side you wish to explicitly designate as a home site. For example, in the following screenshot we configured the listed user to explicitly use the **Hopkinton** as their home site.

# Editing the general settings of a Global Entitlement

To edit a Global Entitlement, open the **Catalog – Global Entitlements** window in the Horizon View Manager Admin console, double-click on the Global Entitlement you wish to edit, and click the **Edit** button shown in the following screenshot to open the **Edit Global Entitlement** window:

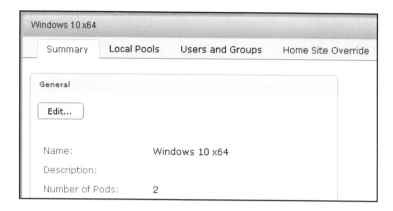

Using the **Edit Global Entitlement** window shown in the following screenshot, we can edit most of the settings we first saw when initially creating the Global Entitlement.

Make changes as needed, and then click **OK** save the updated Global Entitlement.

# Determining the effective home site of a user or security group

While the concept of a Horizon home site is easy enough to understand, owing to home site overrides and the fact that it is possible that a user can be assigned to multiple home sites at once, it is important to have a way to determine what the effective home site should be for a given user. We will use the Horizon home site resolution tool to determine the effective home sites for a user with the following characteristics:

- Member of **Horizon_Homesite_HOP** security group, which is assigned to the **Hopkinton** home site.
- The user account directly assigned to the **Hopkinton** home site (this is in addition to being a member of a security group that is assigned to the home site).
- Home site override in place of the **Windows 10 x64** Global Entitlement that associates the user with the **RTP** home site.

The following steps outline how to use the Horizon home site resolution tool to identify which home site the user will be assigned in this case:

1. Log on to the Horizon View Manager Admin console of any member of the Cloud Pod using an AD account that has administrative permissions within Horizon.
2. Click on **Users and Groups** under **Inventory**, then click the **Home Site** tab, and finally click **Resolution,** as shown in the following screenshot:

3. Click on the field to the left of the **Look Up** button to open the **Find User** window. This window is similar to the one used to find users during the entitlement process, but in this case it can only find individual users and not security groups. Use the window to find the user you wish to investigate, and then click **OK** to return to the **Home Site** tab, as shown in the following screenshot:

4. Click on the **Look Up** button to begin the resolution process; when it has finished, the **Home Site** tab will display the results, as shown in the following screenshot. When a user is assigned to a home site more than once, or is subject to a home site override (in this case both), a triangle will be displayed to the left of the Global Entitlement name. Click on the triangle to expand the results and see all home site assignments that the user was subject to. The effective home site will be displayed at the top of each list, and any others crossed out.

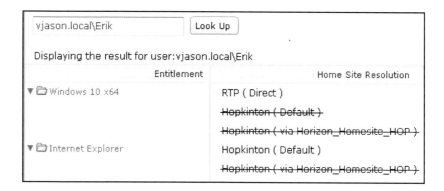

In this case we can see that the **RTP** home site override of the **Windows 10 x64** Global Entitlement has precedence over all other home site assignments. Additionally, the direct assignment of the user account (identified as **Default**) had precedence over the inherited assignment due to being a member of the **Horizon_Homesite_HOP** security group.

# Monitoring Global Entitlement Horizon client sessions

Monitoring a Horizon client session to a Global Entitlement requires a slightly different approach, due to the fact that one Horizon pod could be brokering a connection for desktops in another. Consider the following scenario:

*A user with RTP home site assignment connects to Horizon pod in Hopkinton, and is connected to a desktop in the RTP pod.*

If you reviewed the **Monitoring – Sessions** window in the **RTP** pod, you might expect to see the connection to the desktop. This is not how it works in a Cloud Pod; the session data is maintained by the pod the user initially connected to, not the one where their desktop is hosted (we are assuming they are different for this example). Additionally, the **Monitoring – Sessions** window is not Cloud Pod–aware; unless you know where Horizon pools were actually located you wouldn't know what Horizon pod a user is actually using for their desktop session.

The following screenshot was taken from the **Hopkinton** pod, but the user is connected to a desktop in the **RTP** pod. While the **Pool or Farm** or **DNS Name** identifies the actual location of the desktop the client is using, that is only because I integrated the site name into those values when creating the desktop pools. If I hadn't done that, I might not know the actual location of the desktop the user is connected to. As stated previously, the **Sessions** window in the **RTP** pod will not have any information about this connection.

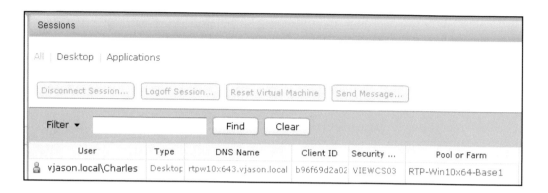

 This is a good time to remind you that it is a good idea to build these types of identifying characteristics into your Horizon pools and desktop or RDS server names, even if you aren't deploying a Cloud Pod.

The following steps outline how to view the full details of a Horizon client session on a Cloud pod:

1. Log on to the Horizon View Manager Admin console of any member of the Cloud Pod using an AD account that has administrative permissions within Horizon.

2. Click on **Search Sessions** under **Inventory** within the console, and then use the left drop-down menu to select **Brokering Pod,** as seen in the following screenshot. Click on the right drop-down menu to select the Horizon pod that is brokering the connections you wish to investigate.

3. Click **Search** to display a list of connections the selected pod is brokering connections for as seen in the following screenshot. Note that this screen is similar to the **Monitoring – Sessions** window, but adds columns for **Brokering Pod**, **Pod**, and **Site** which allows us to easily identify the pod the user is connected to, the pod that contains the resources they are using, and their assigned site. Click on the client session if you wish to perform any of the available actions displayed on the screenshot.

# Summary

In this chapter, we were introduced to Horizon Cloud Pods. We learned how to create a Cloud Pod, which enabled us to create a Cloud Pod Global Entitlement to entitle clients to pools in multiple Horizon pods at once, and allows those clients to log in to any Pod in the Cloud Pod and access the same Horizon pools (without having to know where those pools are).

We discussed the specifics of how a Cloud Pod works, and what the configuration maximums are. We then went through how to enable the Cloud Pod feature, which creates a Pod Federation, at which point we reviewed this to create a Global Entitlement.

We then learned how to use Horizon home sites to control how Horizon assigns desktops, which allows us to leverage a global desktop pool while still favoring specific desktop pools when possible. We finished by reviewing how we administer our Cloud Pod, including the various objects it contains, which is important should we need to modify settings after the initial configuration is complete.

In the next chapter, we will review how to configure **VMware Virtual SAN (VSAN)** to provide storage for our Horizon desktops and Windows RDS servers, as well as the additional configuration options that must be selected when using Horizon pools that use VSAN as the storage target.

# 7
# Using VMware Virtual SAN with Horizon

In this chapter, we will cover the following topics:

- Sizing a Horizon environment for VMware Virtual SAN (VSAN)
- Enabling VMware Virtual VSAN
- Using VSAN with VMware Horizon

## Introduction

VMware **Virtual SAN** (**VSAN**) is a component of VMware vSphere which enables the use of local storage devices on ESXi servers to create a high-performing, replicated, software-defined storage platform that can be used to store Horizon desktop virtual machines. VSAN is included with Horizon Advanced and Enterprise licenses, but may also be purchased as part of vSphere for organizations who wish to use it with non-Horizon ESXi servers.

VSAN is tightly integrated with the vSphere ESXi hypervisor, vCenter Server, and many other VMware products, while requiring minimal ESXi servers overhead. Additionally, VSAN features as a simplified management interface that is integrated with the vSphere Web Client, and offers detailed storage policies that can be applied at the individual **Virtual Machine Disk** (**VMDK**) level.

In this chapter, we will review how to size our Horizon ESXi servers for use with VMware VSAN, understand what resources are available for building VSAN-compatible hosts, walk through the process of enabling VSAN, and review how to use VSAN when creating a VMware Horizon desktop pool.

VMware and EMC have partnered to create the **VxRail** (http://www.vce
.com/products/hyper-converged/vxrail) platform that integrates
vSphere, VSAN, and a purpose-built hardware platform to create a
hyper-converged infrastructure appliance that also includes centralized
management, deduplication, and compression (referred to as **data
efficiency**), **erasure coding** enabled using either RAID-5 and **RAID-6** for
more efficient data protection, **Quality of Service (QoS)**, **stretched
clusters** to span VSAN across multiple datacenters, replication, backup,
and cloud tiering capabilities.

Organizations that are looking to upgrade or implement a vSphere-based
virtualization infrastructure, and who are also considering using VSAN as
their storage platform, might find that a VxRail solution is the ideal
method for rapidly deploying a new Horizon infrastructure.

# Common VMware Virtual SAN terms

The following terms will be used throughout this chapter when discussing VSAN:

- **Components**: This term is used to refer to the virtual machine data files once they
  have been written to a VSAN datastore. The components include the virtual
  machine files, any replicas as defined by the vSphere VSAN SPBM, witness
  components, and metadata. Understanding the number of components required
  is important, as this impacts on the number of vSphere VSAN hosts that are
  required.

- **Data efficiency**: A term used by VMware to refer to the deduplication and
  compression features introduced in version 6.2.

- **Datastore**: A VSAN datastore is similar in appearance to a traditional vSphere
  datastore, but is created using VSAN disk groups rather than local or remote
  storage devices.

- **Disk group**: This is a collection of magnetic hard disks and a flash-based storage
  device within a VSAN cluster.

- **Network**: VSAN uses a vSphere **VMkernel** network adapter to replicate data
  between hosts in the VSAN cluster.

- **Objects**: These are the files that make up a virtual machine; when written to a
  VSAN datastore, these objects comprise multiple components.

- **Storage Policy-Based Management (SPBM)**: This is a component of the vSphere
  VSAN that is applied to individual virtual machine hard disks and influences
  how that data is written, replicated, cached, and striped within the VSAN cluster.
  SPBM provides a framework for all policies related to VSAN.

# Sizing a Horizon environment for Virtual SAN

In this section, we will explore how to properly size our VMware ESXi servers so that they can accommodate VSAN in addition to the Horizon desktops. This section assumes that you are already aware of the storage, networking, and CPU requirements of the Horizon desktops themselves and are only looking to add VSAN as your virtual desktop storage platform.

In this chapter, we will focus on VSAN designs that use a combination of flash and magnetic disks. VSAN 6.2 introduced deduplication and compression capabilities for all-flash VSAN configurations, new monitoring dashboards, and other features. While the price of flash storage continues to drop at a steady rate, it is not yet at a point where it has become the default option for all Horizon deployments.

## ESXi Server CPU requirements

Prior to determining vSphere's host, disk, or flash-based storage requirements, we must first ensure that our hosts have sufficient CPU resources available. VMware recommends that 10 percent of the ESXi server CPU capacity be set aside for VSAN, which is to say that, when determining the number of Horizon desktops, the ESXi server will accommodate and reduce that figure by 10 percent in order to ensure that VSAN will not have to contend with the desktops for ESXi server CPU resources.

The following VMware documents provide additional information on VSAN's sizing, design, and features:

- *VMware Virtual SAN documentation* (https://www.vmware.com/support/pubs/virtual-san-pubs.html)
- *VMware Virtual SAN 6.2 Datasheet* (http://www.vmware.com/files/pdf/products/vsan/VMware_Virtual_SAN_Datasheet.pdf)
- *VMware Virtual SAN 6.2 Space Efficiency Technologies* (http://www.vmware.com/files/pdf/products/vsan/vmware-vsan-62-space-efficiency-technologies.pdf)

# VSAN disk requirements

In this section, we will go over how to determine the number and capacity of magnetic and flash-based storage devices required to support our Horizon infrastructure, as well as the number of ESXi servers our VSAN cluster will require.

# Determining the total number of ESXi server disks required

The following are the sizing recommendations based on the type of Horizon pool deployed in a Virtual SAN cluster.

## Magnetic disk capacity sizing

The recommended total capacity of all magnetic disks in the VSAN cluster should be at least 130 percent of the total size of data to be stored, which will ensure that approximately 30 percent of free space is available for future growth. The following are recommendations concerning the number of magnetic disks that should be used once you have determined the overall capacity required:

- **Linked clone virtual desktops**: It is recommended that you have at least three 10K or 15K RPM SAS disks within each VSAN disk group
- **Dedicated full clone virtual desktops**: It is recommended that you have at least four 10K RPM SAS or 7.2K RPM NL-SAS disks within each VSAN disk group
- **VSAN disk groups**: Create additional VSAN disk groups to scale performance or for capacity reasons

## Flash capacity sizing

In a VSAN cluster that uses a combination of flash and magnetic disks, flash-based storage devices are used as a read/write cache and are not part of the overall VSAN cluster storage capacity.

 All-flash VSAN configurations use dedicated flash disks for a cache, although, in their case, that cache is only used for writes. For VSAN configurations that include magnetic disks, 30 percent of each flash-based storage device in the VSAN cluster is used as a write-back buffer. VSAN also uses 0.4 percent of the ESXi server RAM, up to 1 GB, as an additional cache.

All writes from virtual machines to VSAN datastores are written first to the local flash-based storage device, and later written to the remaining disks for long-term storage. Additionally, based on vSphere's VSAN SPBM settings, these writes are replicated to other flash-based storage devices in the cluster in order to ensure availability in the event of a failure. The data replication settings are discussed later on in the *Number of Failures to Tolerate* section of this chapter.

For VSAN configurations that include magnetic disks, VSAN uses the remaining 70 percent of each flash-based storage device as a read cache. Since the VSAN read cache will only contain blocks of data that are already present in the magnetic disks in the cluster, which means that it is already protected in the event of a failure, the data contained within the flash-based read cache is not replicated between hosts. This has the added benefit of maximizing the amount of flash-based storage available for use as a VSAN read cache.

VMware recommends that, for all desktop pool types, when using magnetic disks with VSAN, the amount of flash-based storage used in the cluster is at least 10 percent of the projected virtual machine storage requirements. The additional 30 percent of storage added to support future virtual machine storage requirements does not need to be considered as part of this calculation. Additionally, we must account for the additional space required for the replicas that VSAN uses in order to provide data protection, as well as the 100 percent space reservation used with full clone desktops and linked clone persistent data disks, as both of these influence the actual amount of space the desktops will require.

 10 percent of flash-based storage is just the minimum required by VMware and might not be applicable in all cases. If it is later determined that additional flash-based storage is required and your ESXi server has sufficient capacity, you can add it to VSAN at a later date by creating a new VSAN disk group. The VMware VSAN documentation (`https://www.vmware.com/support/pubs/virtual-san-pubs.html`) demonstrates the procedure for adding additional storage to a VSAN cluster.

# Sample VSAN storage sizing exercise

The following table shows us the amount of storage required for two different Horizon desktop configurations, including the additional amount of magnetic storage required to support the indicated replicas of the VSAN data. The virtual desktop storage requirements have already been adjusted so that they reflect the total space that will be reserved by VSAN when they are configured:

| Item | Dedicated full clone example | Dedicated linked clone with persistent data disk example |
|---|---|---|
| Virtual desktop storage requirements | 32GB | 7GB |
| Number of virtual desktops | 750 | 1,500 |
| Base amount of space required to store virtual desktops | 24,000GB (approximately 24TB) | 10,500GB (approximately 10.5TB) |
| Additional space added for future growth | 30 percent | 30 percent |
| Base amount of space required to store virtual desktops (with additional space for future growth) | 31,200GB (approximately 31.2TB) | 13,650GB (approximately 13.65TB) |
| Target flash-based storage capacity | 10 percent | 10 percent |
| Number of additional replicas | 2 | 1 |
| Total flash-based storage required in the VSAN cluster | 2,400GB (approximately 2.4TB) | 525MB |
| Total magnetic storage required in the VSAN cluster (includes 30 percent additional capacity for future growth) | 93,600GB (approximately 93.6TB) | 13,650GB (approximately 13.65TB) |

In the examples provided, the total magnetic storage required was determined using the following calculation:

- The base amount of space required to store virtual desktops is 1.3 times the number of replicas
- 3 represents the addition of 30 percent more space to the base figure that supports future storage growth

# Calculating the total number of VSAN objects required

VMware VSAN supports a maximum of 9,000 components per host; this is important as the desktop pool configuration impacts the number of objects that are required, which might influence the number of ESXi servers our cluster must contain.

The information contained in the following two tables was obtained from the **VMware Virtual SAN Design and Sizing Guide** (`http://www.vmware.com/files/pdf/product s/vsan/virtual-san-6.2-design-and-sizing-guide.pdf`), and shows us the different objects created for each VMware Horizon desktop type; the final line of the table shows us the number of each object created. Using these values, we can determine the number of VSAN components that will be required after taking into account the creation of VSAN witnesses and replicas:

| Virtual machine object | Dedicated linked clone with disposable data disk | Floating linked clone with disposable data disk | Floating linked clone | Floating full clone | Dedicated full clone |
|---|---|---|---|---|---|
| Namespace | Required for all Horizon virtual desktops | | | | |
| VMDK | | | | | |
| Swap | | | | | |
| Snapshot | Required for all Horizon linked clone virtual desktops | | | Not applicable | |
| Internal | | | | | |
| Disposable | Required | Required | Not applicable | | |
| Persistent | Required | Not applicable | Not applicable | | |
| Total number of objects per desktop | 7 | 6 | 5 | 3 | 3 |

The right-most column of the following table shows the number of VSAN components that are created for each desktop type, based on the default Horizon VSAN SPBM policies.

| User Assignment Method | Horizon desktop type | Will a desktop disposable data disk be used? | Number of objects per desktop VM | Total number of components per desktop VM with VSAN |
|---|---|---|---|---|
| Floating | Linked clone | No | 5 | 9 replica disks<br>9 per desktop VM |
| | | Yes | 6 | 9 replica disks<br>10 per desktop VM |
| Dedicated | | Yes | 7 | 9 replica disks<br>21 per desktop VM |
| Floating | Full clone | Not applicable | 3 | 7 per desktop VM |
| Dedicated | | Not applicable | 3 | 9 per desktop VM |

The values in the *Total number of VSAN components* row were reached using the following calculations:

- A dedicated full clone example is *750 * 4 = 3,000*
- A dedicated linked clone with persistent data disk example is *(1,500 * 21) + 9 = 31,509*

Based on these results, we see that, while a single ESXi server can host the number of VSAN components required for the proposed number of desktops, owing to the number of components required for the linked clone configuration, we will require at least 11 ESXi servers in our VSAN cluster in order to host these 1,500 desktops.

 Since VSAN requires at least two ESXi servers in a cluster, the full clone configuration will require at least that many hosts even if they aren't required, based on the number of VSAN components the desktops require.

The following limits are strictly related to VSAN clusters as a whole, but by extension, they impact how they can be used with VMware Horizon:

- The maximum number of ESXi servers in a VSAN cluster is *64*
- The maximum number of disks supported in a VSAN host is *35* in the capacity layer (five disk groups of seven disks each) and five for the cache layer
- The maximum number of virtual machines hosted on a VSAN cluster is *6,400*

Note that vSphere HA supports a maximum of *2,048* virtual machines per cluster, although this feature is not typically used with Horizon desktops.

The following table outlines various limits related to the VSAN disk groups, magnetic disks and flash-based storage devices, and the overhead related to the disk-formatting method used by VSAN:

| Object | Minimum | Maximum |
|---|---|---|
| VSAN disk group (per vSphere VSAN host) | 1 | 5 |
| Flash-based storage devices per VSAN disk group (for hybrid configurations) | 1 | |
| Magnetic disks per VSAN disk group | 1 | 7 |
| Disk formatting overhead (VMware VSAN-FS file system) per disk | 1% of capacity plus deduplication metadata (if enabled) | |

While not typically an issue with ESXi servers that are used with VMware Horizon, a minimum of 32 GB of RAM is required in an ESXi server that will support the upper limits of the VSAN platform, be it the number of disk groups, the number of supported magnetic disks, or a combination of both of those items.

# Virtual SAN and the vSphere VSAN SPBM framework

VMware VSAN uses the vSphere VSAN SPBM framework to control how Horizon desktops utilize VSAN storage resources. When a Horizon desktop pool is created on a VSAN datastore, a set of default policies is created based on the recommended VMware guidelines. The policies shown in the following screenshot can be viewed by clicking on the VM Storage Policies icon on the vSphere Web Client home page. Note that these policies will not be created until after you provision a Horizon desktop pool that uses VSAN as a storage target.

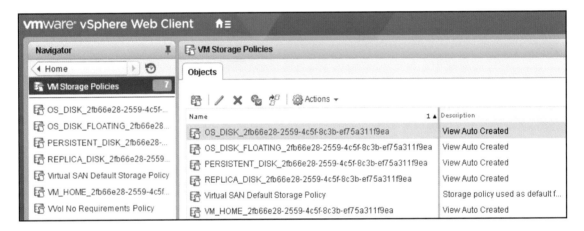

In this figure, we see a number of different policies that were created for both floating and dedicated assignment linked clone desktop pools. The policies are applied automatically to each individual Horizon desktop when it is created, and they are applied directly to the desktop virtual hard disk to which they apply. Policies were created for the desktop OS disk (for persistent desktops), OS floating disk (for floating assignment desktops), desktop replica disk, persistent data disk, and the VM home disk that contains desktop configuration data. The **Virtual SAN Default Storage Policy** is also shown; it is used for virtual machines not provisioned by Horizon that are located on VSAN datastores.

To review or edit these policies, right-click on one of them under the **Objects** window and select **Edit VM Storage Policy** to open the **Edit VM Storage Policy** window. For the default Horizon vSphere VSAN SPBM policies, the policy values are displayed in the **Rule-Set 1** tab, as shown in the following screenshot.

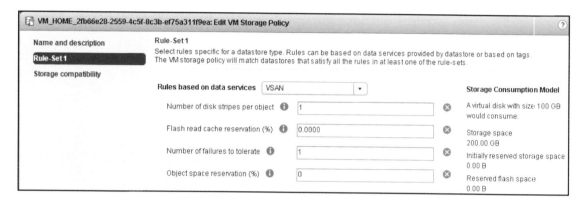

In this section, we will review the default Horizon vSphere VSAN SPBM policies, their impact on VSAN storage utilization, and the default SPBM policies that Horizon creates when configuring desktop pools.

 For additional information on vSphere VSAN SPBM policies, consult the VMware Virtual SAN documentation referenced earlier in this chapter.

# Number of disk stripes per object

VSAN's **number of disk stripes per object** is the number of disks in a VSAN cluster across which each replica of a VSAN storage object will be distributed. Horizon configures the recommended value of 1 for all desktop pool configurations.

# Flash read cache reservation (%)

VSAN's **flash read cache reservation** (%) is the percentage of flash capacity reserved as the read cache for a VSAN storage object, specified as a percentage of the logical size of the object. When configuring linked clone desktop pools, Horizon configures the recommended value of 10 percent for the desktop replica disk object, as this will serve the majority of the read I/O for the pool. All other linked clone and full clone disk objects are set to the recommended value of 0 percent.

# Number of Failures to Tolerate

This vSphere VSAN SPBM **Number of Failures to Tolerate (FTT)** policy defines the number of ESXi servers, disks, or network failures a VSAN storage object can tolerate. The policy states that, for n failures tolerated, *n+1* copies of the object are created, and *2n+1* ESXi servers that contribute storage for VSAN are required.

For example, a VSAN cluster requires a minimum of three ESXi servers with sufficient storage resources. Based on the 2n+1 calculation provided in this section, this configuration will support an FTT policy of either 1 (the default) or 0. If the FTT policy was increased to 2, a minimum of five ESXi servers, as well as the storage required to write an additional copy of each desktop object on the cluster, will be required.

An FTT value of 0 can conceivably be used for the desktop OS virtual hard disks in a linked clone-floating assignment or full clone non-persistent desktop pools. Under these scenarios, if the VSAN cluster experiences the failure of the ESXi server, only the non-persistent data disks will be lost; they should not contain any data of value. However, ensure that additional Horizon desktops are available for the affected clients while the ESXi server or VSAN is being repaired.

The FTT policy has the greatest impact on the capacity of a VSAN cluster owing to, in part, the 3,000 VSAN component limit per ESXi server, as well as the additional storage required for higher policy values. Higher FTT values can increase the storage required by each virtual desktop by up to a factor of four, which is why it is important to consider any changes to the policy beyond the Horizon default of 1.

# Object space reservation (%)

VSAN's **object space reservation** (%) is the percentage of the logical size of the virtual machine storage object that will be reserved using thick provisioning when it is created. The remainder of the virtual machine storage object will be thin provisioned. Horizon configures the following VSAN object space reservation policies by default:

- The linked clone desktop persistent data disks are 100 percent
- The full clone desktop disks are 100 percent
- The linked clone desktop disks (other than the user-persistent data disks) are zero percent

Object space reservation for the Horizon linked clone desktop persistent data disks and full clone desktop disk VSAN components is set to 100 percent by default, in order to ensure that they are evenly balanced across the VSAN cluster when they are deployed. This placement ensures that, as Horizon's desktop storage capacity utilization increases over time, the VSAN datastore is more likely to provide consistent levels of performance.

# VMware Virtual SAN configuration overview

In this section, we will review the procedure used to enable VMware VSAN.

This procedure is only required if you are deploying VSAN on existing server hardware; products such as VxRail are shipped with VSAN already enabled.

To ensure that the VSAN configuration is supported by VMware, it must either be built using hardware that is validated by VMware or selected from a list of validated VMware Virtual San Ready Nodes. The following resources can assist in selecting hardware that is known to be supported by VMware VSAN:

- *VMware Virtual SAN Compatibility Guide* (`https://www.vmware.com/resources/compatibility/pdf/vi_vsan_rn_guide.pdf`)
- *VMware Compatibility Guide* (`http://www.vmware.com/resources/compatibility/search.php?deviceCategory=vsan`)
- *Virtual SAN Hardware Quick Reference Guide* (`http://partnerweb.vmware.com/programs/vsan/Virtual_SAN_Hardware_Quick_Start_Guide.pdf`)

The following are additional items that are either required or recommended in order to enable VMware VSAN.

The required items are as follows:

- At least three ESXi servers with sufficient available storage are required in order to create a VSAN cluster. VSAN can only be configured using the vSphere Web Client, a required component of vCenter Server.

  VSAN can also be configured with just two ESXi servers, provided you also deploy a **VSAN witness appliance**. The example provided in this section will utilize three ESXi servers, which does not require a witness appliance. Consult the VSAN documentation (`https://www.vmware.co m/support/pubs/virtual-san-pubs.html`) for information about the witness appliance.

- VMware VSAN requires a license key that is included by default with the Horizon Advanced and Horizon Enterprise editions. This license key should be installed prior to enabling VSAN, using instructions provided in the VMware vSphere 6 documentation (`http://pubs.vmware.com/vsphere-60/index.js p`).
- A dedicated IP address will be required for the VSAN VMkernel port on each ESXi server.

The recommended items are as follows:

- Consider using a dedicated VSAN VMkernel report, rather than enabling the VSAN VMkernel option on an existing VMkernel port.
- Use a dedicated **Virtual LAN(VLAN)** or another private network for your VSAN network traffic. This is very important for production environments and will ensure that this critical network traffic is not impacted by other traffic on the network.
- The VSAN VMkernel port and the virtual switch it is created on will be configured with a **Maximum Transmission Unit** (**MTU**) value of 9,000, which is commonly referred to as jumbo frames. With jumbo frames enabled, fewer Ethernet frames will be required in order to transmit the VSAN network traffic, which reduces the CPU load on the ESXi server. Prior to changing the MTU value, verify that the networking infrastructure will support it.

The instructions provided in the next section assume that the target vSphere vSwitch and all associated physical network equipment has already been configured with a MTU of 9,000; if not, consult VMware vSphere 6 and network vendor documentation for information on how to edit the vSwitch MTU configuration.

- If dedicated network connections are not being used with VSAN, utilize vSphere **Network I/O Control** (**NetIOC**) in order to ensure that it is guaranteed a minimum of 1GbE of bandwidth, which is the minimum required by VSAN. The VMware vSphere 6 Documentation or VMware Virtual SAN Design and Sizing Guide provide information on how to configure the network I/O control feature. Whenever possible, use NetIOC to guarantee more than the 1 GbE minimum or even use 10 GbE links that are dedicated for use solely with VSAN.

I strongly suggest 10 GbE links for all production Virtual SAN deployments. 1GbE are technically supported, but should be limited to lab or demo use only.

# Deploy VMware Virtual SAN

In this section, we will perform the steps that are required to enable VMware VSAN. These instructions assume that at least three ESXi servers with a VSAN-compatible configuration have been deployed and added to a vSphere cluster in vCenter.

Standard vSphere vSwitches and IPv4 are used in the following example, although distributed vSwitches, as well as IPv6, are supported. Consult the vSphere 6 and VSAN documentation for additional information about how to configure VSAN.

# Configuring the ESXi server Virtual SAN VMkernel adapters

The following steps outline how to configure the VSAN VMkernel adapters required in order to enable VSAN:

1. Access the vSphere Web Client using the default URL of `https://vSphere_Server_ Name_` or `_FQDN:9443/vsphere-client.`
2. On the vSphere Web Client home page, click on the **Hosts and Clusters** icon.
3. On the vSphere Web Client **Hosts and Clusters** page, click on the triangle to the left of the vSphere cluster that contains your VSAN hosts in order to expand it, as shown in the following figure:

4. Click on one of the ESXi servers in the cluster, then click on the **Manage** tab, then select the **Networking** entry, and finally go to the **VMkernel adapters** page, as shown in the following screenshot:

5. Click on the **Add host networking** button that appears as a globe with a green plus sign above the **Device** column, as shown in the previous figure. This opens the **Add Networking** window.

6. Navigate to **Add Networking | Select connection type**, select the **VMkernel Network Adapter** radio button, and then click on **Next**.

7. Navigate to the **Add Networking | Select target device** window, select the **Select an existing standard switch** radio button, click on **Browse**, click on the target switch in the **Select switch** window, and then click on **Next**.

Optionally, configure a new standard switch for use with VSAN if desired, although, if you do, it will interrupt this task and you will most likely be required to start the procedure from the beginning.

8. Navigate to **Add Networking** | **Port properties**, provide the **Network label**, **VLAN ID**, select the **Virtual SAN traffic** checkbox as shown in the following screenshot, and then click on **Next**.

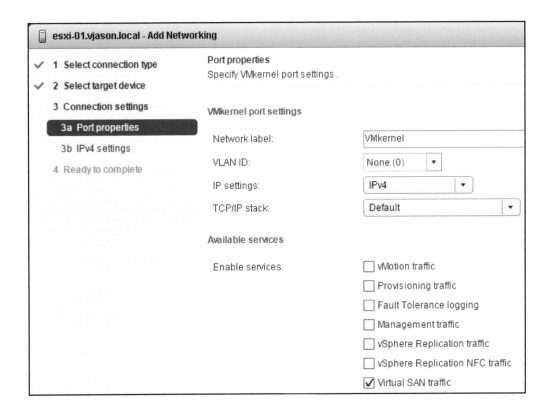

 If IPv6 is not enabled on the ESXi server, the **IP settings** drop-down menu will not be displayed. Use this menu too if you want to enable IPv6 only, or both IPv4 and IPv6, on the VSAN VMkernel interface. By default, IPv4 only will be used; IPv6 is not required to use VSAN.

9. Navigate to **Add Networking** | **IPv4 settings**, select the **Use static IPv4 settings** radio button, provide an unused IP address and subnet mask, and then click on **Next**. This step will not be displayed if you had selected to use only IPv6 in the previous step.

If you enabled IPv6 on the VMkernel interface, you will be prompted to configure it next.

10. Navigate to **Add Networking** | **Ready to complete**, review the settings, and then click on **Finish**. The new VMkernel adapter will now be displayed in the **VMkernel adapters** page, as shown in the following screenshot:

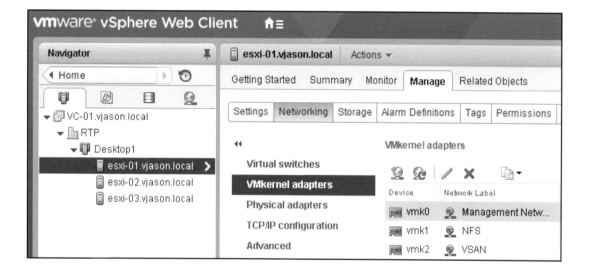

11. Highlight the VSAN **VMkernel adapters**, and then click on the **Edit settings** icon that appears as a yellow pencil above the **Network Label** column shown in the previous figure. This opens the **Edit Settings** window.

12. Go to **Edit Settings** and click on the **NIC settings** tab, change the MTU to 9000, and then click on **OK**. This step is not explicitly required, but it is recommended if the network infrastructure supports it.

13. Repeat steps *4* through *12* for the other ESXi servers in the VSAN cluster using a unique IP address on each during step *9*.

The VMware ESXi servers are now ready for VSAN to be enabled.

# Enabling and configuring VSAN

The following steps outline how to enable and configure the VMware VSAN. In the example provided, we will be configuring an all-flash VSAN cluster, although the process is similar for hybrid configurations:

1. Access the vSphere Web Client using the default URL of `https://vSphere_ Server_Name_` or `_FQDN:9443/vsphere-client.`

2. On the vSphere Web Client home page, click on the **Hosts and Clusters** icon.

3. On the vSphere Web Client's **Hosts and Clusters** page, click on the vSphere cluster that contains the hosts configured for VSAN, then click on the **Manage** tab, and then navigate to **Virtual SAN | General**, as shown in the following screenshot:

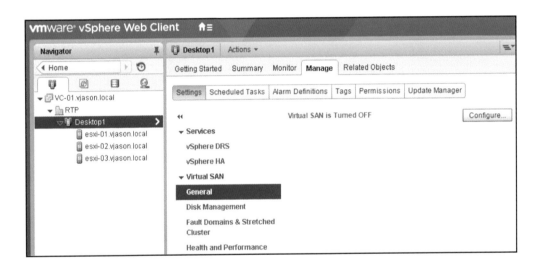

4. Click on the **Configure...** button to open the **Configure Virtual SAN** window.

5. In the **Configure Virtual SAN – Select VSAN capabilities** window, check the **Deduplication and Compression** checkbox, as shown in the following figure, and then click on **Next**. By default, the **Add disks to storage** setting is set to **Manual**, which prevents VSAN from automatically adding new disks that it discovers in the vSphere VSAN hosts; to enable this feature, use the drop-down menu to change the setting to **Automatic**. We will not be using any of the **Fault Domains and Stretched Cluster** features with our Horizon hosts.

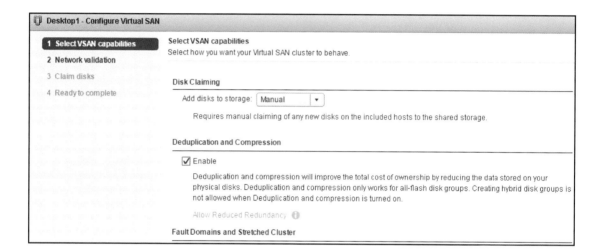

The deduplication and compression feature requires an all-flash VSAN configuration. Additionally, these features tend to provide the most benefit for full clone desktops and the least benefit with linked clone and instant clone desktops, as those types typically have minimal redundant data between them.

6. In the **Configure Virtual SAN | Network validation** window, confirm that the VSAN-enabled VMkernel adapters are enabled and then click on **Next**. If errors are detected on this page, click on **Cancel** and review the configuration of the VMkernel adapters.

7. In the **Configure Virtual SAN | Claim disks** window shown in the following screenshot, verify that the intended disks have been claimed and then click on **Next**.

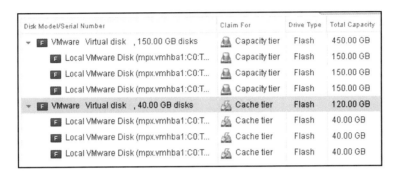

8. In the **Configure Virtual SAN | Ready to complete** window, verify the configuration and then click on **Finish**. VMware VSAN will now be configured, and the configuration process can be monitored using the **Recent Tasks** window of the vSphere Web Client. When the VSAN configuration is complete, the vSphere cluster's **General** page under **Virtual SAN** will get updated, as shown in the following screenshot. The values shown will vary based on the storage configuration of our vSphere VSAN hosts.

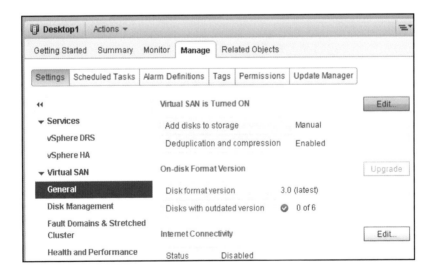

9. The vSphere cluster's **Disk Management** page under **Virtual SAN** now displays the **Disk group** information for each VSAN ESXi server. Select an individual host, as shown in the following screenshot, in order to show which disks from that host are currently being used by VSAN:

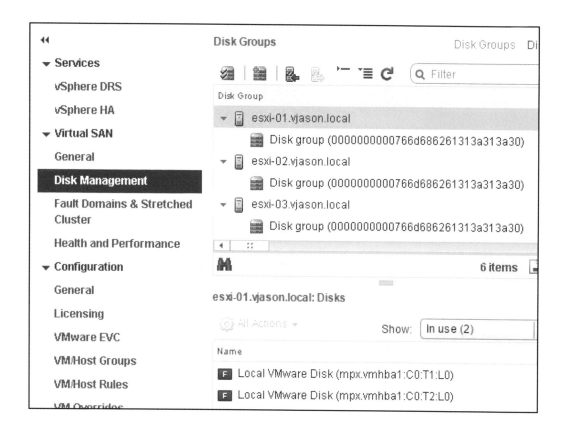

VMware VSAN is now ready for use with VMware Horizon. By default, all VSAN datastores are named `vsanDatastore`; it is recommended to rename them after they are configured to something more meaningful that reflects their intended use. To rename a datastore, browse to the **Related Objects | Datastores** tab on one of the VSAN ESXi servers, as shown in the following screenshot, right-click on the target datastore to open the **Actions** menu, click **Rename…**, enter a new name in the **Datastore | Rename** window, and then click **OK**. The following screenshot shows a VSAN datastore that has been renamed to **Desktop1-VSAN1**.

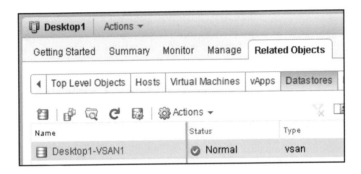

# Using VSAN with VMware Horizon

VMware Horizon requires no additional configuration in order to use VSAN as a target datastore for Horizon desktops. In this section, we will see how to select VSAN when creating a new Horizon desktop pool, a process described in greater detail in `Chapter 10`, *Creating Horizon desktop pools*.

The following steps outline how to use a VSAN datastore to deploy VMware Horizon desktops:

1. Use the Horizon Administrator console to begin the process of creating a Horizon desktop pool, stopping at the **Storage Optimization** window.

2. Navigate to **Add Desktop Pool** | **Storage Optimization**, select the **Use VMware Virtual SAN** radio button, as shown in the following screenshot, and then click on **Next**. This option will ensure that the vSphere VSAN SPBM policies are created and applied to the virtual machines.

3. Navigate to **Add Desktop Pool – vCenter Settings**. Under the **Datastores** step, select the VSAN datastore as the target datastore for the desktops. This process is identical to selecting non-VSAN datastores. By default, the datastore will be named **vsanDatastore**, which can be changed prior to creating the Horizon desktop pool using the vSphere Web Client, via the same process that was used to rename non-VSAN datastores.

4. Complete the Horizon desktop's pool-creation process.

VMware Horizon will now create the desktops, as well as the default vSphere VSAN SPBM policies shown earlier in this chapter.

# Summary

In this chapter, you have been introduced to VMware VSAN, a software-defined storage platform that extends the capabilities of vSphere to provide storage for vSphere virtual machines.

First, we examined the VSAN requirements and limitations, and reviewed a simple VSAN sizing exercise.

Next, we reviewed the vSphere VSAN SPBM framework, which is used to control how VSAN resources are used. We learned how Horizon automatically creates and implements SPBM policies, based on the type of desktop being deployed.

In the remaining sections of the chapter, we reviewed how to configure our ESXi servers to work with VSAN, walked through the process used to enable VSAN on those hosts, and then examined what steps to take when creating a Horizon pool to ensure that it creates the VSAN SPBM policies.

In the next chapter, we will review VMware User Environment Manager, an optional feature of VMware Horizon used to manage and enable portability of users' persona data.

# 8
# Implementing VMware User Environment Manager

VMware **User Environment Manager** (**UEM**) is a standalone component of VMware Horizon Enterprise Edition which provides robust, contextual, dynamic end-user persona management capabilities across different devices and locations. UEM can be used to provide a personalized and consistent desktop experience across Horizon desktops, physical computers, Windows RDS servers, and even virtual desktops managed by other virtual desktop platforms.

While UEM offers a significant number of different options for managing and customizing a users' persona, as we will show in this chapter, a basic installation capable of saving user persona data can be set up and running in less than 30 minutes.

By the end of this chapter, we will learn:

- The UEM pre-installation tasks, including file share and AD group policy requirements
- How to install the UEM Agent
- How to use the UEM Easy Start feature to quickly configure a basic UEM environment
- How to configure the UEM group policies
- How to implement profile folder redirection using UEM
- About some of the advanced UEM settings for user persona customization

The goal of this chapter is to help you stand up a basic UEM version 9 installation for the purpose of managing user persona information within your Horizon infrastructure. Other components of UEM, such as **SyncTool**, **Application Profiler**, and the **Helpdesk Support Tool,** are not explicitly required to use UEM, and sufficiently complex that they cannot be covered in this chapter. Consult the VMware UEM documentation (`htt ps://www.vmware.com/support/pubs/uem-pubs.html`) for information about these UEM components; each has their own separate guide.

# User Environment Manager overview

In early 2015 VMware acquired Immidio, the creators of UEM, and begun offering their persona management product both as a standalone product and as part of Horizon Enterprise Edition. While Horizon already included a persona management utility known as **Horizon Persona Management**, it represented an improvement over traditional Windows roaming profiles, and not a comprehensive user persona management solution with robust customization capabilities. The **VMware UEM FAQ** (`https://www.vmware.c om/files/pdf/products/user-environment-manager/vmware-user-environment-mngr-faq.pdf`) states that the product easily scales to support more than 100,000 users, which is well beyond most Horizon infrastructure sizes.

While UEM improves on Horizon Persona Management in almost every way, it doesn't handle the management of user data, only the settings needed to enable a personalized user experience across UEM client sessions. This feature is certainly a benefit of Horizon Persona Management over UEM, but the truth is that, unless managed carefully, the movement of this user data by Horizon Persona Management between the remote file share and the Horizon desktop can cause frequent performance issues, particularly with profiles that have large amounts of user data.

Already using Horizon Persona Management? While UEM and Persona Management aren't meant to be used side by side on an ongoing basis, migrating from Persona Management to UEM requires little more than running both at the same time for as long as is needed for all of your users to log in. VMware KB article 2118056 (`http://kb.vmware.com/selfser vice/microsites/search.do?language=en_US&cmd=displayKC&ex ternalId=2118056`) provides an outline of the steps required to migrate to UEM.

Like App Volumes, UEM provides the most benefit in non-persistent desktop environments. The combination of UEM and App Volumes enables users to leverage two of the most desirable architectural possibilities of VMware Horizon:

- Non-persistent desktopsâ∘∘UEM and App Volumes provide a persistent experience in a non-persistent environment. When compared to persistent desktops, non-persistent desktops typically require less effort to manage over the long term, as well as less physical storage.
- Fewer virtual desktop master images with seamless migration between eachâ∘∘UEM enables application personalization across Windows OS versions, while App Volumes decouples applications from the desktop image. The combination of both means that you only need one basic image for each Windows OS, which you can then customize using App Volumes, to then provide a personalized user experience using UEM, regardless of which OS they happen to log in to.

Please note that App Volumes cannot roam user-installed applications between Windows OS versions; it will create distinct user-writable volumes for each. You will learn more about this in `Chapter 9, Implementing VMware App Volumes`.

The following diagram shows the combination of UEM and App Volumes layered on top of a Windows OS, presenting the user with a personalized experience while actually abstracting each of the components that makes that personalization possible.

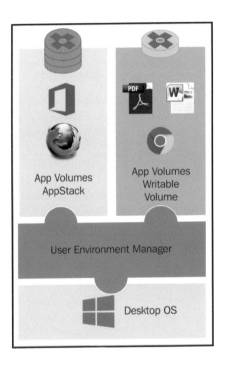

# User Environment Manager pre-installation tasks

This section will outline what infrastructure resources are required prior to configuring UEM in your environment. For the purpose of this chapter, we will be using the following AD security groups and Windows file share names:

- UEM administrators AD security groupâ©©UEM_Admins
- UEM users AD security groupâ©©UEM_Users
- UEM configuration file share locationâ©©\\FS1\UEM
- * UEM configuration file share locationâ©©\\FS1\UEMUsers

While the purpose of each resource is in most cases self-explanatory, the specific function of each will be explained later on in this chapter.

# Configuration share

UEM stores its configuration, in a Windows-based file share. This share has minimal storage requirements, but must be accessible to all clients and any individuals who will use the UEM management console. The share and underlying folder requires the following permissions to be configured:

- Share-level permissions:
    - UEM Administrators (UEM_Admins)â©©change
    - UEM Users (UEM_Users)â©©read
- Folder-level permissions
    - UEM Administrators (UEM_Admins)â©©full control
    - UEM Users (UEM_Users)â©©read and execute

If you will be using the UEM Helpdesk Support Tool, additional share-level permissions will be required in order to for users of that tool. Consult the VMware *User Environment Management Helpdesk Support Tool Administrator's Guide* (https://www.vmware.com/support/pubs/uem-pubs.html) for details about the permissions required.

# Persona share

UEM stores user persona data in a Windows-based file share, and must be accessible to all clients and any individuals who will use the UEM management console. It is recommended to create a new share for this purpose, and not attempt to use an existing file share used for general file storage.

The amount of persona space required per user will vary greatly based on the UEM configuration, the amount of customization that was done, and the number of profile archives that are kept. It is suggested to start with at least 100 MB of storage per user during a pilot phase, and as the pilot progresses, monitor if additional storage is required. The UEM share should be able to be expanded as needed if additional storage per user is required, as well as to support additional users.

The share and underlying folder requires the following permissions to be configured:

- Share-level permissions:
    - UEM Administrators (`UEM_Admins`)—change
    - UEM Users (`UEM_Users`)—change
- Folder-level permissions
    - UEM Administrators (`UEM_Admins`)—full control; apply to **This folder, subfolders and files**
    - UEM Users (`UEM_Users`)—read and execute and **Create folders/append data**; apply to **This folder only**
    - Creator-owner (default Windows security principle)—full control; apply to **Subfolders and files only**

If you will be using the UEM Helpdesk Support Tool, additional folder-level permissions will be required in order for users of that tool. Consult the VMware *User Environment Management Helpdesk Support Tool Administrator's Guide* (`https://www.vmware.com/support/pubs/uem-pubs.html`) for details about the permissions required.

# Windows user folder redirection share

Windows user profile folder redirection is not an explicit requirement of UEM, but for Horizon environments that require user data to be retained between non-persistent desktop sessions, it is one of multiple methods we can use. We will demonstrate folder redirection later on in this chapter, but only because many Horizon environments require some way to transparently persist user files across Horizon client sessions.

If you intend to use a single instance of UEM with Horizon pods across multiple sites, you will probably want to consider using AD **Distributed File System** (**DFS**) namespaces to ensure users are redirecting folders to file servers located within the same datacentre as their UEM client. The Microsoft TechNet article titled *Deploy Folder Redirection with Offline Files* (`https://technet.microsoft.com/en-us/library/jj649078.aspx`) mentions some important things to consider when using DFS with folder redirection. Keep in mind, when reviewing that article, that our primary interest is using DFS and folder redirection together, as UEM itself will handle the task of actually implementing folder redirection.

The share and folder-level permissions for Windows-based file shares that will host redirected user folders should mimic those of any existing user home directories, which in most cases when created allow access only to the folder owner, along with any administrative and backup accounts. I am not providing specific permissions recommendations for these folders in this chapter, as each organization may have their own requirements for the security of the data of individual users, and given that these folders are used for exactly that, it is important you determine what your own needs are.

> Microsoft KB article 274443 (https://support.microsoft.com/en-us /kb/274443) provides examples of how to create shares to host-redirected folders that meet most common security requirements. Additionally, the share and folder-level permissions referenced in the *Persona share* section of this chapter may also be used as a reference to creating root file shares that automatically protect individual folders created within.

# Group policy files

UEM is enabled at the client level using AD group policy objects, which are provided in the **XML-based GPO template (ADMX)** format. Six templates are provided by default for the following UEM components:

- **VMware UEM FlexEngine** (VMware UEM FlexEngine.admx)âۥused to enable UEM at the client level
- **VMware UEM Helpdesk Support Tool** (VMware UEM Helpdesk Support Tool.admx)âۥused to configure the UEM Helpdesk Support Tool, which provides for the management of UEM profile archives
- **VMware UEM Management Console** (VMware UEM Management Console.admx)âۥused to automatically configure the UEM environment settings in the management console, or to lock down what items the target users can access
- **VMware UEM SyncTool – Computer** (VMware UEM SyncTool COMPUTER.admx)âۥused to configure UEM SyncTool, which is designed to sync UEM profiles to physical clients who have only intermittent connectivity to the UEM shares; this GPO template is for AD computer objects
- **VMware UEM SyncTool – User** (VMware UEM SyncTool USER.admx)âۥsame function as the UEM SyncToolâۥcomputer policy object, but for AD user objects
- **VMware UEM** (VMware UEM.admx)âۥRoot UEM GPO folder object for the AD Group Policy Management Console; contains no configurable policies

The VMware UEM FlexEngine GPO template is the only one needed to enable UEM, and the only UEM GPO template we will use in this chapter. For information about the remaining policy templates and the features they enable, consult the VMware UEM documentation (`https://www.vmware.com/support/pubs/uem-pubs.html`).

Prior to performing the examples required in this chapter, the UEM ADMX files and their associated `en-US` directory were copied to the replicated `PolicyDefinitions` folder on the domain controller, located at `c:\windows\sysvol\domain\Policies\PolicyDefinitions`, which ensures that they will be replicated to and available on all domain controllers in the domain.

The Microsoft Developer Network article **Managing Group Policy ADMX Files Step-by-Step Guide** (`https://msdn.microsoft.com/en-us/lib rary/bb530196.aspx`) explains where to place ADMX files on a domain control to ensure they are accessible to remote users of the AD Group Policy Management Console.

# Installing the User Environment Manager Agent

The UEM Agent software is used to enable UEM on client computers, which may include Horizon desktops, Windows RDS servers, physical computers, or desktops used with other VDI solutions. The installation process is the same regardless of where the agent software is being installed, so only one example will be provided.

The UEM installer files are provided by VMware (`https://my.vmware.com/web/vmware /evalcenter?p=uem`) as a single *ZIP* file; extract the files prior to beginning the installation process. The UEM Agent software is named in a format similar to `VMware User Environment Manager X.y xYY.exe`, where `X.y` is the current UEM version number, and `xYY` represents which processor type (`x86` or `x64`) the installer is for. A UEM demo license is also available as a separate download; you will need that license or your permanent one during the installation of the UEM Agent software.

The following steps outline the UEM Agent installation process; this process should be performed on a virtual desktop or Windows RDS server master image prior to deployment, a linked or instant clone master image prior to being updated for redeployment or deployed to users for the first time, or as stated previously, an existing or new physical computer.

1. Double-click the `VMware User Environment Manager X.y xYY.exe` (32 and 64-bit versions are available) to launch the **VMware User Environment Setup** wizard. Click **Next** and proceed through the steps until you reach the **Choose License File** window, selecting a **Typical** installation when prompted.

2. In the **Choose License File** window, the installer should detect that it is being used with Horizon and allow you to move on to the next step by clicking on **Next**. If it does not and you are prompted for one, click **Browse...** to open the **Open** window, then select the UEM license file, and then click **Open** to return to the **Choose License File** window. Click **Next** to continue.

3. In the **Ready to Install VMware User Environment Manager** window, click **Install**, and when completed, click **Finish**.

The UEM Agent software is now ready to use. The updated image is now ready to be deployed, although it will not function until we complete the steps outlined in the next section, *Configuring User Environment Manager*.

# Configuring User Environment Manager

Assuming that we have configured the UEM shares and uploaded the GPO templates as described previously in the section of this chapter titled *User Environment Manager pre-installation tasks*, we are ready to configure UEM itself. In this section of the chapter, we will complete the initial configuration of UEM, which includes installing the UEM management console, implementing the required AD GPOs, and, while optional, we will also enable Windows folder redirection.

# Installing the User Environment Manager management console

The UEM management console software may be installed wherever it is needed to facilitate UEM management. The actual UEM configuration is stored in the UEM configuration share; the console does nothing more than connect to and manage the UEM configuration data stored on it. In the examples provided in this chapter, administrative access to UEM is controlled using the UEM_Admins AD security group. Only members of that group have the necessary access rights to make changes to the UEM configuration share, which is what is required to administer UEM.

The following steps outline the UEM management console installation process. The console is installed using the same installer file as the UEM Agent. In the example provided, we are installing the console while logged in as a user who is a member of the UEM_Admins AD security group:

1. Double-click the VMware User Environment Manager X.y xYY.exe to launch the **VMware User Environment Setup** wizard. Click **Next** to proceed through the initial installation steps, including accepting the license agreement.
2. In the **Destination Folder** window, accept the default software **Destination Folder**, or update as needed and then click **Next**.
3. In the **Choose Setup Type** window, click **Custom**.
4. In the **Custom Setup** window, uncheck the **VMware UEM FlexEngine** components and sub-components, check the **VMware UEM Management Console** component as shown in the following screenshot, and then click **Next**.

5. In the **Ready to Install VMware User Environment Manager** window, click **Install**.

6. When the install process completes, click **Finish**.

7. In the Windows start menu, click the **VMware UEM** folder, and then click **Management Console** to open the UEM management console for the first time.

8. The UEM management console will open up the **UEM configuration share** window. Provide the FQDN **Location:** of the UEM configuration (`\\fs1.vjason.local\UEM` in the example provided) share as shown in the following screenshot, and then click **OK** to return to the UEM management console main window.

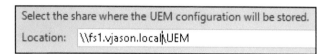

9. If this is the first time the UEM configuration share was accessed using the UEM management console, you will be prompted in the **Settings** screen to check which features you want to enable in the console. As shown in the following screenshot, enable all of the features and then click **OK**.

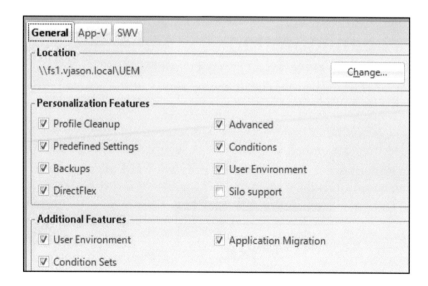

These settings can be changed at any time using the **Configure** button in the UEM management console; this button is shown in the screenshot provided next.

The UEM management console is shown in the following screenshot and is ready to be used to customize the UEM installation. Since we have not yet configured the UEM client GPO objects, we are free to configure the UEM without the risk of impacting our clients.

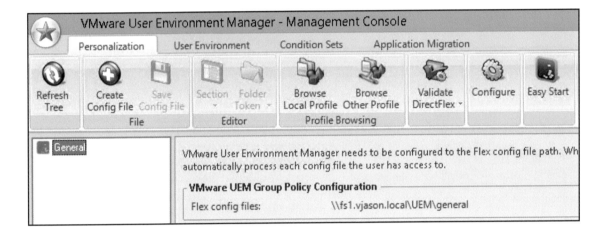

# Easy Start configuration

The **Easy Start** feature of the UEM is used to quickly get it up and running, and is a good starting point for a basic installation. The following steps outline how to perform the initial UEM configuration using Easy Start.

1. Log in to a computer that has the UEM management console installed as a user who is a member of the UEM_Admins AD security group.
2. In the Windows start menu, click the **VMware UEM** folder, and then click **Management Console** to open the UEM management console.
3. In the UEM management console, click **Easy Start** to open the **Easy Start** window.

4. In the UEM **Easy Start** window shown in the following screenshot, click the versions of Microsoft Office you are using in your environment, and then click **OK**.

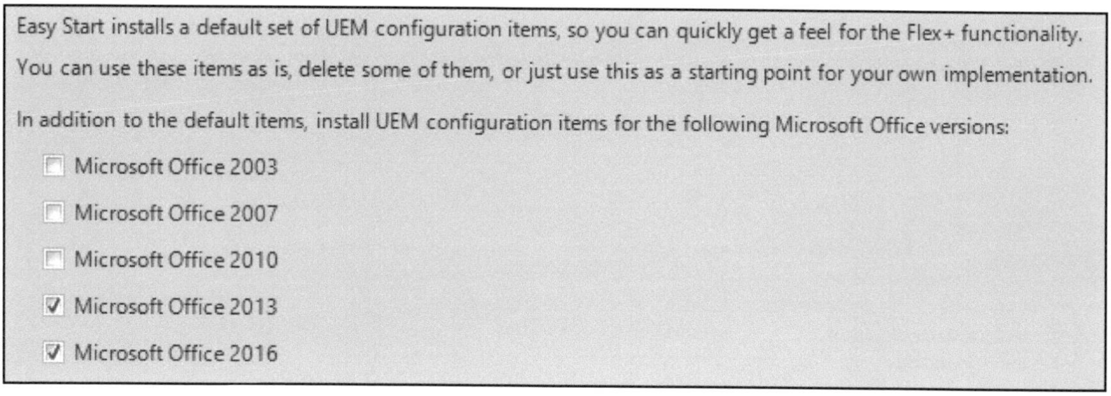

Easy Start installs a default set of UEM configuration items, so you can quickly get a feel for the Flex+ functionality.

You can use these items as is, delete some of them, or just use this as a starting point for your own implementation.

In addition to the default items, install UEM configuration items for the following Microsoft Office versions:

☐ Microsoft Office 2003

☐ Microsoft Office 2007

☐ Microsoft Office 2010

☑ Microsoft Office 2013

☑ Microsoft Office 2016

5. The **Easy Start** window will now update to confirm a successful installation. Click **OK** to close the window and complete the initial configuration of UEM.
6. UEM is now configured for use by clients; all that remains is to configure the required GPOs and instruct our users to log in as they normally would. In the next section we will configure the GPOs needed to enable UEM.

# Easy Start defaults

UEM Easy Start creates a number of sample items which are helpful in understanding the basics of how the software works, but should be removed prior to activating the software using the GPOs referenced in the next section of this chapter.

The UEM Easy Start setup configures a number of different Windows settings, but among those there are ones specific to users that will in most cases need to be removed before the UEM is placed into production.

The initial settings are created under the UEM management console **User Environment** tab, which is shown in the following figure and contains settings related to the Windows profile itself.

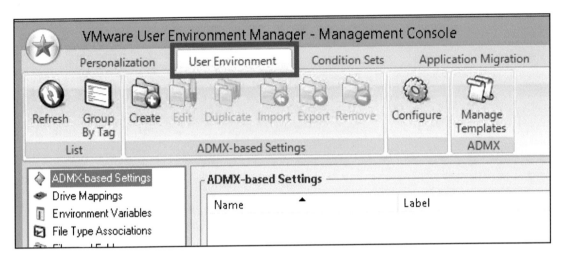

The following User Environment settings are among those configured by default, and are recommended to be removed or customized prior to placing the UEM into production:

- **Files and Folders**: Used to create the README file on the desktop and adds a VMware website entry to the Favorites folder
- **Registry Settings**: Used to creates registry keys in `HKCU\Software\VMwareUEMDemo`
- **Shortcuts**: Used to create shortcuts for various default Windows applications, a shortcut to the VMware website, as well as UEM features such as Self-Support and User Environment Refresh
- **Triggered Tasks**: Used to display an information message when the user unlocks the computer

Consult the UEM documentation (`https://www.vmware.com/support/pubs/uem-pubs .html`) for information about the other settings available, and refer to the *Advanced configuration – examples* section of this chapter for examples of how some of these and other settings may be used in a UEM deployment.

# User Environment Manager group policy settings

UEM is enabled and client options are set using GPOs applied at both the computer and user level. In the examples provided in this chapter, we will be using the following AD security groups and **organizational units(OUs)**:

- UEM_Users AD security group
- Horizon – Computers AD OU
- Horizon – Users AD OU

## UEM user policies

The following steps will provide instructions on the configuration of the user AD GPOs needed to enable UEM:

1. While logged in as a user who has privileges to create and edit GPOs in the AD domain, open the AD **Group Policy Management console (GPMC)**.
2. Create and link an AD GPO object to the **Horizon – Users** OU. In the example provided, we will name the AD GPO **UEM_Users**.

3. Edit the **UEM_Users** GPO object, and navigate to **User Configuration – Policies – Administrative Templates – VMware UEM – FlexEngine** as shown in the following screenshot.

   - The full name of the **Administrative Templates** folder is actually **Administrative Templates: Policy definitions (ADMX files) retrieved from the central store**; to make the instructions easier to read, the shortened name will be used throughout this chapter.

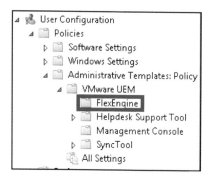

4. Configure the **Flex config files** policy as shown in the following screenshot. Provide the **Central location of Flex config files:**, check the **Process folder recursively** checkbox, and then click **OK**. In the example provided, the UEM Flex config file location is set to **\\fs01.vjason.local\UEM\general**, where **general** is the default Flex config file folder created by the UEM management console during the initial configuration.

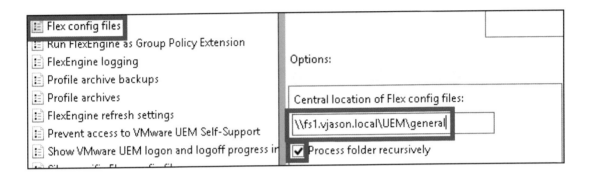

While not shown in the screenshot, when selected, each UEM GPO setting (along with almost every other GPO setting) is explained in detail within the AD GPMC itself. Refer to this information under **Help:** for a more detailed explanation of what it is you are configuring. You can also refer to the UEM documentation (`https://www.vmware.com/support/pubs/uem-pubs.html`) for information about the different UEM GPO settings.

5. Configure the **Profile archives** policy as shown in the following screenshot. Provide the **Location for storing user profile archives:**, check the **Compress profile archives** and **Retain file modification dates** checkboxes, and then click **OK**. In the example provided, the UEM profile archive file location is set to `\\fs01.vjason.local\UEMUsers\%username%\Archives`, which will create it within the logged on users UEM profile folder.

We won't be setting any of the *hide folder* options in any of these UEM GPOs, to make it easier to validate that UEM is functioning as intended. I recommend hiding both UEM folders and their shares by default in a production environment, to help prevent them from being discovered and subsequently modified, even by authorized users.

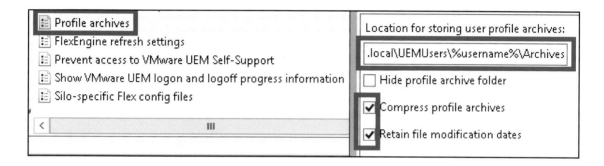

5. Configure the **Profile archive backups** policy as shown in the following screenshot. Provide the **Location for storing user profile archive backups:**, set the **Number of backups per profile archive:** to **1**, check the **Create single backup per day** checkbox, and then click **OK**. In the example provided, the UEM profile archive file location is set to `\\fs01.vjason.local\UEMUsers\%username%\Backups`, which will create it within the logged-on user's UEM profile folder.

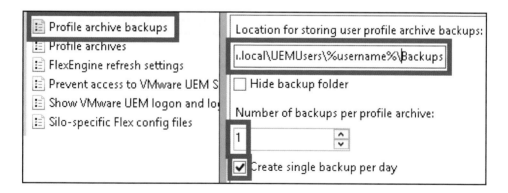

6. Click the **Run FlexEngine as Group Policy Extension** radio button, as shown in the following screenshot, and then click **OK**.

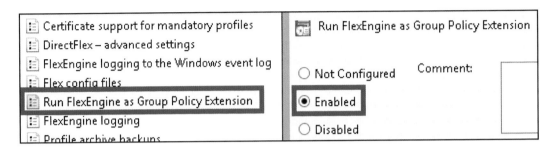

The UEM user GPOs have now been created. Proceed to the next section to create the required user GPOs.

# UEM computer policies

The following steps will provide instructions on the configuration of the computer GPOs needed to enable UEM:

1. Create and link a GPO object to the **Horizon – Computers** OU. In the example provided, we will name the GPO **UEM_Computers**.
2. While logged in as a user who has privileges to create and edit GPOs in the AD domain, open the AD **GPMC**.

   The policy we create here would need to be applied to all UEM client computers.

3. Edit the **UEM_Computers** GPO object, and navigate to **Computer Configuration** | **Policies** | **Windows Settings** | **Scripts** | **Logon/Logoff**, as shown in the following screenshot.

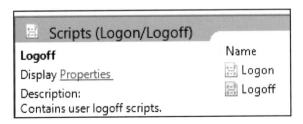

4. Double-click on **Logoff** to open the **Logoff Properties** window, and then click **Add...** to open the **Add a Script** window.

5. In the **Add a Script** window **Script Name:** field, type the full path to the `FlexEngine.exe` executable and in the Script Parameters field, type **-s** as shown in the following screenshot. Click **OK** when finished, and **OK** again to close the **Logoff Properties** window.

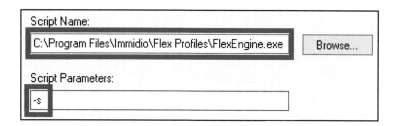

You may run the `FlexEngine.exe -s` command at logoff using other techniques if you wish; this isn't your only option for doing so.

6. Navigate to **Computer Configuration | Policies | Administrative Templates | System–Logon**.

7. Edit the **Always wait for the network at computer startup and logon** policy, and click the **Enabled** radio button, as shown in the following screenshot. Click **OK** when finished.

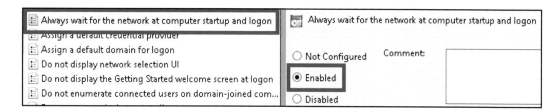

The UEM computer GPOs have now been created and, assuming the previous steps were completed successfully, UEM will now be activated within the client computers. In the next section, we will redirect some of the user profile directories.

# Windows folder redirection

In this section, we will use UEM to enable Windows folder redirection. When deploying folder redirection in production deployments, it is recommended to use a dedicated share that meets your users' aggregate performance and capacity requirements for their data.

> As stated previously, folder redirection is optional and not required for UEM to function. In some cases, you may prefer to instruct users to save critical files to mapped network drives, rather than use the redirected profile folders.
>
> Folder redirection will not move existing data when enabled; if implementing within an existing environment you must have a method to deal with any existing data on the target desktop or RDS server.

The following steps will provide instructions on configuring UEM to redirect user profile folders:

1. Log in to a computer that has the UEM management console installed as a user who is a member of the **UEM_Admins AD** security group.
2. In the Windows start menu, click the **VMware UEM** folder, and then click **Management Console** to open the UEM management console.
3. In the UEM management console, click the **User Environment** tab, then the **Folder Redirection** section, as shown in the following screenshot, and then click **Create** to open the **Folder Redirection** window:

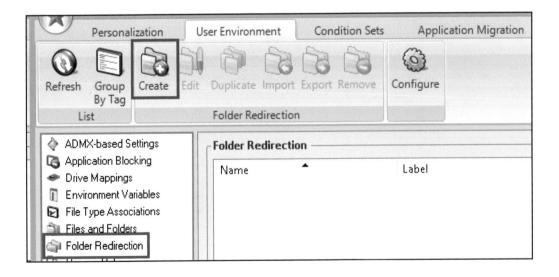

4. Provide a **Name:** for the policy, and a **Remote path:** where the folders will be directed to. The path must include a variable for the user ID, such as `%username%`. In the example provided, our remote path is `\\fs1.vjason.local\FolderRedir\%username%`. Click on the checkboxes next to the folders you want redirected, as shown in the following screenshot, and then click **Save**.

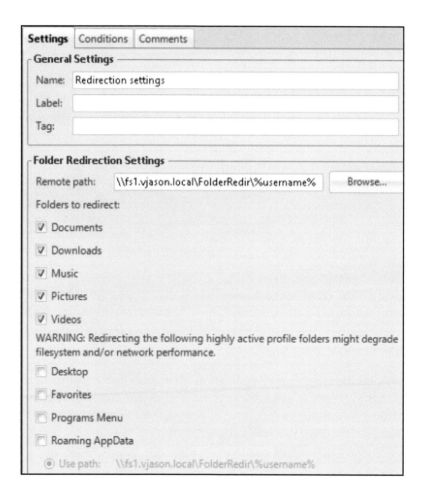

We won't use them here, but like other UEM policies you can use the **Conditions** tab to control who this policy is applied to. This is typically used when you need to create multiple policies, each with a unique configuration that should only apply to specific users.

The UEM folder redirection settings have now been configured, and will apply to users the next time they log in to a computer that has the UEM agent installed. If data currently exists in the target folders on the computer, it will remain there and the user will be redirected to an empty folder. In the next section, we will review some of the different advanced configuration options for UEM.

# Advanced UEM configuration examples

In this section, we will review each of the UEM management console configuration tabs, and provide examples of how some of the more common items are used. The configuration tabs are broken down into four sections:

- **Personalization**: Settings related to individual applications, Windows settings for various hardware devices (mouse, keyboard, and so on), or other system applications, such as the screensaver:
  - The VMware Community forum for UEM Documents page is regularly updated with new UEM Application Templates (`https://communities.vmware.com/community/vmtn/user-environment-manager/content?filterID=contentstatus[published]~objecttype~objecttype[document]`)
- **User Environment**: Settings related to a user's Windows profile configuration
- **Condition Sets**: Used to create conditions that control how and when a Personalization, User Environment, and Application Migration feature is used
- **Application Migration**: Used to enable UEM to migrate user settings between different versions of an application

> The Condition Sets and Application Migration features are considered advanced topics which are not discussed in this chapter; refer to the UEM documentation (`https://www.vmware.com/support/pubs/uem-pubs.html`) for details concerning these features.

# Personalization

The UEM management console Personalization tab can be used to customize Windows application settings. By default, UEM includes templates for various default Windows applications, multiple versions of Microsoft Office, Adobe Acrobat, and WinZip. Additionally, the UEM Application Profiler can be used to generate templates for additional applications as needed.

The VMware blog post titled *VMware User Environment Manager and Application Profile Settings* (`https://blogs.vmware.com/consulting/2015/07/vmware-user-environment-manager-application-profile-settings.html`) provides an example of how the Application Profiler tool is used.

## Application profile Import / Export feature

One of the most common options that will be configured when using UEM within the application profile is the **Import / Export** feature, which determines which registry trees, folder trees, and even individual folders will be retained by UEM for use in subsequent client sessions.

The following screenshot shows the default **Import / Export** screen for Microsoft **Word** 2013, which is one of the application templates included by default with UEM. By default, no settings are retained, something we will change in the next screenshot.

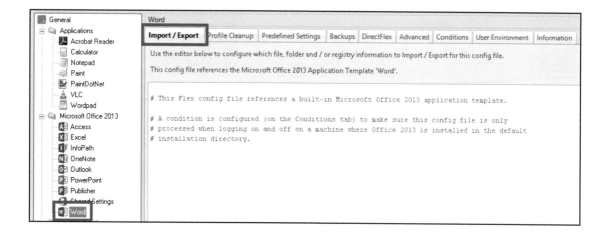

The following is what we must enter in the application template screen to retain the registry trees, folder trees, and files that we have determined we will need to retain across client sessions. To retain additional items, we would simply need to follow the same syntax and add those items to the template.

Note that Windows environment variables are used, bracketed by < and > symbols instead of % signs, rather than providing full paths to any file references.

```
[IncludeRegistryKeys]
HKCU\Software\Microsoft\Office\Word
HKCU\Software\Microsoft\Office\15.0\Word
[IncludeFolderTrees]
<AppData>\Microsoft\Word
[IncludeFiles]
<LocalAppData>\Microsoft\Office\Word.officeUI
```

Careful research and analysis is required to determine what, if any, registry settings or application files you need UEM to retain across client sessions. The VMware Community Forum for UEM is a good resource for this (`https://communities.vmware.com/community/vmtn/user-env ironment-manager`), but in some cases you may just need to experiment to get the results you want. Resist the temptation to copy every application configuration item you can find, and instead use Windows mandatory profiles or GPOs to set those values on a global basis so UEM isn't forced to manage more than it needs to.

UEM assists you in adding items to this screen by validating your entries whenever possible, be it by validating the text entry itself or by popping up a list of potential selections. The following screenshot shows the popup for the possible items to include or exclude, but a similar popup is displayed for user environment variables.

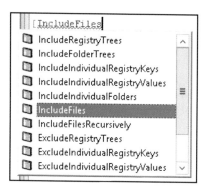

The following screenshot shows the completed entry. Click the **Save Config File** option to update the settings and apply them to UEM users. The next time the user logs off, the registry keys and files specified will be retained by UEM for use with subsequent client sessions.

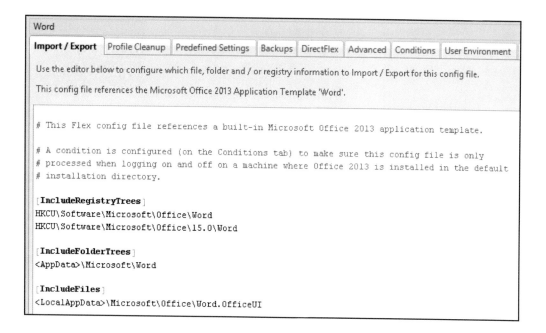

As shown in each screenshot in this section, each application template has several options that control how and when it runs, sets limits that control what files are exported, and many other options. Consult the UEM documentation (`https://www.vmware.com/support/pubs/uem-pubs.html`) for information about these options, and how they can be used to enable even more granular control over the Personalization settings.

# User Environment

The UEM management console User Environment tab can be used to customize user profile settings. UEM offers several different built-in options for managing the profile, as shown in the following screenshot, although, given that it includes the ability to update the registry virtually, any Windows option can be configured, assuming you know the proper syntax.

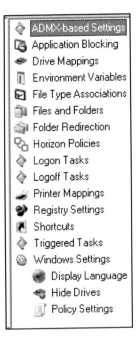

Most of the settings are self-explanatory for anyone with basic Windows knowledge. These include: **Drive Mappings**, **Environment Variables**, **File Type Associations**, **Logon Tasks**, **Logoff Tasks**, **Printer Mappings**, **Registry Settings**, **Shortcuts**, and common **Windows Settings**. Each of these represent items you can customize using traditional Windows GPOs, but the advantage of using UEM is that you don't need permissions in AD to configure these settings. The following remaining items can be set using the User Environment tab:

- **ADMX-based settings**: Using the Manage Templates button in the UEM management console, you can import AD ADMX files and use them to implement virtually any GPO setting using UEM.

- **Application Blocking**: Authorize or block applications within the desktop using detailed conditional policies, without the need to use an overhead of Windows group policies.

- **Files and Folders**: Copy files or folders to the UEM client, including items such as Internet shortcuts.

- **Horizon Policies**: Apply common policies to Horizon desktops, including PCoIP bandwidth policies, USB redirection, and so on. When combined with the policy **Condition** tab, this enables very granular control over Horizon settings, without the need to use an overhead of Windows group policies.

- **Triggered Tasks**: Used to perform different tasks, including custom commands, when a UEM client computer is locked, unlocked, disconnected from, or reconnected to. You can also apply UEM Condition Sets to further control when these tasks are performed.

As stated previously, in many cases the actions these settings perform are something you can do using GPOs or even custom scripts, but the power of UEM is that it is all done from a central console, without the need to make changes to the AD domain itself. Additionally, given the power of features such as UEM condition sets, you can exercise complete control over how and when a given configuration item is applied.

# Shortcut management feature

The following screenshot shows one example of the level of control provided by UEM. This is an example of a UEM-created shortcut, and you can see the different options that exist for where the shortcut is created, the **Conditions** tab which allows us to control when it is created (if required), and other settings related to the application execution parameters and appearance.

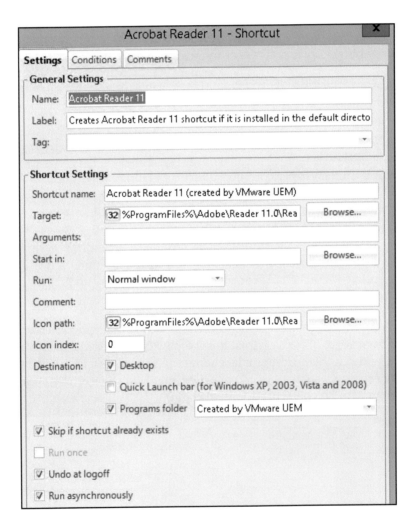

As shown in each screenshot in this section, each UEM has the ability to manage the entirely of a user's profile configuration without the need to make any changes to AD itself. Consult the UEM documentation (`https://www.vmware.com/support/pubs/uem-pubs.html`) for information about how to fully customize user profiles to suit your exact needs.

# Summary

In this chapter, you have been introduced to a very useful component of Horizon: User Environment Manager. You learned what is required to deploy UEM and the UEM client agent, perform the initial configuration, and implement the AD GPOs required to enable the feature in the clients.

We then discussed UEM user profile folder redirection, which may be required in environments where you must be certain that user data files are retained across client sessions.

Finally, you were introduced to some of the more advanced features of UEM, which provide you with total control over user profile and Windows settings without the need to edit the existing AD GPO configuration.

In the next chapter, we will discuss VMware App Volumes, which can be used to provide on-demand application delivery to desktops, potentially eliminating the need to create multiple virtual-desktop master images with customized application loads.

# 9
# Implementing VMware App Volumes

VMware App Volumes is a standalone component of VMware Horizon Enterprise edition that extends two new capabilities to virtual desktops:

- Deliver natively installed applications on demand, independent of the desktop image, using shared App Volumes AppStacks.
- Seamlessly roam user-installed applications between Horizon client sessions, even in non-persistent desktop environments using App Volumes Writable Volumes.

App Volumes uses vSphere VMDK files to enable transparent, on-demand, application portability without making any permanent changes to the virtual desktop. Applications are delivered and maintained using the App Volumes function and appear as if they were natively installed, because technically speaking they were. When used in combination with the software described in Chapter 8, *Implementing VMware User Environment Manager*, you have the ability to provide a persistent desktop experience using non-persistent desktops, without having to buy any third-party software to do so.

This chapter will discuss the installation, configuration, backup, and recovery of the App Volumes manager servers and their associated AppStacks and user Writable Volumes.

By the end of this chapter, we will learn:

- An overview of VMware App Volumes AppStacks, Writable Volumes, and the App Volumes Manager server
- App Volumes prerequisites
- How to install and configure an App Volumes Manager server
- How to add additional App Volumes Manager servers to a single-vCenter environment
- What is required when deploying App Volumes in a multi-site or multi-vCenter environment
- How to install the App Volumes Agent and AppCapture software
- How to create and assign an AppStack to users
- How to update an AppStack
- How to assign Writable Volumes to users
- How to delete Writable Volumes
- Additional App Volumes resources for review

This chapter is not meant to convey all possible App Volumes use cases or configurations. The goal is to help you stand up a basic App Volumes environment, and leverage its core features within your Horizon environment. I will provide several external resources that I recommend for anyone intending to make heavy use of App Volumes in their organization to review.

# App Volumes overview

Chapter 1, *VMWare Horizon View Infrastructure Overview*, provided an overview of most of the key features of VMware App Volumes. To summarize that information, VMware App Volumes can be used to decouple applications from Horizon desktops and Windows RDS servers, be they user-installed or ones packages and assigned by App Volumes administrators. The following diagram explains the conceptual relationship between the Horizon desktop and the Windows RDS server OS, the App Volumes Agent, and the AppStacks and Writable Volumes.

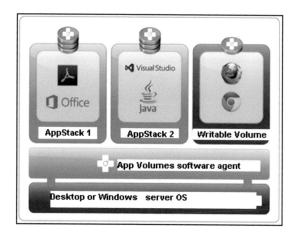

 RDS servers used with Horizon application streaming cannot use Writable Volumes, nor would they need them since Horizon clients using that feature don't have the ability to install applications on the hosting server.

The capabilities enabled by App Volumes are transparent to the client, as shown in the following screenshot, which shows the client view from Windows Explorer for a Horizon desktop, next to the virtual desktop hard disk configuration as seen in the vSphere web client. In the web client, we see **Hard disk 4**, which is the writable volume, and **Hard disk 5**, which is a single App Volumes AppStack (the remaining disks are all part of the Horizon non-persistent desktop). These disks are silently and transparently integrated in to the OS at login, and detached when the client session is ended.

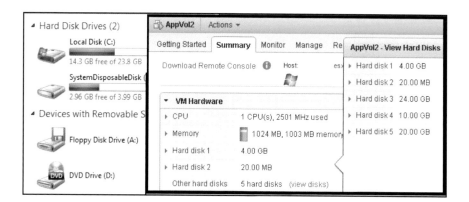

When combined with a user persona management solution, such as the one discussed in `Chapter 8`, *Implementing VMware User Environment Manager*, App Volumes enables Horizon customers to provide a persistent desktop experience while leveraging non-persistent desktops (using Writable Volumes), and while also reducing the number of virtual desktop master images to support, since we have decoupled their applications (using AppStacks).

In the remainder of this chapter we will learn how to implement and administer VMware App Volumes.

# App Volumes prerequisites

A production installation of App Volumes will require the following items:

- App Volumes appliance **Open Virtualization Alliance(OVA)** file, license file, client agent installers, and AppCapture installer
- Static IP addresses and pre-created DNS entries for each of the App Volumes Manager servers
- A provisioning computer, deployed as a virtual machine, running the same OS as the App Volumes clients; multiple provisioning computers will be required if you use more than one desktop or Windows RDS OS version
- App Volumes Agent supported OSs
    - Windows 7 or newer (for use as a desktop OS)
    - Windows 2008 R2 or newer (for use as an RDS server)
- A local account with the required permissions on each Horizon desktop ESXi host; the App Volumes Manager uses this account to mount VMDK files to desktops
    - The same password must be used on all accounts, and for security purposes it is not recommended to use the ESXi root account
    - An account named `appvol` will be used in the examples provided.
    - The permissions required for these accounts are listed in the *Problem: ESX Hosts Not Accessible* section of the *VMware App Volumes 3.0 Installation and Administration guide* (`https://www.vmw are.com/support/pubs/app-volumes-pubs.html`)

- Two AD user accounts, or one account that has been granted both sets of the following permissions:
  - Read access to Active Directory
  - vCenter permissions as outlined in the next section of this chapter titled vCenter permissions
  - In the examples provided we will use an account named `svc-appvolumes`
- A file share that will be used to store AppStacks; the App Volumes Manager server imports AppStacks from this share in to the assigned vSphere datastores
  - The `svc-appvolumes` account should be granted read and write permissions to this share
  - In the examples provided the share will be located at `\\vc-01.vjason.local\AppCapture`, and we will refer to it as **VC-01 AppStack Share** in the **App Volumes Manager** console
  - This share can be used with multiple App Volumes installations, even those located in other datacenters
- One AD group who you will grant administrative access to App Volumes
  - In the examples provided we will use a group named **AppVolumes_Admins**
- One AD group to assign AppStacks to
  - In the examples provided we will use a group named `AppVolumes_NotepadPlus`
- One vSphere datastore per 1,000 Writable Volumes
  - The default Writable Volume template is 10 GB in size, so these volumes could require as much as 10 TB of space each
  - These datastores should be named using the same prefix, in the same case; **AVW** will be used in the examples provided
- One vSphere datastore for every 2,000 clients who will attach to AppStacks
  - The size of these AppStack datastores will vary based on the number of AppStacks that will be created
  - These datastores should be named using the same prefix, in the same case; **AVA** will be used in the examples provided

The figures provided with regard to number of App Volumes Manager appliances, and number of users per vSphere datastore is subject to change. Consult the VMware App Volumes product documentation (http s://www.vmware.com/support/pubs/app-volumes-pubs.html) and other resources listed throughout this chapter for updated information on the recommended infrastructure configuration.

While not explicitly required, we will be using AD security groups to entitle users to AppStacks and Writable Volumes. It is possible to assign each directly to users using the same methods that will be demonstrated in this chapter.

# vCenter permissions

The App Volumes vCenter service account (svc-appvolumes in the example provided) requires the following permissions to each of the Horizon vCenter Servers. These permissions may be granted using the same technique referenced in the *Create a vCenter role and grant permissions* section of Chapter 2, *Implementing Horizon Connection Server*.

- **Datastore**: Allocate space, Browse datastore, Low level file operations, Remove file, and Update virtual machine files
- **Folder**: Create folder and Delete folder
- **Global**: Cancel task
- **Host**: Local operationsâ©©reconfigure virtual machine
- **Sessions**: View and stop sessions
- **Tasks**: Create task
- **Virtual machine configuration**: Add existing disk, Add new disk, Add or remove device, Change resource, Remove disk, Settings, and Advanced
- **Inventory**: Create new, Move, Register, Remove, and Unregister
- **Provisioning**: Promote disks
- Deploying an App Volumes Manager appliance

App Volumes are deployed using the product OVA file, which is named in a format similar to `VMware_appvolumes_ovf-x.x.x-yyy.ova`. This Linux-based appliance is preconfigured with the App Volumes Manager server software. The following steps outline the installation process:

1. Identify the vCenter Server that manages the ESXi servers where App Volumes will be deployed, and log on to the vSphere Web Client using an account that has administrative permissions.

2. Click on the vSphere cluster or host where the appliance will be deployed, then click the **Actions** drop down menu as shown in the following screenshot, and then click **Deploy OVF Template...** to open the **Deploy OVF Template** window.

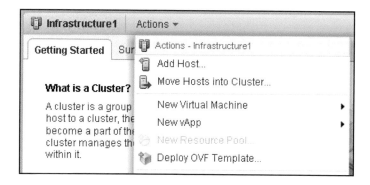

3. In the **Deploy OVF Template** | **Select source** window, click the **Browse** button, select the App Volumes appliance OVA file, and then click **Next**.

4. In the **Deploy OVF Template** | **Select source** window, review the details and then click **Next**.

5. In the **Deploy OVF Template** | **Accept License Agreements** window, review the license agreement, click the **Accept** button, and then click **Next**.

6. In the **Deploy OVF Template** | **Select name and folder** window, provide a name for the App Volumes appliance (**RTPAPPV01** in the example provided), select a destination vCenter Server VM folder, and then click **Next**.

7. In the **Deploy OVF Template** | **Select storage** window, click on a destination vSphere datastore for the appliance, update the virtual disk format (**Thin Provisioned** in our example), apply a **VM Storage Policy** if desired, and then click **Next**.

8. In the **Deploy OVF Template** | **Select network** window, select the virtual machine network the appliance will communicate on, and then click **Next**.

The desktops, RDS servers, and vCenter Servers must all be able to reach this network.

9. In the **Deploy OVF Template** | **Customize template** window, complete the details needed to configure the appliance networking settings as shown in the following screenshot, and then click **Next**.

| ▼ Networking Properties | 6 settings |
|---|---|
| Default Gateway | The default gateway address for this VM. Leave blank if DHCP is desired. |
| | 172.16.100.1 |
| Domain Name | The domain name of this VM. Leave blank if DHCP is desired. |
| | vjason.local |
| Domain Search Path | The domain search path (comma or space separated domain names) for the DHCP is desired. |
| | vjason.local |
| Domain Name Servers | The domain name server IP Addresses for this VM (comma separated). Lea desired. |
| | 172.16.100.6 |
| Network 1 IP Address | The IP address for this interface. Leave blank if DHCP is desired. |
| | 172.16.100.30 |
| Network 1 Netmask | The netmask or prefix for this interface. Leave blank if DHCP is desired. |
| | 255.255.224.0 |

10. In the **Deploy OVF Template** | **Ready to complete** window, review the configuration, use the **Back** button as needed to make any changes, click the **Power on after deployment check box**, and then click **Finish** to deploy the OVA file.

11. Repeat steps *2* through *10* to deploy redundant App Volumes Manager servers, including those located in other datacenters.

The App Volumes Manager appliance has been deployed, and an initial configuration performed, and is ready for final configuration steps. To replace the default self-signed SSL certificate, refer to the procedure found in `Chapter 14`, *Managing Horizon SSL Certificates*.

App Volumes version 3 introduced a new management layer that sits on top of the one used with previous versions (2.10 and earlier). While those familiar with the original management interface may still use it by accessing the web interface over HTTPS and using port `3443`, VMware recommends using the new version, as using both at the same time will likely lead to corruption in the App Volumes Manager database.
The state of the new management interface is only maintained on the App Volumes Manager server where it resides, so changes made on one interface will not be reflected on another, which is one of the reasons why App Volumes Manager database corruption can occur.

# Configuring App Volumes Manager

App Volumes is configured using a web-based GUI accessed on the App Volumes Manager appliance. For information about options not used, or otherwise referenced, during the configuration process, consult the *VMware App Volumes documentation* (`https://www.vmwa re.com/support/pubs/app-volumes-pubs.html`). The following steps outline the App Volumes configuration process:

1. Log on to the console of the App Volumes Manager server using the username `root` and password `123`, and change the password when prompted. The password requirements are similar to those of ESXi local accounts, and are outlined in the App Volumes documentation.

By default, App Volumes Manager servers will not trust vCenter or vRealize Operations Servers that have self-signed SSL certificates. Three options are available to address this, and one must be performed prior to linking the vCenter Server in the next step:

1. Replace these scripts with ones signed by a root certificate authority trusted by the App Volumes Manager; this is the preferred option.
2. Import the scripts in to the App Volumes Manager server where they will be trusted; this procedure is detailed in the SSL Certificate Validation section of the product documentation (`ht tps://www.vmware.com/support/pubs/app-volumes-pub s.html`)
3. Disable the SSL certificate validation by running the following script on the App Volumes Manager server, which will address the issue but is not recommended for production installs: `/etc/wemi/utils/disable_ssl_validation.sh`

2. Log in to the App Volumes Manager web portal using the web browser, and the FQDN of the App Volumes Manager server. In the example provided, the URL is `https://rtpappv01.vjason.local`. No log in is required during the initial configuration process.
3. In the **General Setup** | **Active Directory** section of the initial configuration page, click **Configure** to open the **Register Active Directory** window.

4. In the **Register Active Directory** window, complete each of the fields shown in the following screenshot, and then click **Domain Bind** to open the **Add Super Administrator** window.

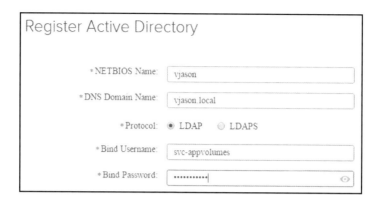

5. In the **Add Super Administrator** window, search for and select the AD security group that contains the App Volumes administrators (**AppVolumes_Admins** in the example provided), as shown in the following screenshot, and then click **Save**. You will then be logged out of the App Volumes Manager, and prompted to log in using an administrator account.

If this App Volumes Manager server is being added to an existing deployment, you may stop the configuration process at this point. Refer to the *Deploying additional App Volumes Manager servers* section of this chapter for the procedure used to add a new App Volumes Manager server to an existing deployment.

6. Log in to the App Volumes Manager using an account that is a member of the administrators group selected in the previous step (**svc-appvolumes** in the example provided).

7. In the **Customer Experience Improvement Program** window, make changes as needed and then click **Save**.

When navigating the web portal during the next few steps you may see a screen that mentions configuring the integration with **vRealize Operations** (**vROps**). This is only used with customers using App Volumes with **Citrix XenDesktop**, not Horizon.

8. Click on the **App Assignment** section of the initial configuration page to display the selections, and in the **vCenter Location** section click **New** to open the **New vCenter** window.

9. In the **New vCenter** window, complete each of the fields shown in the following screenshot, keeping in mind that the datastore prefixes are case sensitive, and then click **Save** to return to the previous window.

New vCenter

|  |  |
| --- | --- |
| * Name: | VC-01 |
| * Hostname: | vc-01.vjason.local |
| City Name: | City Search |
|  | Raleigh |
| * vCenter Username: | vjason\svc-appvolumes |
| * vCenter Password: | •••••••••• |
| * ESX Username: | appvol |
| * ESX Password: | ••••••••••• |
| AV Managers: |  |
| * Appstack Datastore Prefix: | AVA |
| * Writable Datastore Prefix: | AVW |

Note that this screen is where you specify the datastore prefixes and ESXi root account mentioned in the *App Volumes Prerequisites* section of this chapter. If App Volumes does not include your datacenter **City Name** in its database of locations, select any city you can find that is nearby. This information is used to display App Volumes Manager installations on a map in the interface.

10. Repeat steps *8* and *9* as needed to add additional vCenter Servers.

11. In the **Getting Started** window shown in the following screenshot, click on **SETTINGS**, then **Locations**.

12. In the **Locations** window | **AV MANAGER** tab, click the check box to the left of the App Volumes Manager server as shown in the following screenshot, and then click **Edit**.

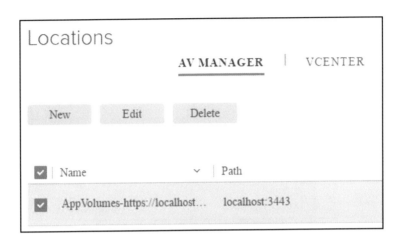

13. In the **Edit AV Manager** window, edit the **Name:** and **Path:** fields to match the appliance name and FQDN as shown. In the **Destination vCenter:** field, use the down arrow key and select the vCenter Server added in in step 9. Click **Save** when you have finished to return to the previous window.

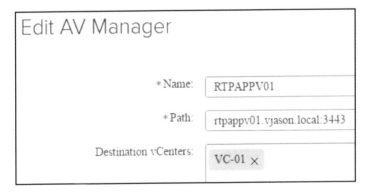

If you ever need to link additional vCenter Servers to your App Volumes Manager servers you would do so using this screen.

14. In the **Locations** window | **AV Manager** tab shown in the following screenshot, verify that the App Volumes Manager now appears with the new name and FQDN as configured in the previous step:

15. In the **Locations** window | **FILE SHARE** tab, click the **New** button to open the **New File Share** window.

16. In the **New File Share** window, complete each of the fields shown in the following screenshot. In the **Destination vCenter:** field, use the down arrow key and select the vCenter Server added in in step 9, and then click **Save** to return to the previous window.

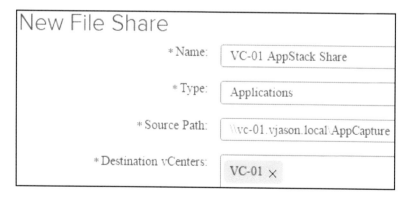

If you want to replicate AppStacks to vSphere datastores, managed by multiple vCenter Servers, add them all here. Once the replication finishes, the AppStacks will be available for use by Horizon desktops or RDS servers managed by those vCenter Servers. This assumes that AppStack datastores can be identified based on the prefix specified in step 9.

17. App Volumes is now configured, although at this point we only have one App Volumes Manager deployed. For redundancy purposes we will want to provision at least one additional appliance in each site where we deployed App Volumes.

18. The procedure used to add an additional App Volumes Manager server to our existing deployment will be outlined in the next step.

# Deploying additional App Volumes Manager servers

The procedure used to deploy additional App Volumes Manager servers differs based on how many vCenter Servers that you have; specifically, if you have only one, or you have more than one. In this section, we will review the procedures used for each scenario.

When adding additional App Volumes Managers servers to an existing deployment, or performing administrative tasks, do not forget that you must always use the web portal of the first server you installed.

# Deploy additional App Volumes Manager servers in a single vCenter environment

The following steps outline how to add additional App Volumes Manager servers to an existing installation that uses only one vCenter Server. For installations that use more than one vCenter Server, which includes those that span multiple sites, you must use the procedure outlined in the next section of this chapter:

1. Deploy and configure the new App Volumes Manager server using the following procedures:

    Deploying an App Volumes Manager appliance

    Configuring App Volumes Managerâ®®Steps *1* through *5* only

2. Log in to the App Volumes Manager web portal of the first server that was deployed using an account that is a member of the administrators group. In the example provided, this would be `https://rtpappv01.vjason.local`.

3. In the **Getting Started** window, click on **SETTINGS**, then **Locations**.

4. In the **Locations** window | **AV MANAGER** tab, click the **New** button to open the **New AV Manager** window.

5. In the **New AV Manager** window, fill in the information for the new App Volumes Manager server in the **Name:** and **Path:** fields, and in the **Destination vCenters:** field use the down arrow key to add the vCenter Server as shown on the following screenshot. Click on **Save** when finished to return to the previous window.

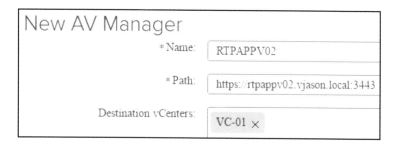

The new App Volumes Manager server has been added to the existing installation, and can now service client requests. If you will be using a load balancer in front of your App Volumes Manager Servers, you should configure that at this time.

In the next section we will add App Volumes Manager servers to an installation that has more than one vCenter Server, which requires additional steps.

# Deploying App Volumes in Multi-site and Multi-vCenter Environments

If you have more than one datacenter that requires App Volumes, or more than one vCenter Server in a single datacenter, you are required to deploy a new installation in each location, as with Horizon. However, all datacenters can use the `\\vc-01.vjason.local\AppCapture` share configured in steps *15* and *16* of the *Configuring App Volumes Manager* section of this chapter, which makes it much easier to distribute new and updated AppStacks to all datacenters.

If you are deploying App Volumes in a multi-site or multi-vCenter environment, I recommend using unique prefixes for your AppStack and Writable Volume datastores. This should reduce the likelihood of conflicts related to similar datastore names when VMware introduces a global App Volumes administration layer that can manage multiple installations as one.

The following is a high level overview of the sections of this chapter you must repeat when deploying an additional vCenter Server for Horizon (be it in the same datacenter as your existing one, or another site entirely) to deploy and configure App Volumes:

- *Deploying an App Volumes Manager appliance*
- *Configuring App Volumes Manager* (use the existing `\\vc-01.vjason.local\AppCapture` share)
- *Deploying additional App Volumes Manager servers*
- *Installing the App Volumes Agent*
- *Assigning AppStacks*
- *Deleting AppStacks Assignments*
- *Enabling Writable Volumes*
- *Disabling Writable Volumes*
- *App Volumes Backup and Recovery*

Future releases of App Volumes 3 are intended to support multi-site and multi-vCenter installations that share the same App Volumes Manager web portal, which should greatly simplify setup and administration. If this happens, the procedure used to implement App Volumes will be different than what I describe here.

# Installing the App Volumes Agent

The App Volumes Agent software is used to enable communication between App Volumes clients and the App Volumes Manager servers, and is typically installed in one of two places:

- Horizon desktop virtual desktop master image
- Horizon Windows RDS server master image

The installation process is the same regardless of where the agent software is being installed, so only one example will be provided.

The following steps outline the App Volumes Agent installation process:

1. Double click the `VMware-appvolumes-unifiedagent-xYY-y.y.y-zzz.exe` agent installer to launch the **App Volumes Unified Agent Installation Wizard**. Click **Next >** to proceed through the initial installation steps, including accepting the license agreement.

   VMware provides individual installers for 32 and 64-bit OSs.

2. In the **Setup Type** window, accept the default **Complete** install and then click **Next >**.

3. In the **Configure App Volumes** window, enter the FQDN for one of the local App Volumes Manager servers (`rtpappv01.vjason.local` in the example provided) and default port (`3443`) and then click **Next >**.

   If you are going to use a load balancer with your App Volumes Manager servers, you should provide the load-balanced URL here instead. If you intend to use the native App Volumes Agent failover capabilities, you will need to add additional App Volumes Manager server addresses using the method outlined in the next section of this chapter.

4. In the **Ready to Install the Program** window, use the **< Back** button as needed to make any changes to the configuration, and then click **Install**.

5. In the **InstallShield Wizard Completed** window, click **Finish**.

The App Volumes Agent is now installed, and is ready for use with the App Volumes Manager named in step 3. In the next section, we will edit the agent software configuration so that the agent software can still use more than one App Volumes Manager server, an important step if a load balancer is not being used.

# Configuring native load balancing for the App Volumes Agent software

The App Volumes Agent includes the ability to support low-level fault tolerance by utilizing more than one App Volumes Manager server. The primary difference between the agent-based load balancing, versus using a load balancer to transparently balance client connections, is that the agent-based method must wait for a timeout to occur to attempt to contact the next App Volumes Manager server.

Many dedicated load balancers can perform ongoing checks of downstream server availability, even when no client connections are occurring, ensuring that when an App Volumes client request is made, they will be immediately connected to a known functioning server.

The following steps outline the necessary registry changes that must be made to implement native App Volumes Agent load balancing:

1. Open the Windows Registry Editor on the computer that has the App Volumes Agent software installed.

2. Expand the computer registry to reach `Computer\HKEY_LOCAL_MACHINE\SYSTEM\CurrentControlSet\services\svservice\Parameters`.

3. Right click on the **Parameters** registry key, and, in the menu that opens, click **New – String Value**. Name the string **Manager2**, and in the **Data** field provide the `FQDN:port number` for the second App Volumes Manager server as shown in the following screenshot.

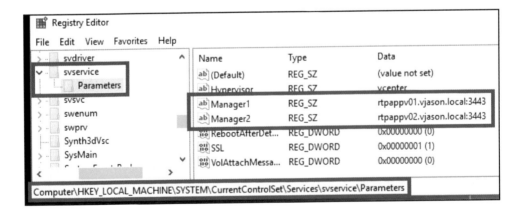

4. Repeat as needed for additional App Volumes Manager servers, adding keys named **Manager3**, **Manager4**, and so on.

 If you have multiple virtual desktop master images, use a different order for the App Volumes Manager servers in the `ManagerX` registry string values. For example, image 1 should use App Volumes Manager server 1 and 2 in that order, while image 2 would use them in the reverse order. This will help distribute the client load across all of your App Volumes Servers, instead of just a single one.

5. Reboot the computer or alternatively use the Windows **Services** management console to restart the **App Volumes Service**.

The load-balancing settings may also be edited using AD Group Policies to add the required registry keys, or by importing the registry file (file with a `.reg` extension) with the updated settings, in a format similar to the following example:

```
Windows Registry Editor Version 5.00
[HKEY_LOCAL_MACHINESYSTEMCurrentControlSetservicessvserviceParameters]
Manager2=rtpappv01.vjason.local:3443
Manager3=rtpappv02.vjason.local:3443
```

Regardless of the method used to add the needed registry keys, once finished, the App Volumes Agent will now be able to use each of the servers specified in the updated settings.

# Installing the AppCapture program

The App Volumes AppCapture program is used on the provisioning computer to capture and create AppStacks. The following steps outline the App Volumes AppCapture program installation process:

1. Double click the `VMware-appvolumes-appcapture-y.y.y-zzz.exe` agent installer to launch the **AppCapture Program Installation Wizard**. Click **Next >** to proceed through the initial installation steps, including accepting the license agreement.
2. In the **Ready to install the program** window, click **Install**.
3. In the last **AppCapture Program Installation Wizard** screen, click **Finish**.
4. Disable **User Account Control (UAC)** on the provisioning computer.

The App Volumes AppCapture program is now installed, and is ready to use to capture and create AppStacks. A snapshot should be taken of the provisioning computer prior to creating an AppStack.

 You will need to create a provisioning computer for each OS version you use with Horizon, including both Windows desktops and RDS server, and install the AppCapture program on each.

# Creating an AppStack

App Volumes uses a very simple process to create an AppStack, requiring very little more from the administrator than executing a few commands and installing the target application. In this section we will create an AppStack for **Notepad++**, although the process is similar for other applications, or even collections of applications.

 Where possible, combine multiple applications in to a single AppStack. The more AppStacks you assign to a user, the more likely it is that additional time will be required for them to log in due to the time required to attach multiple AppStack VMDK files.

The following steps outline the procedure used to create an AppStack. It assumes that the provisioning computer being used is running the same OS and patch level as the target App Volumes clients, is a member of the target domain, has not been used as an App Volumes client, and has the AppCapture program installed. Additionally, a snapshot should be taken of this computer prior to installing the application, as you will revert to this snapshot once the AppStack has been created.

 For compatibility reasons, you will need to use multiple provisioning computers, one for each OS you intend to use with App Volumes. You will need to repeat the AppStack capture process on each of these computers, and only assign the resulting AppStack to Horizon desktops or RDS servers running the same OS.

1. Log in to the App Volumes provisioning computer using an account with local administrator permissions.
2. Open a windows command prompt, and navigate to the `C:\Program Files (x86)\VMware\AppCapture` directory.

3. Execute the command `AppCapture.exe /n AppStackName`, replacing `AppStackName` with a name representing the application you are capturing (`NotepadPlus` in the example provided) as shown in the following screenshot. Do not include spaces in the name.

```
c:\Program Files (x86)\VMware\AppCapture>AppCapture.exe /n NotepadPlus

VMware AppCapture Program
Version 3.0.0.340 (with App Volumes Agent v3.0.0.0)
Copyright (c) 2016 VMware, Inc.

INFO : creating output disk (copying 100 % done)
INFO : preparing output virtual disk for capture
INFO : attaching virtual disk for capture
INFO : disk attachment complete
INFO : waiting to become capture-ready: 8

  Ready to capture application(s):
  ----------------------------------------------------------------------
  Run installers to install applications. If an installer requires a machine
  reboot, allow the reboot to proceed. When the installation is complete, hit
  ENTER at the prompt below, to begin reboot and finalize capture.

  Use "CTRL+C" to cancel and begin a new session.

  After all application installs are complete, hit ENTER here :
```

4. Install the target application, or applications, along with any required patches, accept any license agreements, and then make any needed changes to the default configuration. The provisioning computer may be rebooted as many times as is needed. When you have finished, hit *Enter* within the command prompt, and when prompted again, as seen in the following screenshot, hit *Enter* again to reboot the provisioning computer and finalize the capture process.

```
  After all application installs are complete, hit ENTER here :

  System will now reboot to finalize capture. Hit ENTER again to confirm :
```

5. Log in to the provisioning computer to complete the capture process. The following screenshot shows the results of the AppStack creation process:

```
Virtual disks with captured application(s) are now available at:

C:\ProgramData\VMware\AppCapture\appvhds\NotepadPlus.vhd
C:\ProgramData\VMware\AppCapture\appvhds\NotepadPlus.vmdk
```

Although not listed, a third file with the same name and a JSON extension was also created.

6. Copy the three files that were created to the AppStack share (\\vc-01.vjason.local\AppCapture in the example provided).
7. In the App Volumes Manager web portal **Getting Started** window, click on **SETTINGS**, then **Locations**, then the **FILE SHARE** tab.

Remember to use the first App Volumes Manager server when accessing the portal.

8. In the **FILE SHARE** tab, click the check box to the left of the file share (**VC-01 AppStack Share** in the example provided).
9. Click on the **...** drop down menu shown in the following screenshot and then click **Sync Now** to immediately import the AppStack.

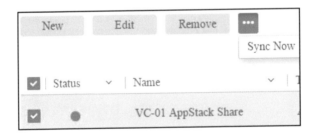

8. Click on **INVENTORY**, then **Applications**. Verify that the AppStack has been imported as seen in the following screenshot. You may click on the AppStack to view additional details.

The initial release of App Volumes 3.0 does not offer the ability to remove AppStacks from the App Volume Manager; you must contact VMware support to remove them. This issue will be fixed in a future release.

11. Revert the provisioning computer to the virtual machine snapshot that was taken prior to the installation of the application or applications.

The AppStack creation process has now been completed, and the AppStack imported. We can now assign the AppStack to your end users or associated AD security groups. The AppStack assignment process is outlined in the section of this chapter titled *Assigning AppStacks*.

If you have an application that has been captured using VMware **ThinApp**, that has been packaged as a **Microsoft Installer (MSI)** file, you may use that to create an AppStack. Simply install the MSI as you would a normal application, and App Volumes will capture the application and the ThinApp virtualization layer. This is useful when you need the application virtualization capabilities of ThinApp, but want to leverage App Volumes to seamlessly, and transparently, deliver that application to your end users.

# Updating an AppStack

The process used to update an AppStack is similar to that of creating one, with the exception that you will be making changes to an existing AppStack, rather than installing the software from scratch. When you initiate the AppStack update process, App Volumes mounts the source AppStack, prompts you to make any needed changes, and when finished builds a new AppStack that includes those changes. From there, we upload the new AppStack to the AppCapture share, perform a manual sync, and can then assign the new version to our clients.

The following steps outline the procedure used to update an AppStack. It assumes that a snapshot was taken of the provisioning computer, that it is now powered on, and a user with local administrator privileges has logged in.

1. Open a windows command prompt, and navigate to the `C:\Program Files (x86)\VMware\AppCapture` directory.
2. Create a folder on the provisioning workstation (`C:\NotepadPlus` in the example provided) and copy the target AppStack files from the `AppCapture` share to it.
3. Execute the command `AppCapture.exe /n AppStackName-1 /s "C:\AppStackDir\AppStack.vhd"`, replacing `AppStackName` with a AppStack (`NotepadPlus` in the example provided), `AppStackDir` with the location of the files you copied in the previous step, and `AppStack` with the name of the VHD file in that directory, and then hit *Enter*. The completed command is shown in the following screenshot:

```
c:\Program Files (x86)\VMware\AppCapture>AppCapture.exe /n NotepadPlus-1 /s "C:\NotepadPlus\NotepadPlus.vhd"
```

The `-1` is used to indicate that this is a new version of an AppStack; you can use something else if you wish.

4.  When the provisioning computer is ready for the application to be updated, it will display text similar to the following screenshot. You can now update or make changes to the application as needed; you may even install additional applications if you want. When you have finished, return to the command prompt and hit *Enter* twice to reboot the provisioning computer and finalize the AppStack update process.

```
Ready to capture application(s):
-------------------------------------------------------------------------
Run installers to install applications. If an installer requires a machine
reboot, allow the reboot to proceed. When the installation is complete, hit
ENTER at the prompt below, to begin reboot and finalize capture.

Use "CTRL+C" to cancel and begin a new session.

After all application installs are complete, hit ENTER here :
```

5.  Log in to the provisioning computer to complete the capture process. The following screenshot shows the results of the AppStack creation process:

```
-------------------------------------------------------------------------
Virtual disks with captured application(s) are now available at:

C:\ProgramData\VMware\AppCapture\appvhds\NotepadPlus-1.vhd
C:\ProgramData\VMware\AppCapture\appvhds\NotepadPlus-1.vmdk
-------------------------------------------------------------------------
```

Although not listed, a third file with the same name and a JSON extension was also created.

6. If you did not update the software version contained within the AppStack, when imported it would be listed using the same name and version within the App Volumes Manager web portal. You would only be able to identify which AppStack was the updated version by clicking on the AppStack to view its details, and then looking at the **Template:** field, which would show the new file name with the -1 appended to edit. To customize the application**name** or **version**, edit the AppStack JSON file as shown in the following screenshot (in the example provided we added -Rev2 to the version). Save the changes prior to continuing onto the next step.

```
NotepadPlus-1.json - Notepad

"apps" : [
            {
                          "name" : "Notepad++",
                    "version" : "6.8.3-Rev2",
                  "publisher" : "Notepad++ Team",
```

This step is not required if you updated to a new version of the software as the version number should have changed. Regardless, you should verify that prior to copying the files in the next step.

7. Copy the three files that were created to the AppStack share and perform a manual sync of the AppStack share using the procedure outlined in steps *6* through *9* of the section of this chapter titled *Creating an AppStack*.

8. Click on **INVENTORY**, then **Applications**. Verify that the AppStack has been imported as seen in the following screenshot. You may click on the AppStack to view additional details.

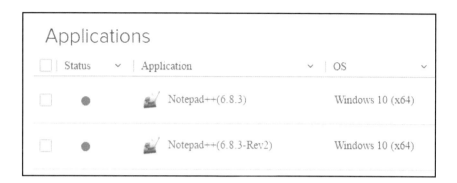

Remember to use the first App Volumes Manager server when accessing the portal.

9. Revert the provisioning computer to the virtual machine snapshot that was taken prior to the installation of the application or applications.
10. Update or replace your assignments using the technique using the procedure found in the next section of this chapter titled *Assigning AppStacks*.

The AppStack update process has now been completed.

# Assigning AppStacks

App Volumes AppStacks may be assigned to individual users or AD security groups that contain user accounts. Additionally, the prefix of the computer name can be used to further restrict the AppStack assignments.

The following steps outline the procedure used to assign an AppStack.

1. Log in to the App Volumes Manager web portal of the first server that was deployed using an AD account that has administrative permissions. In the example provided, the URL of the server is `https://appvolmgr1.vjason.local.`

2. In the **Getting Started** window, click on **ASSIGN**, then click the **New** button to open the **New Assignment** window.

3. In the **New Assignment** window, under the **Applications** section, click the **Get Started!** button to open the **New Applications Assignment** window.

4. In the **New Applications Assignment** window **DEFINITON** screen, provide an **Assignment Name: (NotepadPlus** in the example provided), select the **OS:** if required, and provide an optional case sensitive **Computer Name Prefix:** if you wish to limit the assignment only to specific computers. Click **Next >** to continue.

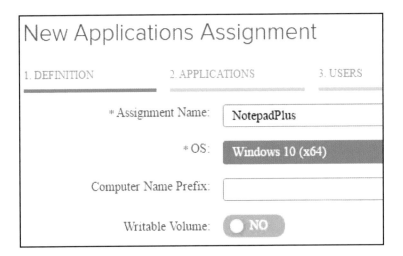

 We will talk about Writable Volumes in the section of this chapter titled Creating a **Writable Volume**, do not enable them at this time.

5. In the **New Applications Assignment** window **APPLICATIONS** screen, check the box to the left of the AppStack you wish to assign (**Notepad++(6.8.3)** in the example provided) as shown in the following screenshot and then click **Next >**.

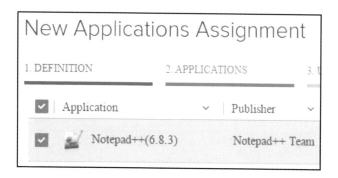

6. In the **New Applications Assignment** window **USERS** screen, search for and click on the AD user or security group you wish to assign the AppStack to (the security group **AppVolumes_NotepadPlus** in the example provided), and then click **Next >**.

7. In the **New Applications Assignment** window **SUMMARY** screen, use the **< Back** button to make any changes if required, and when finished click on **Submit** to return to the **Assignments** window.

8. Verify that the new assignment is displayed as shown in the following screenshot.

The AppStack assignment process has now been completed, and the selected clients will attach to the AppStack the next time they log in. In the next section we will delete AppStacks assignments.

# Deleting AppStacks assignments

The following steps outline the procedure used to delete an AppStack assignment:

1. Log in to the App Volumes Manager web portal of the first server that was deployed using an AD account that has administrative permissions. In the example provided, the URL of the server is `https://appvolmgr1.vjason.local`.

2. In the **Getting Started** window, click on **ASSIGN**, then click the checkbox to the left of the AppStack assignment to delete as shown in the following screenshot.

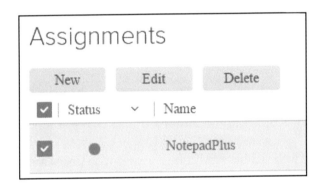

- Click the **Delete** button, and in the confirmation window that is displayed click **Delete** again to delete the AppStack assignment.

The AppStack assignment has now been deleted, and the affected clients will no longer attach the target AppStack.

# Enabling Writable Volumes

Writable Volumes are enabled as part of an AppStack assignment, and are used with Horizon clients who are accessing traditional desktops, not RDS servers.

 Future versions of App Volumes will likely restore the ability to enable Writable Volumes separately from AppStacks. Refer to the release notes and documentation for future releases to see if the option returns.

To enable a writable volume, when creating an AppStack assignment you click on the slider next to the **Writable Volume:** option to set it to **Yes** as seen in the following screenshot. This option occurs during step 4 of the procedure outlined in the section of this chapter titled *Assigning AppStacks*.

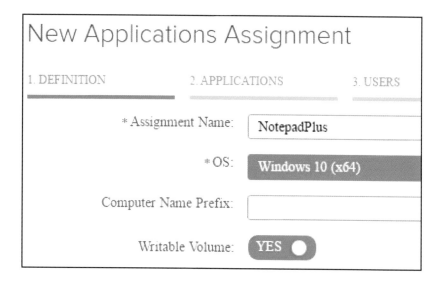

# Disabling Writable Volumes

There are two options for disabling Writable Volumes:

- Delete the AppStack assignment that has the **Writable Volume** feature enabled.
- Edit the AppStack assignment and disable the Writable Volume feature using the following procedure:
    1. Log in to the App Volumes Manager web portal of the first server that was deployed using an AD account that has administrative permissions. In the example provided, the URL of the server is `https://appvolmgr1.vjason.local`.
    2. In the **Getting Started** window, click on **ASSIGN**, click the checkbox to the left of the AppStack assignment to edit as shown in the following screenshot, and then click the **Edit** button to open the configuration page for the assignment.

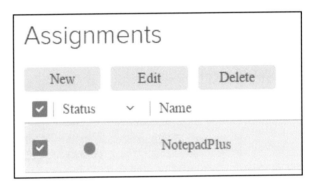

3. Click on the slider next to the **Writable Volume:** option to set it to **No** as seen in the following screenshot, and then click the **Save & Exit** button to save the changes.

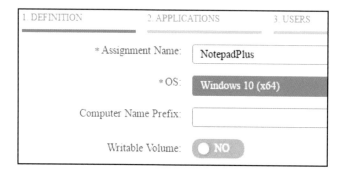

Writable volumes are now disabled for clients who are assigned the selected AppStack. The volumes will not be deleted, enabling them to be used again if required.

Future versions of App Volumes will likely restore the ability to delete Writable Volumes when disabled. Refer to the release notes and documentation for future releases to see if the option returns.

# App Volumes backup and recovery

App Volumes stores all configuration information in the App Volumes database, and the App Volumes Manager servers operate independently of one another. Owing to this, there is no critical information to back up on the App Volumes Managers servers themselves, although if custom SSL certificates were installed you may wish to retain backups of those.

If your environment uses Writable Volumes, it is important to be able to recover the underlying storage configuration and contents. App Volumes manages writable volume assignments based on where the volume was first created, and, if those Writable Volumes are restored to an alternate location, their connection to the clients would be lost until they are imported and manually assigned.

# What to backup

The following items should be backed up to ensure that App Volumes can be recovered in the event of a disaster or other scenario:

- App Volumes Manager servers appliances
- AppStacks can be backed up from and restored to anywhere; what is most important is getting a reliable backup
- App Volumes Writable Volumes, including their underlying storage configuration if possible
- App Volumes Manager server appliance custom SSL certificates (if used)

> VMware Engineers have developed a utility that can be used to backup AppStacks and Writable Volumes. While the **App Volumes Backup Utility** (https://labs.vmware.com/flings/app-volumes-backup-utility) is not an official component of App Volumes, and offers no formal support, it may be useful for smaller environments that require a simple process for backing up critical App Volumes files.

# Recovery process

The following provides a basic overview of App Volumes recovery. For more complex recovery scenarios, you will need to refer to the VMware App Volumes documentation (https://www.vmware.com/support/pubs/app-volumes-pubs.html), or in some cases even VMware product support. The following outlines the basic tasks that must be accomplished:

1. If needed, restore the Horizon vCenter Servers, and any other components of the Horizon infrastructure including Horizon Connection Servers, desktops, and RDS servers
2. Restore the AppStacks and Writable Volumes to their original locations
3. Restore the App Volumes Manager servers

The steps will return most App Volumes installations to a fully functional state, assuming Horizon itself is functional. As previously mentioned, if the recovery is more complex, certain items may need to be reconfigured, or manually updated, either with the assistance of the App Volumes documentation or with VMware product support.

# App Volumes references

The following resources will help you extend your knowledge of App Volumes, and understand some of the options not explored in this chapter in greater depth. If you intend to use App Volumes in your Horizon infrastructure I recommended you review these resources.

- **VMware App Volumes Documentation** (`https://www.vmware.com/support/pubs/app-volumes-pubs.html`)
- **VMware Community Forums for App Volumes** (`https://communities.vmware.com/community/vmtn/appvolumes`)

# Summary

In this chapter, you have been introduced to the very useful component of Horizon: App Volumes. You learnt what is required to deploy and configure App Volumes Manager servers and their associated client agent software, and how to build, deploy, and manage user access to AppStacks and Writable Volumes.

We then discussed how to create and assign Writable Volumes, which are used to enable the persistence of user-installed applications in linked and instant clone desktop-based Horizon environments.

Finally, we discussed what is required when backing up or recovering an App Volumes installation, including the AppStacks and Writable Volumes.

In the next chapter, we will discuss how to create the different Horizon pool types, which include those that provide access to desktops as well as Windows RDS servers.

# 10

# Creating Horizon Desktop Pools

A **Horizon desktop pool** is a collection of desktops that users select when they log in using the Horizon client. A pool can be created based on a subset of users, such as finance, but this is not explicitly required unless you will be deploying multiple virtual desktop master images. The pool can be thought of as a central point of desktop management within Horizon: from it you create, manage, and entitle access to Horizon desktops. This chapter will discuss how to create a desktop pool using the Horizon Administrator console, an important administrative task.

By the end of this chapter we will learn:

- An overview of Horizon desktop pools
- Desktop pool common terms
- How to create three different types of Horizon desktop pools
- How to monitor the provisioning of Horizon desktop pools
- Common problems encountered when provisioning a Horizon desktop pool
- How to manage entitlements to Horizon desktop pools

 A number of storage array vendors have given their products the ability to provision desktops outside the Horizon environment and then register them directly within Horizon. If you choose to use this method to create your virtual desktops, you should review the vendor documentation carefully to understand the impact it has on managing your Horizon environment. For example, you will need to know how virtual desktop maintenance, discussed in Chapter 12, *Performing Horizon Desktop Pool Maintenance*, differs if the desktops were not deployed using Horizon.

# Horizon desktop pool overview

Creating a Horizon desktop pool is commonly the final step in the process of deploying virtual desktops. In most cases, when you are ready to deploy your first desktop pool you have done at least the following:

- Created the necessary infrastructure services needed for your virtual desktop deployment, such as DHCP, DNS, Active Directory, and so on
- Deployed or identified the **vCenter** Server you will use with Horizon
- Deployed at least one ESXi server to host your virtual desktops
- Deployed and configured at least one Horizon Connection Server
- If linked clones will be used, you will have deployed Horizon Composer either on the Horizon vCenter Server or on a dedicated server.
- Created a virtual desktop master image, as discussed in `Chapter 13`, *Creating a Master Horizon Desktop Image*

Each of these items will be required in order to deploy your first desktop pool. Prior to placing your Horizon environment into production, it is important to verify that you have deployed sufficient resources to meet your scalability and availability needs.

 This chapter will focus on using the Horizon Administrator console to create your desktop pools. You also have the option of using PowerShell to create and manage your desktop pools: this is discussed in `Chapter 15`, *Using Horizon PowerCLI*.

# Desktop pool common terms

There are a number of options that must be selected when creating a Horizon desktop pool. Understanding what these options mean is important, as they will impact not only on how the desktops are deployed, but also on what options users have when they attempt to access those desktops.

Later on in the chapter, we will go through the deployment of two different desktop pools, but prior to that it is important to familiarize yourself with some of the terminologies that will come up during that process. Once you understand these terms, you will be able to create any type of desktop pool, something which we cannot demonstrate in this book due to the sheer number of options that exist.

| Term | Definition |
|------|-----------|
| Access group | Used to organize desktop pools within a Horizon pod, for reasons such as delegated administration. |
| Adobe Flash Settings for Sessions | Pool settings that control Adobe Flash quality and throttling for Horizon Clients, both of which affect connection bandwidth utilization. |
| Automated Desktop Pool | A pool that uses desktops provisioned using Horizon. |
| Automatic assignment | Used with Dedicated desktop assignment: if a user does not already have a desktop assigned, they will automatically be assigned a free one from the desktop pool. |
| Blackout times | Used to set when the View Storage Accelerator and VM disk space reclamation will not run. |
| Connection Server restrictions | Used to restrict what Connection Servers can be used to access a desktop pool: commonly used to assign pools to a Connection Server that has specific security settings. |
| Dedicated (assignment) | A desktop from the pool is assigned to a user, and from then on it is available only to that user unless the assignment is manually removed. |
| Desktop pool ID | The unique identifier for a desktop pool within a Horizon pod. |
| Display name | The desktop pool name that will be displayed in the Horizon Client login window. |
| Disposable file redirection | Used with a linked clone desktop to redirect disposable files to a non-persistent disk rather than the OS disk. |
| Floating (assignment) | Desktops are not assigned to any one user: if not in use, they are available to anyone that is entitled to access the desktop pool. |
| Full virtual machines (desktops) | Full virtual machine clones of a vCenter template created from the virtual desktop master image. |
| Guest customization | The process of preparing a Horizon desktop for placement within an Active Directory domain. |
| Instant Clones | Instant Clone desktops share the same base virtual desktop master image as linked clones, but can only be deployed using floating assignment pools. After every logoff, Instant Clone desktops are rapidly recreated using **vSphere vmFork** technology. |

| Manual Desktop Pool | A pool that uses desktops that already exist within vCenter, such as those configured using storage array-based cloning technologies. |
|---|---|
| Naming pattern | Used by Horizon to generate names for the virtual machines that it creates. |
| Non-persistent disk | Optional part of a Horizon Composer linked clone desktop: used to store disposable files that will be deleted automatically when the user's session ends. |
| Persistent disk | Optional part of a Horizon Composer linked clone desktop: used to retain user profile data during a Horizon Composer refresh, recompose, or rebalance operation. |
| QuickPrep | Similar to Microsoft Sysprep: optional method offered by Horizon for customizing and then joining linked clone desktops to an Active Directory domain. |
| Reclaim VM disk space | Reclaims blocks that are no longer being used by the virtual machine operating system. |
| Replica disk | Part of a Horizon Composer linked clone desktop: the replica disk is a read-only copy of the virtual desktop master image virtual hard disk that is shared among the desktops in the pool. |
| Storage Overcommit | Determines how Horizon places new VM on selected data stores. The more aggressive the setting, the more VM Horizon will place on the data store while reserving less space for sparse disk growth. |
| RDS Desktop Pool | A pool that provides access to Windows RDS servers: these servers are typically used to host multiple simultaneous Horizon client sessions. |
| Use native NFS snapshots (VAAI) | This feature eliminates the need for the **ESXi servers** to read and write data during the creation of Horizon Composer linked clones by using the built-in capabilities of the storage array to create the virtual machines. |
| View Composer linked clones | Clones of a virtual desktop master image that share the same base disk. Changes to linked clone desktops are written to a dedicated virtual hard disk attached to the linked clone virtual machine. |
| View Storage Accelerator | Uses up to 2GB of ESXi server RAM to cache frequently used blocks of virtual desktop data. |
| VM folder location | The location where Horizon will place the virtual machines it creates in the vCenter VM and Templates view. |

# Horizon desktop pool options

There are multiple decisions that must be made prior to configuring your first desktop pool. These choices will have an impact on your infrastructure and how your virtual desktops work, which is why they must be considered in advance.

Horizon can provision three different desktop types: Horizon Composer linked clones, Instant Clones, and full clones. From the perspective of an end user, each of these desktop types look exactly the same, although their underlying configuration is quite different. The master image for both is prepared using the same tuning techniques discussed in `Chapter 13`, *Creating a Master Horizon Desktop Image*, but how that image is used differs greatly based on the type of desktop you choose to deploy.

Deciding on what type of clone type to use is not an easy task. While instant and linked clones have some definite advantages, which I will describe in detail, to maintain that advantage you must adopt new ways of performing desktop maintenance.

# Horizon Composer linked clones

**Horizon Composer linked clone** desktops are created from a virtual desktop master image. While a full clone is created from a vSphere template, creating linked clones requires a virtual desktop master image that is in the standard virtual machine format. Once the image is ready for deployment, the only requirement is that it is powered down and a snapshot of the image is created. A snapshot is required so that Horizon Composer can create the replica of the virtual desktop master image. This replica will be used as the base image for all of the linked clone desktops in the pool.

In addition, as the virtual desktop master image has a snapshot the Horizon administrator will be able to power it on and make changes to it, while still retaining the ability to deploy additional desktops based on the condition of the desktop when the snapshot was taken. When it is time to deploy the updated image, you would simply take a second snapshot and recompose the desktops using the techniques described in `Chapter 12`, *Performing Horizon Desktop Pool Maintenance*. Assuming you left the initial snapshot in place, you could even recompose the desktops to that snapshot as well as the second one that you created.

# Instant Clone desktops

**Instant Clone desktops** are very similar to linked clone desktops in that they are provisioned from and share the same virtual desktop master image. However, Instant Clones are deployed using the vSphere vmFork technology, which utilizes a powered on virtual desktop master image replica VM on each ESXi server so that the clones can copy its disk and memory state during the provisioning process. This enables Instant Clones to be deployed or replaced in a matter of seconds as they require no additional reboots to configure, while linked clones require multiple reboots to complete the customization process. Similar to linked clones, the Instant Clone replica image can be replaced at any time with an updated version, and App Volumes may be used to manage applications independent of the virtual desktop master image.

Consult the VMware blog post **VMware Instant Clone Technology for Just-In-Time Desktop Delivery in Horizon 7 Enterprise Edition** (`http:/`
`/blogs.vmware.com/euc/2016/02/horizon-7-view-instant-clon`
`e-technology-linked-clone-just-in-time-desktop.html`) for
more information about how vmFork works, and why it is much faster
than deploying using linked clones.

Instant Clone desktops differ from linked clones in that they do not use Horizon Composer to deploy and manage the desktops, do not support dedicated user assignment, and there are no options for desktop persistence. All Instant Clone desktops utilize floating user assignment, and when the Horizon client logs off, the desktop is deleted and immediately deployed again using the vmFork functionality. If you require user persona data and personal files to persist, you must use tools such as User Environment Manager and folder redirection, discussed in `Chapter 8`, *Implementing VMware User Environment Manager*. Similar to linked clone desktop pools, a snapshot is required so that Horizon can create the replica of the master image.

# Full clone desktops

**Full clone Horizon desktops** are created using a virtual desktop master image that has been converted to the vSphere template format. A full clone is an independent copy of that template, managed separately from other desktops and the template on which it was based. Aside from the fact that it was created from a template, from a conceptual standpoint it is very similar to the physical desktop that it may have replaced. As a result, the life cycle of the full clone desktop is typically managed using the same techniques used with a physical desktop.

# Linux desktops

Horizon supports the use of Linux virtual desktops, although it contains no automated method to deploy them, and can only act as a connection broker for Horizon clients. Linux desktops must be deployed and managed outside of Horizon, and then added to **Horizon Manual Desktop Pools**. This process is much more complex than what is required to deploy Windows-based desktop pools, which makes it prohibitive to discuss further within this chapter.

The VMware document **Setting Up Horizon 7 for Linux Desktops** (`http://pubs.vmware .com/horizon-7-view/topic/com.vmware.ICbase/PDF/horizon-70-linux-deskto ps.pdf`) provides examples of the scripts you can use to deploy and customize Linux desktops, and then register them with Horizon for use in manual desktop pools. Once the desktops have been deployed, configured, registered with Horizon, added to Horizon Manual Desktop Pools, and entitlements assigned, they will be available for use by Horizon clients.

Experience with both Linux and vSphere **PowerCLI** is a recommended prerequisite to deploying Linux desktops for use with Horizon.

# QuickPrep versus Sysprep

Windows**Sysprep** is a utility included with the Windows operating system that is used to personalize a Windows image. Rather than install Windows on each machine individually, organizations can apply a preconfigured image to a machine and then use Sysprep to generate the identifiers that make that installation of Windows unique.

> Instant Clone desktop pools use a dedicated customization method called **ClonePrep**, which is similar to QuickPrep. There is no option to select Sysprep when creating Instant Clone desktop pools.

When deploying linked clone desktops, you have the option of using Sysprep or the included VMware**QuickPrep** tool to customize the operating system. The tools do not perform all of the same tasks, so it is important to understand what differs when you choose one over the other.

The following table details the differences between Sysprep and QuickPrep:

| Task | QuickPrep | Sysprep |
|---|---|---|
| Change security identifiers on the parent image | No | Yes |
| Change the computer name | Yes | Yes |
| Join the new virtual machine to the domain | Yes | Yes |
| Remove local accounts | No | Yes |
| Remove parent image from the domain | No | Yes |
| Reuse preexisting AD computer accounts | Yes | Yes |
| Generate a new **System Identifier (SID)** | No | Yes |
| Update language, regional, data, and time settings | No | Yes |
| Reboots required | 0 | 1 |
| Requires a configuration file and Sysprep utility | No | Yes |

Like QuickPrep, ClonePrep retains the replica Windows OS SID and application **Globally Unique Identifiers (GUID)** during the cloning process. Unlike QuickPrep, ClonePrep cannot reuse existing AD computer accounts.

It is important to consider the differences between Sysprep and QuickPrep when determining which method to choose. In some environments, it may be that QuickPrep cannot be used because it does not generate a new SID for the guest operating system. In other environments, it may be that there are no issues with using QuickPrep. Generally speaking, QuickPrep enables faster desktop deployment, which affects not only desktop pool creation but recompose operations as well. Regardless of which method you choose, it is important to monitor the behavior of the desktop during a pilot program to ensure that the desktops are functioning as expected.

You should use Microsoft **Key Management Services (KMS)** to license and activate your Horizon Desktops. This is particularly important when using linked clones, as nearly every Horizon Composer maintenance task will initiate a license activation request, regardless of whether ClonePrep, QuickPrep, or Sysprep was used. These requests would quickly exhaust ordinary **Multiple Activation Key (MAK)** license keys. Microsoft typically provides both KMS and MAK keys to organizations that purchase volume licensed versions of their Windows and Office products.

# Advantages of linked or Instant Clone desktops

Linked clone and Instant Clone desktops have a number of advantages over full clone desktops. Some of these advantages include:

- Linked clone and Instant Clone desktops share the same parent virtual disk for read operations, therefore the amount of disk space they require is greatly reduced.
- Linked clone desktops can be recomposed, which is a process where their replica disks are replaced with an updated version that has software updates or other changes applied. Rather than apply updates to individual desktops, you can update the master image once, and then use a recompose operation to update the replica disks, which applies those changes to the entire desktop pool.
    - Instant Clone desktops support a similar operation named **Push Image**.
    - These procedures are described in Chapter 12, *Performing Horizon Desktop Pool Maintenance*.

Using a recompose to upgrade the operating system version is not supported.

- Linked clone desktops can be refreshed, a process that deletes the contents of the linked clone OS and disposable data disks, which returns them to the same state they were in when initially deployed. This enables you to discard any changes that were made after the desktop was deployed, allowing for tight control over the end user experience. Desktops can be refreshed at a specific time, when a specified amount of disk space has been used, or even after every logoff. The refresh process is described in Chapter 12, *Performing Horizon Desktop Pool Maintenance*.
    - Instant Clone desktops are automatically deleted every time a Horizon client logs off; manual refresh operations are not required.
- A linked clone desktop pool can be rebalanced, which redistributes linked clone storage evenly across data stores. Individual linked clone disk utilization will vary over time, leading to an imbalance in storage utilization across all the data stores. A rebalance operation addresses this by moving relocating linked clone storage. The rebalance process is described in Chapter 12, *Performing Horizon Desktop Pool Maintenance*.
    - Instant Clone desktop pools do not require or support a rebalance operation.

Storage vMotion is not supported with linked clone desktops. You must use a rebalance operation to relocate or rebalance linked clone desktop storage.

# Considerations for linked and Instant Clone desktops

Owing to how linked and Instant Clone desktops work, it is important to remember that they should not be managed using the same techniques as a typical virtual machine. Some examples of this include:

- If you were to apply software patches to linked clones individually, rather than using a recompose operation, the linked clone virtual hard disks would grow significantly over time. This defeats the storage efficiency that are one of the primary reasons for choosing linked clones. Additionally, deploying patches to Instant Clone desktops would be pointless as any changes are erased when the user logs off

- Recompose, refresh, and rebalance operations all change the state of the linked clone virtual desktop, which can affect utilities such as indexing programs. If these operations lead to resource-intensive operations, such as a file index, every time they occur, it may be that they need to be disabled or their behavior altered. This topic is discussed further in Chapter 13, *Creating a Master Horizon Desktop Image*.

 For performance reasons, Windows indexing features should be disabled in Instant Clone master images.

- Instant Clones currently support Windows 7 and Windows 10 only, require that View Storage Accelerator be enabled, and the Instant Clone option must have been selected during the Horizon agent installation process described in Chapter 13, *Creating a Master Horizon Desktop Image*.

Generally speaking, you should approach managing Instant and linked clone desktops from the master image wherever possible as this enables you to realize most of the advantages of linked clones. If a proposed change can be done on the master image, and then rolled out to users using a recompose operation, that is the preferred method of working with linked clones, and the only way to work with Instant Clones. Chapter 12, *Performing Horizon Desktop Pool Maintenance* will provide more information about how to manage linked and Instant Clone desktops.

# Creating a Horizon desktop pool

This section will provide an example of how to create two different Horizon dedicated assignment desktop pools, one based on Horizon Composer linked clones and another based on full clones. Horizon Instant Clone pools only support floating assignment, so they have fewer options compared to the other types of desktop pools. Also discussed will be how to use the Horizon Administrator console and the vSphere client to monitor the provisioning process.

The examples provided for full clone and linked clone pools created dedicated assignment pools, although floating assignment may be created as well. The options will be slightly different for each, so refer to the information provided earlier in this chapter, as well as the Horizon documentation (`https://www.vmware.com/support/pubs/view_pubs .html`), to understand what each setting means. Additionally, the Horizon Administrator console often explains each setting within the desktop pool configuration screens.

# Creating a pool using Horizon Composer linked clones

The following steps outline how to use the Horizon Administrator console to create a dedicated assignment desktop pool using Horizon Composer linked clones. As discussed previously, it is assumed that you already have a virtual desktop master image that you have created a snapshot of. During each stage of the pool creation process, a description of many of the settings is displayed in the right-hand side of the **Add Desktop Pool** window. In addition, a question mark appears next to some of the settings; click on it to read important information about the specified setting.

1. Log on to the Horizon Administrator console using an AD account that has administrative permissions within Horizon.
2. Open the **Catalog – Desktop Pools** window within the console.
3. Click on the **Add...** button in the **Desktop Pools** window to open the **Add Desktop Pool** window.

4. In the **Desktop Pool Definition** | **Type** window, select the **Automated Desktop Pool** radio button as shown in the following screenshot, and then click on **Next >**:

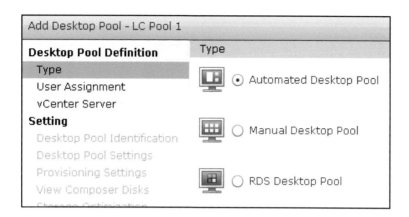

5. In the **Desktop Pool Definition** | **User Assignment** window, select the **Dedicated** radio button and check the **Enable automatic assignment** checkbox as shown in the following screenshot, and then click on **Next >**:

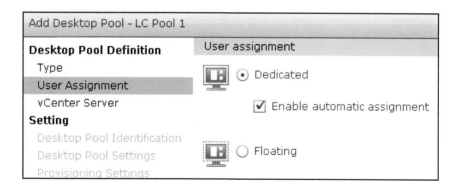

6. In the **Desktop Pool Definition | vCenter Server** window, select the **View Composer linked clones** radio button, highlight the vCenter server as shown in the following screenshot, and then click on **Next >**:

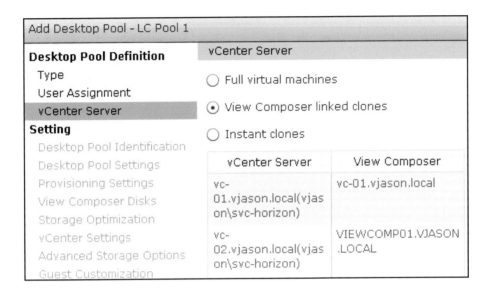

7. In the **Setting | Desktop Pool Identification** window, populate the pool **ID:** as shown in the following screenshot, and then click on **Next >**. Optionally, configure the **Display Name:** field. When finished, click on **Next >**:

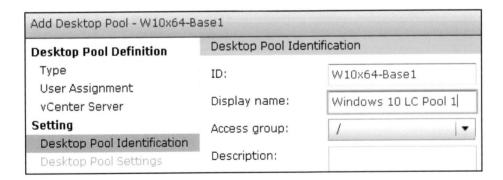

8. In the **Setting** | **Desktop Pool Settings** window, configure the various settings for the desktop pool. Many of these options are self-explanatory; those that are not are described in the *Desktop pool common terms* section of this chapter. These settings can also be adjusted later if desired. When finished, click on **Next >**:

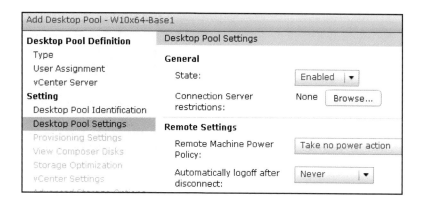

9. In the **Setting** | **Provisioning Settings** window, configure the various provisioning options for the desktop pool that include the desktop naming format, the number of desktops, and the number of desktops that should remain available during Horizon Composer maintenance operations. When finished, click on **Next >**:

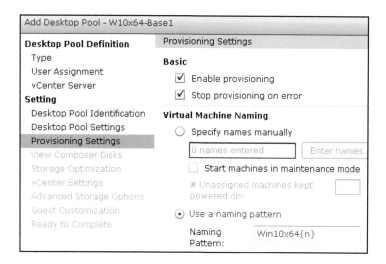

When creating a desktop naming pattern, use a {n} to instruct Horizon to insert a unique number in the desktop name. For example, using Win10x64{n}, as shown in the preceding screenshot, will name the first desktop Win10x641, the next Win10x642, and so on.

10. In the **Setting** | **View Composer Disks** window, configure the settings for your optional linked clone disks. By default, both a **Persistent Disk** for user data and a non-persistent disk for **Disposable File Redirection** are created. When finished, click on **Next >**:

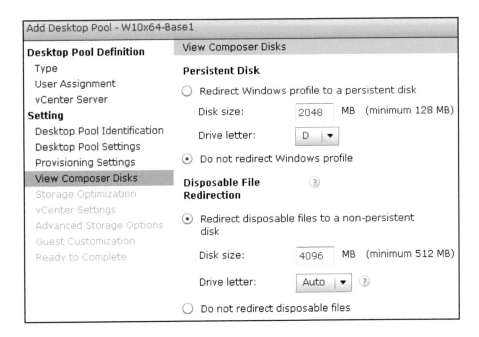

11. In the **Setting | Storage Optimization** window, we configure whether or not our desktop storage is provided by VMware Virtual SAN, and, if not, whether or not to separate our Horizon desktop replica disks from the individual desktop OS disks. In our example, we have checked the **Use VMware Virtual SAN** radio button as that is what our destination vSphere cluster is using. When finished, click on **Next >**:

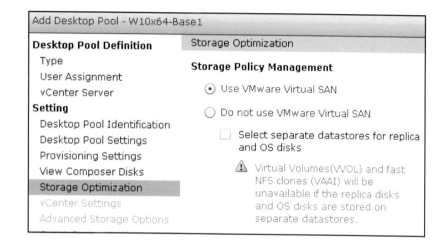

 As all-flash storage arrays or all-flash or flash-dependent **Software Defined Storage (SDS)** platforms become more common, there is less of a need to place the shared linked clone replica disks on separate, faster data stores than the individual desktop OS disks.

12. In the **Setting | vCenter Settings** window, we will need to configure six different options that include selecting the parent virtual machine, which snapshot of that virtual machine to use, what vCenter folder to place the desktops in, what vSphere cluster and resource pool to deploy the desktops to, and what data stores to use. Click on the **Browse...** button next to the **Parent VM:** field to begin the process and open the **Select Parent VM** window:

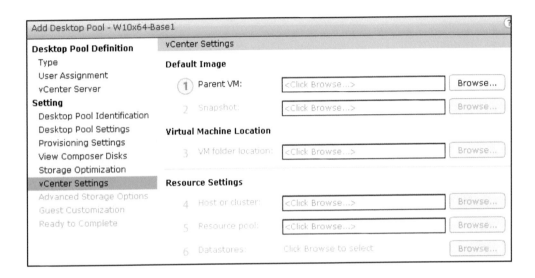

13. In the **Select Parent VM** window, highlight the virtual desktop master image that you wish to deploy desktops from, as shown in the following screenshot. Click on **OK** when the image is selected to return to the previous window:

The virtual machine will only appear if a snapshot has been created.

14. In the **Setting | vCenter Settings** window, click on the **Browse...** button next to the **Snapshot:** field to open the **Select default image** window. Select the desired snapshot, as shown in the following screenshot, and click on **OK** to return to the previous window:

15. In the **Setting | vCenter Settings** window, click on the **Browse...** button next to the **VM folder location:** field to open the **VM Folder Location** window, as shown in the following screenshot. Select the folder within vCenter where you want the desktop virtual machines to be placed, and click on **OK** to return to the previous window:

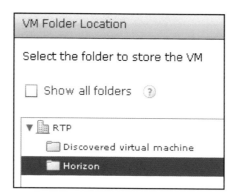

16. In the **Setting** | **vCenter Settings** window, click on the **Browse...** button next to the **Host or cluster:** field to open the **Host or Cluster** window, as shown in the following screenshot. Select the cluster or individual ESXi server within vCenter where you want the desktop virtual machines to be created, and click on **OK** to return to the previous window:

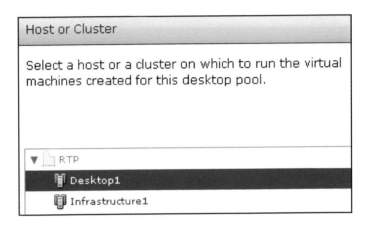

17. In the **Setting** | **vCenter Settings** window, click on the **Browse...** button next to the **Resource pool:** field to open the **Resource Pool** window, as shown in the following screenshot. If you intend to place the desktops within a resource pool you would select that here; if not select the same cluster or ESXi server you chose in the previous step. Once finished, click on **OK** to return to the previous window:

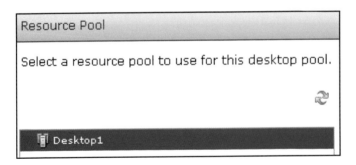

18. In the **Setting | vCenter Settings** window, click on the **Browse...** button next to the **Datastores:** field to open the **Select Linked Clone Datastores** window, as shown in the following screenshot. Select the datastore or datastores where you want the desktops to be created, and click on **OK** to return to the previous window:

---

**Select Linked Clone Datastores**

Select the linked clone datastores to use for this desktop pool. Only datastores that can be us selected host or cluster can be selected.

☐ Show all datastores (including local datastores)  ⑦  🖥 Local datastore  🖳 Shared dat

| | Datastore | Capacity (GB) | Free (GB) | FS Type |
|---|---|---|---|---|
| ☑ | 🖳 Desktop1-VSAN1 | 426.18 | 420.67 | vsan |

---

If you were using storage other than VMware Virtual SAN, and had opted to use separate datastores for your OS and replica disks in step 11, you would have had to select unique datastores for each here instead of just one. Additionally, you would have had the option to configure the storage overcommit level.

19. The **Setting | vCenter Settings** window should now have all options selected, enabling the **Next >** button. When finished, click on **Next >**:

20. In the **Setting** | **Advanced Storage Options** window, if desired select and configure the **Use View Storage Accelerator** and **Other Options** check boxes to enable those features. In our example, we have enabled both the **Use View Storage Accelerator** and **Reclaim VM disk space** options, and configured **Blackout Times** to ensure that these operations do not occur between 8 A.M. (**08:00**) and 5 P.M. (**17:00**) on weekdays. When finished, click on **Next >**:

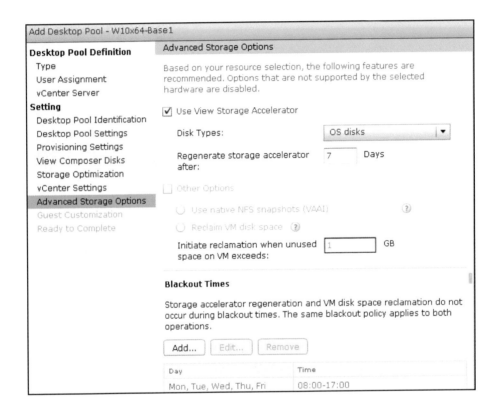

 The **Use native NFS snapshots (VAAI)** feature enables Horizon to leverage features of a supported NFS storage array to offload the creation of linked clone desktops. If you are using an external array with your Horizon ESXi servers, consult the product documentation to understand if it supports this feature. Since we are using VMware Virtual SAN, this and other options under **Other Options** are greyed out as these settings are not needed. Additionally, if View Storage Accelerator is not enabled in the vCenter Server settings the option to use it would be greyed out here.

21. In the **Setting** | **Guest Customization** window, select the **Domain:** where the desktops will be created, the **AD container:** where the computer accounts will be placed, whether to **Use QuickPrep** or **Use a customization specification (Sysprep)**, and any other options as required. When finished, click on **Next >**:

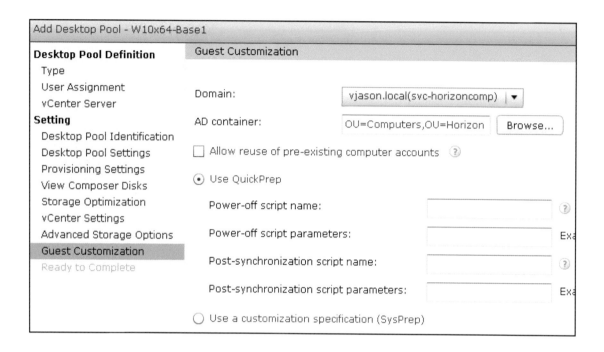

22. In the **Setting** | **Ready to Complete** window, verify that the settings we selected were correct, using the **< Back** button, if needed, to go back and make changes. If all the settings are correct, click on **Finish** to initiate the creation of the desktop pool.

The Horizon desktop pool and virtual desktops will now be created. To monitor the creation of the desktops, review the *Monitoring the desktop creation process* section of this chapter. Also located in this chapter is the *Managing Horizon Desktop Pool Entitlements* section, which outlines how to grant clients access to the desktop pools that we have created.

# Creating a pool using Horizon Instant Clones

The process used to create an Instant Clone desktop pool is similar to that used to create a linked clone pool. As discussed previously, it is assumed that you already have a virtual desktop master image that has the Instant Clone option enabled in the Horizon agent, and that you have taken a snapshot of that master image.

 A master image can have either the Horizon Composer (linked clone) option or Instant Clone option enabled in the Horizon agent, but not both. To get around this restriction you can configure one snapshot of the master image with the View Composer option installed, and a second with the Instant Clone option installed.

The following steps outline the process used to create the Instant Clone desktop pool. Screenshots are included only when the step differs significantly from the same step in the *Creating a pool using Horizon Composer linked clones* section.

1. Log on to the Horizon Administrator console using an AD account that has administrative permissions within Horizon.
2. Open the **Catalog | Desktop Pools** window within the console.
3. Click on the **Add...** button in the **Desktop Pools** window to open the **Add Desktop Pool** window.

4. In the **Desktop Pool Definition | Type** window, select the **Automated Desktop Pool** radio button as shown in the following screenshot, and then click on **Next >**.
5. In the **Desktop Pool Definition | User Assignment** window, select the **Floating** radio button (mandatory for Instant Clone desktops), and then click on **Next >**.
6. In the **Desktop Pool Definition | vCenter Server** window, select the **View Composer linked clones** radio button as shown in the following screenshot, highlight the vCenter server, and then click on **Next >**:

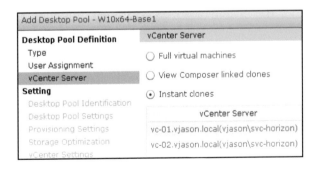

If **Instant Clones** is greyed out here, it is usually because you did not select **Floating** in the previous step.

7. In the **Setting** | **Desktop Pool Identification** window, populate the pool **ID:**, and then click on **Next >**. Optionally, configure the **Display Name:** field.

8. In the **Setting** | **Desktop Pool Settings** window, configure the various settings for the desktop pool. Many of these options are self-explanatory; those that are not are described in the *Desktop pool common terms* section of this chapter. These settings can also be adjusted later if desired. When finished, click on **Next >**.

9. In the **Setting** | **Provisioning Settings** window, configure the various provisioning options for the desktop pool that include the desktop naming format, the number of desktops, and the number of desktops that should remain available during maintenance operations. When finished, click on **Next >**.

Instant Clones are required to always be powered on, so some options available to linked clones will be greyed out here.

10. In the **Setting** | **Storage Optimization** window, we configure whether or not our desktop storage is provided by VMware Virtual SAN, and if not whether or not to separate our Horizon desktop replica disks from the individual desktop OS disks. When finished, click on **Next >**.

11. In the **Setting** | **vCenter Settings** window, we will need to configure six different options that include selecting the parent virtual machine, which snapshot of that virtual machine to use, what vCenter folder to place the desktops in, what vSphere cluster and resource pool to deploy the desktops to, and what datastores to use. Click on the **Browse...** button next to the **Parent VM:** field to begin the process and open the **Select Parent VM** window.

12. In the **Select Parent VM** window, highlight the virtual desktop master image that you wish to deploy desktops from. Click on **OK** when the image is selected to return to the previous window.

13. In the **Setting** | **vCenter Settings** window, click on the **Browse...** button next to the **Snapshot:** field to open the **Select default image** window. Select the desired snapshot, and click on **OK** to return to the previous window.

14. In the **Setting** | **vCenter Settings** window, click on the **Browse...** button next to the **VM folder location:** field to open the **VM Folder Location** window. Select the folder within vCenter where you want the desktop virtual machines to be placed, and click on **OK** to return to the previous window.

15. In the **Setting | vCenter Settings** window, click on the **Browse...** button next to the **Host or cluster:** field to open the **Host or Cluster** window. Select the cluster or individual ESXi server within vCenter where you want the desktop virtual machines to be created, and click on **OK** to return to the previous window.

16. In the **Setting | vCenter Settings** window, click on the **Browse...** button next to the **Resource pool:** field to open the **Resource Pool** window. If you intend to place the desktops within a resource pool you would select that here; if not select the same cluster or ESXi server you chose in the previous step. Once finished, click on **OK** to return to the previous window.

17. In the **Setting | vCenter Settings** window, click on the **Browse...** button next to the **Datastores:** field to open the **Select Instant Clone Datastores** window. Select the datastore or datastores where you want the desktops to be created, and click on **OK** to return to the previous window.

18. The **Setting | vCenter Settings** window should now have all options selected, enabling the **Next >** button. When finished, click on **Next >**.

19. In the **Setting | Guest Customization** window, select the **Domain:** where the desktops will be created, the **AD container:** where the computer accounts will be placed, and any other options as required. When finished, click on **Next >**.

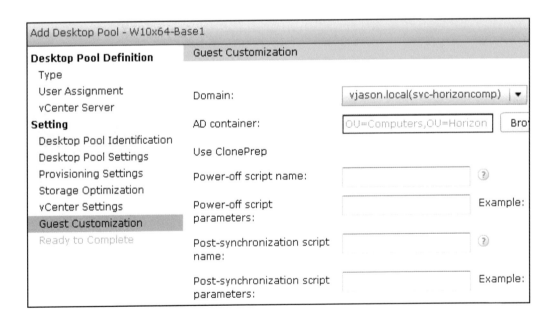

Instant Clones only support ClonePrep for customization, so there are fewer options here than seen when deploying a linked clone desktop pool.

20. In the **Setting** | **Ready to Complete** window, verify that the settings we selected were correct, using the **< Back** button if needed to go back and make changes. If all the settings are correct, click on **Finish** to initiate the creation of the desktop pool.

The Horizon desktop pool and Instant Clone virtual desktops will now be created. To monitor the creation of the desktops, review the *Monitoring the desktop creation process* section of this chapter. Also located in this chapter is the *Managing Horizon Desktop Pool Entitlements* section, which outlines how to grant users access to the desktop pools that we have created.

# Creating a pool using full clones

The process used to create full clone desktop pools is similar to that used to create a linked clone pool. As discussed previously, it is assumed that you already have a virtual desktop master image that you have converted to a vSphere template.

In addition, if you wish for Horizon to perform the virtual machine customization, you will need to create a Customization Specification using the vCenter Customization Specifications Manager. The Customization Specification is used by the Windows Sysprep utility to complete the guest customization process. Visit the VMware vSphere virtual machine administration guide (`http://pubs.vmware.com/vsphere-60/index.jsp`) for instructions on how to create a Customization Specification.

The following steps outline the process used to create the full clone desktop pool. Screenshots are included only when the step differs significantly from the same step in the Creating a pool using Horizon Composer linked clones section.

1. Log on to the Horizon Administrator console using an AD account that has administrative permissions within Horizon.
2. Open the **Catalog** | **Desktop Pools** window within the console.
3. Click on the **Add...** button in the **Desktop Pools** window to open the **Add Desktop Pool** window.

4. In the **Desktop Pool Definition** | **Type** window select the **Automated Pool** radio button and then click on **Next**.
5. In the **Desktop Pool Definition** | **User Assignment** window, select the **Dedicated** radio button, check the **Enable automatic assignment** checkbox, and then click on **Next**.
6. In the **Desktop Pool Definition** | **vCenter Server** window, click the **Full virtual machines** radio button, highlight the desired vCenter server, and then click on **Next**.
7. In the **Setting** | **Desktop Pool Identification** window, populate the pool **ID:** and **Display Name:** fields and then click on **Next**.
8. In the **Setting** | **Desktop Pool Settings** window, configure the various settings for the desktop pool. These settings can also be adjusted later if desired. When finished, click on **Next >**.
9. In the **Setting** | **Provisioning Settings** window, configure the various provisioning options for the desktop pool that include the desktop naming format and number of desktops. When finished, click on **Next >**.
10. In the **Setting** | **Storage Optimization** window, we configure whether or not our desktop storage is provided by VMware Virtual SAN. When finished, click on **Next >**.

11. In the **Setting** | **vCenter Settings** window, we will need to configure settings that set the virtual machine template, which vSphere folder to place the desktops in, which ESXi server or cluster to deploy the desktops to, and which datastores to use. Other than the **Template** setting described in the following step, each of these settings is identical to those seen when creating a Horizon Composer linked clone pool. Click on the **Browse...** button next to each of the settings in turn and select the appropriate options.

- To configure the **Template:** setting, select the vSphere template that you created from your virtual desktop master image as shown in the following screenshot, and then click **OK** to return to the previous window:

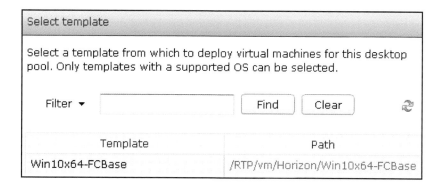

A template will only appear if one is present within vCenter.

12. Once all the settings in the **Setting** | **vCenter Settings** window have been configured, click on **Next >**.

13. In the **Setting** | **Advanced Storage Options** window, if desired, select and configure the **Use View Storage Accelerator** radio buttons and configure **Blackout Times**. When finished, click on **Next >**.

14. In the **Setting | Guest Customization** window, select either the **None – Customization will be done manually** or **Use this customization specification:** radio button, and if applicable select a customization specification. When finished, click on **Next >**. In the following screenshot, we have selected the **Win10x64-HorizonFC** customization specification that we previously created within vCenter:

Add Desktop Pool - W10x64-Base1

| **Desktop Pool Definition** | Guest Customization |
| --- | --- |
| Type | ○ None - Customization will be done manually |
| User Assignment | |
| vCenter Server | ☐ Do not power on virtual machines after cre |
| **Setting** | |
| Desktop Pool Identification | ⊙ Use this customization specification: |
| Desktop Pool Settings | ☐ Show all customization specifications ② |
| Provisioning Settings | |
| Storage Optimization | |
| vCenter Settings | |
| Advanced Storage Options | |
| Guest Customization | |

| Name | Guest OS | |
| --- | --- | --- |
| Win10x64-HorizonFC | Windows | |
| Win2012R2 | Windows | |

Manual customization is typically used when the template has been configured to run Sysprep automatically upon start up, without requiring any interaction from either Horizon or VMware vSphere.

15. In the **Setting | Ready to Complete** window, verify that the settings we selected were correct, using the **< Back** button if needed to go back and make changes. If all the settings are correct, click on **Finish** to initiate the creation of the desktop pool.

The desktop pool and virtual desktops will now be created. To monitor the creation of the desktops, review the *Monitoring the desktop creation process* section of this chapter. Also located in this chapter is the *Managing Horizon Desktop Pool Entitlements* section that outlines how to grant users access to the desktop pools that we have created.

# Monitoring the desktop creation process

The amount of time it takes to create the desktop pool varies based on a number of factors. There are multiple locations within the Horizon Administrator console and the vSphere Client where you can monitor the progress of the desktop deployment.

# Horizon Administrator console

Horizon desktops are displayed throughout the Horizon Administrator console as soon as they are initially created within vCenter. This section details two areas of the console where you can view the current status of the desktops.

- **Dashboard**: As desktops move through the deployment and configuration process, their status on the Desktop Status dashboard will change. The following screenshot shows how the Desktop Status dashboard window changes as desktops move from Preparing stage (left) to the Prepared for use stage (right).

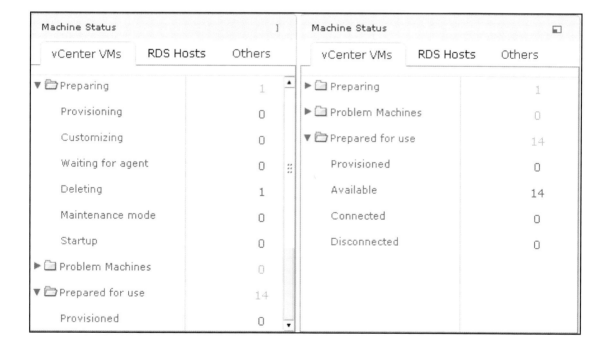

- **Desktops**: This option appears under **Inventory**. This window will display each of the Horizon desktops, along with their current status.

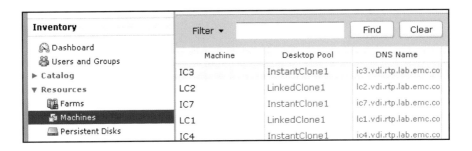

# The vSphere Web client task window

Creating virtual desktops will generate a number of vCenter tasks, during which the desktops will begin to appear within the vCenter Console. Monitor the following areas of the vSphere Web client to verify that the desktop pool is being created.

- **Task Console**: This window is shown in the following screenshot and will display the tasks associated with the creation and configuration of the virtual desktops:

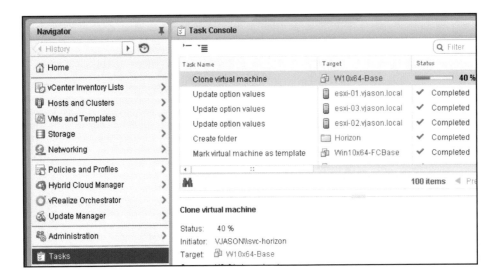

- **VMs and Templates or Hosts and Clusters**: Horizon desktops will appear in these views of the vSphere client just as with any other virtual machine. The following screenshot shows Horizon desktops as seen in the VMs and Templates view, within the folder we specified during the creation of the desktop pool:

# Common provisioning problems

There are a number of different issues that can arise during the deployment of desktop pools. While it is impossible to try and list them all, the following represent some of the more common issues that can occur:

- **Undersized or misconfigured DHCP address pool**: This is more common with linked clones, which change MAC addresses when redeployed; this can exhaust a DHCP pool. Linked clone environments typically work best when the DHCP lease time is very short. Desktops cannot complete the provisioning process without access to the network.
- **Issues with Windows operating system activation**: If Windows KMS services are not functioning within the domain, the provisioning process will fail.
- **Insufficient permissions within vCenter**: If the accounts used by Horizon and Horizon Composer do not have the required permissions within vCenter, the provisioning process will fail.
- **DNS not functioning properly**: DNS is integral to desktop provisioning. If the desktops cannot resolve the IP addresses or infrastructure services including Active Directory and Horizon components, the provisioning process will fail.

The Horizon event log, located in the **Monitoring – Events** window of the Horizon Administrator console, contains detailed information that can be used to troubleshoot the provisioning process.

# Managing Horizon Desktop pool entitlements

The following steps outline how to grant users or AD security groups access to a Horizon desktop pool, a necessary task since no access is granted by default. This can be done while the pool is still being provisioned.

1. Log on to the Horizon Administrator console using an AD account that has administrative permissions within Horizon.
2. Open the **Catalog | Desktop Pools** window within the console.
3. Highlight the pool you wish to entitle, as shown in the following screenshot, and navigate to the **Entitlements… | Add entitlement…** to open the **Add Entitlements** window:

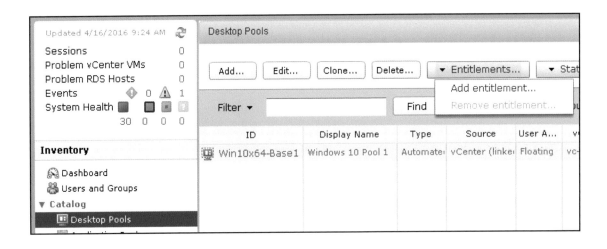

4. In the **Add Entitlements** window shown in the following screenshot, click on the **Add…** button to open the **Find User or Group** window:

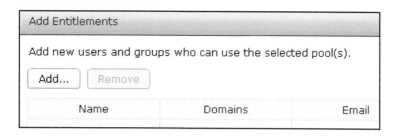

5. In the **Find User or Group** window shown in the following screenshot, use the **Name/User name:** or **Description:** fields to search for the user or group to which you wish to grant access. In the following example, we used the **Find** button to search for a security group that was created specifically for a Horizon named **Horizon_DTPool_Win10NP**. Highlight the desired user or group, and click on **OK** to return to the **Add Entitlements** window:

6. Repeat steps 4 and 5 as needed to entitle additional users or groups.
7. If all the required users and groups have been added, click on the **OK** button in the **Add Entitlements** window to complete the action.

The selected users and groups now have access to the available desktops within the desktop pool. Now that we have entitled a user or group to do the desktop pool, the **Remove Entitlement…** option shown in step 3 will no longer be greyed out, and we can use it to remove entitlements if needed.

Removing an entitlement to a dedicated assignment linked clone or full clone desktop pool does not remove any assignments to the desktops themselves, which occurs when a user logs in for the first time or when set manually by a Horizon administrator. To fully remove the entitlement, you must also highlight the desktop in the Horizon Administrator console **Resources – Machines** window, open the **More Commands** drop down menu as shown in the following screenshot, click **Unassign User…** to open the **Unassign User** window, and then click **OK**. The desktop will not be available for new logins until this is performed.

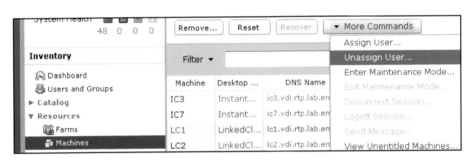

Alternatively, you may use the **Remove…** button to delete the desktop and force the creation of a new, unassigned desktop. Both methods require the entitlement to be removed as well; if this is not done the user will be able to log in again and be assigned a new desktop.

# Summary

In this chapter, we have learned about Horizon desktop pools. In addition to learning how to create three different types of desktop pools, we were introduced to a number of key concepts that are part of the pool creation process.

We discussed the difference between Instant Clone, linked clone, and full clone virtual desktops, how Sysprep differs from QuickPrep, how to monitor the provisioning of a Horizon desktop pool, the types of issues that can prevent a pool from provisioning successfully, and how to grant users or security groups access to desktop pools using desktop pool entitlements.

In Chapter 11, *Implementing Horizon Application Pools*, we will examine how to stream individual applications directly to the Horizon client using Microsoft Windows RDS servers.

# 11
# Implementing Horizon Application Pools

VMware Horizon includes the ability to stream individual Windows applications to clients using Microsoft Windows **Remote Desktop Services** (**RDS**), a feature formally known as Terminal Services. Application streaming is particularly useful to those clients that require access only to applications, as the application appears to them as it would if it were installed on their device, even if they are using a tablet-based Horizon client. For those clients, this is typically a much more efficient means of accessing their applications than navigating a traditional desktop GUI on a tablet device. While application streaming is not in itself a new feature, after all even ThinApp has a streaming mode, this feature enables individual applications to be accessed directly from the Horizon client.

 In this book, the terms Remote Desktop Services (RDS) and **Remote Desktop Session Hosts** (**RD Session Host**) are used interchangeably; they both refer to the same Windows server feature.

By installing the Horizon Agent directly onto a supported Windows server with the RDS feature installed, we can entitle applications to users just as we would entitle desktops. An additional benefit is that on a per-client basis, for users that use a very small number of applications, or for a small number of applications concurrently, fewer resources will be required to deploy streamed applications, in many cases, when compared to deploying individual desktops for each client.

In this chapter, we will review all the steps required to implement, configure, and administer RDS application streaming using VMware Horizon. By the end of this chapter, we will learn:

- Configuring the Windows Remote Desktop Services (RDS) server for use with Horizon
- Creating a linked clone based RDS farm in Horizon
- Creating an RDS application pool in Horizon
- Using the Horizon client to access RDS-streamed applications
- Monitoring the status of RDS servers and Horizon client sessions
- Modifying an RDS application pool in Horizon
- Modifying an RDS farm or server in Horizon

# Configuring a Windows RDS server for use with Horizon

This section will detail outline the minimum steps required to configure Windows RDS to use with Horizon. For a more in-depth discussion on Windows RDS optimization and management, consult the Microsoft TechNet page for Windows Server 2012 R2 (`http://te chnet.microsoft.com/en-us/library/hh801901.aspx`).

VMware Horizon supports the following versions of Window server for use with RDS:

- Windows Server 2008 R2: Standard, Enterprise, or Datacentre, with SP1 or later installed
- Windows Server 2012: Standard or Datacentre
- Windows Server 2012 R2: Standard or Datacentre

The examples shown in this chapter were performed on Windows Server 2012 R2.

 If you intend to use Microsoft Office on RDS, note that it has specific licensing requirements for that use case. Consult Microsoft's **Licensing of Microsoft Desktop Application Software for Use with Windows Server Remote Desktop Services** document (`https://www.microsoft.com/en -us/licensing/learn-more/brief-remote-desktop-services.as px`), for additional information.

# Windows RDS licensing

The Windows RDS feature requires a licensing server component called the **Remote Desktop Licensing role service**. For reasons of availability, it is not recommended that you install it on the RDS host itself, but rather on an existing server that performs some other function, or even on a dedicated server if possible. Ideally, the RDS licensing role should be installed on multiple servers for redundancy reasons.

The Remote Desktop Licensing role service is different from the Microsoft Windows **Key Management System** (**KMS**), as it is used solely for Windows RDS servers. Consult the Microsoft TechNet article, **RD Licensing Configuration on Windows Server 201**2 (`https://blogs.technet.microsoft.com/askperf/2013/09/20/rd-licensing-configuration-on-windows-server-2012/`), for the steps required to install the Remote Desktop Licensing role service. Additionally, consult Microsoft document **Licensing Windows Server 2012 R2 Remote Desktop Services** (`https://www.microsoft.com/en-us/Licensing/learn-more/brief-windows-server-2012-rds.aspx`) for information about the licensing options for Windows RDS, which include both per-user and per-device options.

# Windows RDS host recommended hardware configuration

The following resources represent a starting point for assigning CPU and RAM resources to Windows RDS servers. The actual resources required will vary based on the applications being used, and the number of concurrent users, so it is important to monitor server utilization and adjust the CPU and RAM specifications if required. The following are the recommended requirements:

- Four vCPUs to support a maximum of 50 RDS sessions (per server)

 While it is possible to assign more vCPUs to support more sessions, this configuration offers a fairly predictable performance, regardless of the ESXi host server CPU configuration. If you decide to configure your RDS servers with more than four vCPUs, monitor ESXi host **CPU Ready** statistics, which will reveal if there are any delays in scheduling VM vCPU requests to the ESXi server CPU. A CPU Ready value of greater than five percent will usually impact performance of the VM, and the only way to alleviate the issue is to add more physical CPUs to the ESXi host, or remove vCPUs from the VM experiencing the issue.

- 24GB RAM
- A minimum of 40GB hard disk space for the RDS server itself, plus sufficient hard drive space to store RDS user profiles (if storing locally). Consider one of the following options to help better manage user profiles:
  - **VMware User Environment Manager (UEM)** may be used to manage profiles for users of Horizon application pools; refer to `Chapter 8`, *Implementing VMware User Environment Manager* and the UEM documentation (`https://www.vmware.com/support/pubs/uem-pubs.html`) for further details.
  - **Horizon Persona Management**, which is not discussed in this book, is not supported for use with Windows RDS servers. Even if it were, owing to its more advanced capabilities, UEM is a better choice for user profile management.
  - Windows RDS includes multiple native options to control user profile configuration and growth, including a RD user home directory, RD roaming user profiles, and mandatory profiles. For information about these and other options, consult the Microsoft TechNet article, **Manage User Profiles for Remote Desktop Services** (`https://technet.microsoft.com/en-us/library/cc742820.aspx`).

While the vCPU and RAM requirements might seem excessive at first, remember that to deploy a virtual desktop for each of these 50 users we would need at least 50 vCPUs, 100 GB of RAM, and 2TB of hard disk space, which is much more than our single Windows RDS host requires.

By default, Horizon allows unlimited RDS user sessions for each Windows RDS host in the farm. Based on the RDS server specification provided, we will need to deploy multiple RDS servers if we anticipate having more than 50 connections, plus additional hosts for redundancy purposes. It is recommended to set the default sizing to 50 as that is what recommended RDS server configuration is optimized for.

# Importing the Horizon RDS AD group policy templates

Some of the settings configured throughout this chapter are applied using AD group policy templates. Prior to using the RDS feature, these templates should be distributed to either the RDS servers, in order to be used with the Windows local group policy editor, or to an AD domain controller where they can be applied using the domain. Complete the following steps to install the RDS group policy templates:

 When referring to VMware Horizon installation packages, `y.y.y` refers to the version number and `xxxxxx` refers to the build number. When you download packages, the actual version and build numbers will be in a numeric format. For example, the filename of the current Horizon 7 GPO bundle is `VMware-Horizon-Extras-Bundle-4.0.0-3616726.zip`.

Obtain the `VMware-Horizon-Extras-Bundle-x.x.x-yyyyyyy.zip` file, unzip it, and copy the `en-US` folder, the `vmware_RDS.admx` file, and the `vmware_RDS_server.admx` file to the `C:\Windows\PolicyDefinitions` folder on either an AD domain controller or your target RDS host, based on how you wish to manage the policies. Make note of the following points while doing so:

- If you want to set the policies locally on each RDS host, you will need to copy the files to your RDS server master image
- If you wish to set the policies using domain-based AD group policies, you will need to copy the files to the domain controllers, the group policy Central Store (described in the Microsoft KB article titled **How to create and manage the Central Store for Group Policy Administrative Templates in Windows** available at `https://support.microsoft.com/en-us/kb/3087759`), or to the workstation from which we manage these domain-based group policies

The following steps outline the procedure to enable RDS on a Windows Server 2012 R2 host. Note that the host used in this section has already been connected to the domain, and has been logged in using an AD account that has administrative permissions on the server.

1. Open the **Windows Server Manager** utility and go to **Manage** | **Add Roles and Features** to open the **Add Roles and Features Wizard**.
2. On the **Before you Begin** page, click on **Next**.

3. On the **Installation Type** page, select **Remote Desktop Services** installation and click on **Next** as shown in the following screenshot:

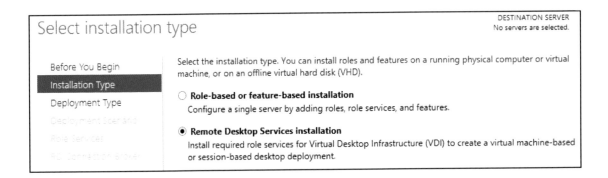

4. On the **Deployment Type** page, select **Quick Start** and click on **Next**.

You can also implement the required roles using the standard deployment method outlined in the Deploy the session virtualization standard deployment section of the Microsoft TechNet article, **Test Lab Guide: Remote Desktop Services Session Virtualization Standard Deployment** (https://technet.microsoft.com/en-us/library/hh831610.asp x). If you use this method, you will complete the component installation and proceed to step 9 in this section.

5. On the **Deployment Scenario** page, select **Session-based desktop deployment** and click on **Next**.

6. On the **Server Selection** page, select a server from the list under **Server Pool**, click the red, highlighted button to add the server to the list of selected servers, and click on **Next** as shown in the following screenshot:

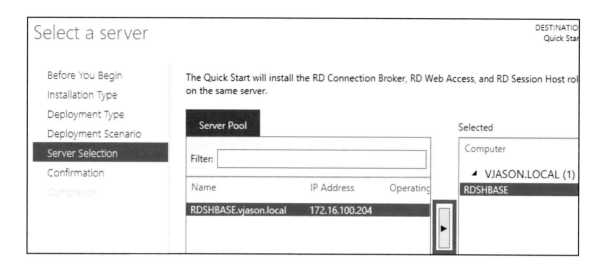

7. On the **Confirmation** page, check the box marked **Restart the destination server automatically if required** and click on **Deploy**.

8. On the **Completion** page, monitor the installation process and click on **Close** when finished in order to complete the installation. If a reboot is required, the server will reboot without the need to click on **Close**. Once the reboot completes, proceed with the remaining steps.

9. Set the RDS licensing server using the `Set-RDLicenseConfiguration` Windows PowerShell command. In this example, we are configuring the local RDS host to point to redundant license servers (`RDS-LIC1` and `RDS-LIC2`) and setting the license mode to `PerUser`. This command must be executed on the target RDS host. After entering the command, confirm the values for the license mode and license server name by answering `Y` when prompted. Refer to the following code:

```
Set-RDLicenseConfiguration -LicenseServer @("RDS-
LIC1.vjason.local","RDS-LIC2.vjason.local") -Mode PerUser
```

- This setting might also be set using group policies applied either to the local computer or using **Active Directory (AD)**. The policies are shown in the following screenshot, and you can locate them by going to **Computer Configuration** | **Policies** | **Administrative Templates** | **Windows Components** | **Remote Desktop Services** | **Remote Desktop Session Host** | **Licensing** when using AD-based policies. If you are using local group policies, there will be no Policies folder in the path:

| Setting | State |
|---|---|
| Use the specified Remote Desktop license servers | Not configured |
| Hide notifications about RD Licensing problems that affect t... | Not configured |
| Set the Remote Desktop licensing mode | Not configured |

10. Use local computer or AD group policies to limit users to one session per RDS host using the **Restrict Remote Desktop Services users to a single Remote Desktop Services session** policy. The policy is located at **Computer Configuration** | **Policies** | **Administrative Templates** | **Windows Components** | **Remote Desktop Services** | **Remote Desktop Session Host** | **Connections**, and should be set to **Enabled**.

11. Use local computer or AD group policies to enable **Time zone redirection**. The policy is located at **Computer Configuration** | **Policies** | **Administrative Templates** | **Windows Components** | **Horizon View RDS Services** | **Remote Desktop Session Host** | **Device and Resource Redirection** when using AD-based policies. If you are using local group policies, there will be no **Policies** folder in the path. To enable the setting, set **Allow time zone redirection** to **Enabled**.

12. Use local computer or AD group policies to enable **Windows Basic Aero-Styled Theme** to minimize the RDS server resources required to deliver each client session. The policy is located at **User Configuration** | **Policies** | **Administrative Templates** | **Control Panel** | **Personalization** when using AD-based policies. If you are using local group policies, there will be no Policies folder in the path. To configure the theme, set **Force a specific visual style file or force Windows Classic** to **Enabled** and set **Path to Visual Style** to `%windir%\resources\Themes\Aero\aero.msstyles`.

13. Use local computer or AD group policies to start `Runonce.exe` when the RDS session starts. The policy is located at **User Configuration | Policies | Windows Settings | Scripts (Logon/Logoff)** when using AD-based policies. If you are using local group policies, there will be no `Policies` folder in the path. To configure the logon settings, double-click on **Logon**, then click on **Add**, enter `runonce.exe` in the **Script Name** box, and then enter `/AlternateShellStartup` in the **Script Parameters** box.

The recommended AD group policies for the Windows RDS server have now been configured, and the server is ready for the Horizon agent software to be installed.

# Installing the Horizon Agent on the Windows RDS host

The following steps outline how to install the Horizon Agent software on a Windows RDS host. These steps assume we will be deploying linked clone RDS servers as described previously in this chapter. These steps should be performed on the RDS server master image, and the master image should be joined to the domain and have the RDS feature installed prior to beginning the agent installation process.

1. On the Windows RDS host, double-click on the 64-bit Horizon Agent installer to begin the installation process. The installer should have a name similar to `VMware-viewagent-x86_64-y.y.y-xxxxxx.exe`. On the **Welcome to the Installation Wizard for VMware Horizon Agent** page, click on **Next**.

2. On the **License Agreement** page, select the **I accept the terms in the license agreement** radio check box and click on **Next**.

3. On the **Network protocol configuration** page, select your preferred protocol and click on **Next**.

4. On the **Custom Setup** page, enable the **VMware Horizon View Composer Agent** option to enable the deployment of linked clone RDS servers, make changes as needed to the other agent options and click on **Next**.

5. On the **Ready to Install the Program** page, click on **Install** to begin the installation.

6. When the installation completes, reboot the server if prompted.

The RDS server is now able to be used to deploy linked clone-based Horizon application pools. Any applications that are needed may now be installed, and then the VM should be shut down and a snapshot taken.

# vSphere customization specification for the Windows RDS servers

To deploy linked clone based Windows RDS servers using Horizon you will first need to create a **customization specification** in vCenter. Customization specifications are used to customize the Windows OS during the deployment process, and include information such as the product key, local administrator passwords, and other basic information.

The VMware vSphere document **Creating and Managing Customization Specifications** (h ttp://pubs.vmware.com/vsphere-60/topic/com.vmware.vsphere.vm_admin.doc/ GUID-EB5F090E-723C-4470-B640-50B35D1EC016.html) provides details on how to create and manage customization specifications in vCenter. The only customization specification setting explicitly required by Horizon in order to deploy RDS servers is the **Computer Name** setting; it should be set to **Use the virtual machine name**.

# Additional resources related to using Windows RDS servers

The following resources provide additional information about the configuration of the RDS server master image:

- The Microsoft TechNet article titled **Set-RDLicenseConfiguration** (https://tec hnet.microsoft.com/en-us/library/jj215465.aspx) provides the complete syntax of the PowerShell command used to configure the RDS licensing settings.
- The Microsoft TechNet article titled **Remote Desktop Services Client Access Licenses (RDS CALs)** (http://technet.microsoft.com/en-us/library/cc 753650.aspx) explains the different RDS license types and reveals that an RDS per-user **Client Access License** (**CAL**) allows our Horizon clients to access the RDS servers from an unlimited number of endpoints while still consuming only one RDS license.
- The Microsoft TechNet article titled **Remote Desktop Session Host Licensing** (ht tp://technet.microsoft.com/en-us/library/ee791926(v=ws.10).asp x) provides additional information on the group policies used to configure the RDS licensing options.

- The VMware document **Enable Windows Basic Theme for Applications** (`http://pubs.vmware.com/horizon-7-view/topic/com.vmware.horizon-view.desktops.doc/GUID-931FF6F3-44C1-4102-94FE-3C9BFFF8E38D.html`) explains that the Windows Basic aero-styled theme is the only theme supported by Horizon, and demonstrates how to implement it.
- The VMware document **Enable Time Zone Redirection for RDS Desktop and Application Sessions** (`http://pubs.vmware.com/horizon-7-view/topic/com.vmware.horizon-view.desktops.doc/GUID-443F9F6D-C9CB-4CD9-A783-7CC5243FBD51.html`) explains why time zone redirection is required, as it ensures that the Horizon client session will use the same time zone as the client device.
- The VMware document **Configure Group Policy to Start Runonce.exe** (`http://pubs.vmware.com/horizon-7-view/topic/com.vmware.horizon-view.desktops.doc/GUID-85E4EE7A-9371-483E-A0C8-515CF11EE51D.html`) explains why we need to add the `runonce.exe /AlternateShellStartup` command to the RDS logon script. This ensures that applications that require Windows Explorer will work properly when streamed using Horizon.

# Creating a Windows RDS farm in Horizon

This section will discuss the steps that are required to create a linked clone based RDS farm in Horizon. An RDS farm is a collection of Windows RDS servers, and serves as the point of integration between the Connection Server and the individual applications installed on each RDS server. Additionally, key settings concerning client session handling and client connection protocols are set at the RDS farm level within Horizon.

Many of the options seen in this section are similar to those seen when deploying linked clone desktops in `Chapter 10`, *Creating Horizon Desktop Pools*. Owing to this, not every setting will be explained like it was in that chapter. Refer to `Chapter 10`, *Creating Horizon Desktop Pools*, as well as the VMware Horizon documentation (`https://www.vmware.com/support/pubs/view_pubs.html`) for a more detailed explanation of the different options we will see in this section.

To create an RDS farm in Horizon, we need to have at least one RDS host master image configured using the steps described previously in this chapter. This includes taking a VM snapshot of that image once the configuration is complete; if that is not done you will not be able to select the master image when creating the RDS farm. The following steps outline the procedure used to create a Windows RDS farm.

1. Log onto the Horizon Administrator console using an account that has administrative privileges.
2. Navigate to **Resources** | **Farms** and click on **Add…**, as shown in the following screenshot:

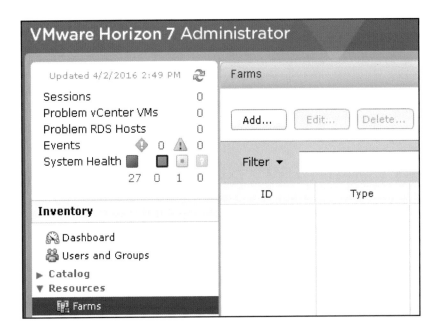

3. On the **Add Farm** | **Type** page, click the **Automated Farm** radio button and then click **Next**.
4. On the **Add Farm** | **vCenter Server** page, click on the vCenter Server where the RDS master image resides and the RDS servers will be deployed and then click **Next**.

5. On the **Add Farm | Identification and Settings** page, shown in the following screenshot, provide a farm **ID**, enter a **Description** if desired, make any desired changes to the default settings, and then click on **Next**.

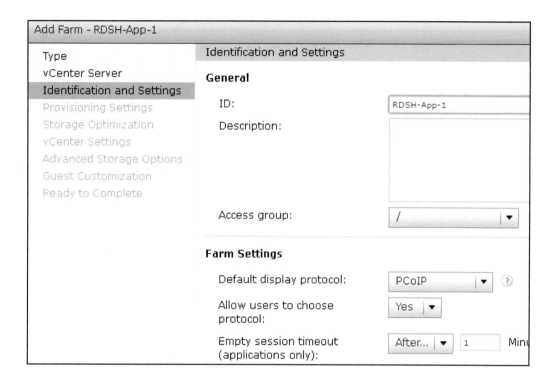

These settings may also be edited after the application pool is created, as with desktop pools. Refer to the section titled *Modifying Windows RDS farms* later on in this chapter for further details about how to modify existing RDS farms.

6. On the **Add Farm** | **Provisioning Settings** page, provide a desktop **Naming Pattern** and the **Max number of machines** (RDS servers) to deploy and click on **Next**. You should deploy sufficient RDS servers so that you are able to accommodate RDS server maintenance tasks or even unplanned outages.

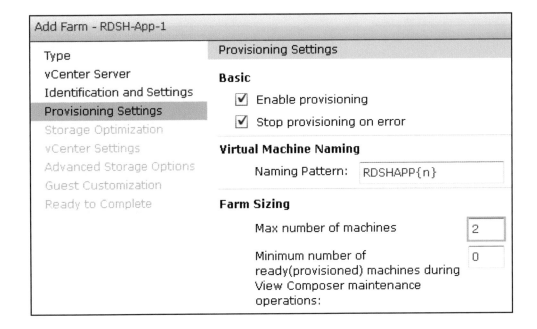

To add more RDS servers to the farm at a later date, you can edit the pool and update the value for **Max number of machines**. As is the case with desktop pools, as soon as you update that value, Horizon will provision the additional number of VMs required.

7. On the **Add Farm** | **Storage Optimization** page, edit the settings as required, selecting the **Use VMware Virtual SAN** radio button if applicable, and click on **Next**.

8. On the **Add Farm** | **vCenter Settings** page, select the RDS server **Parent VM**, **Snapshot**, **VM folder location**, vSphere **Host or cluster**, **Resource pool**, and **Datastores** as shown in the following screenshot, and then click on **Next**.

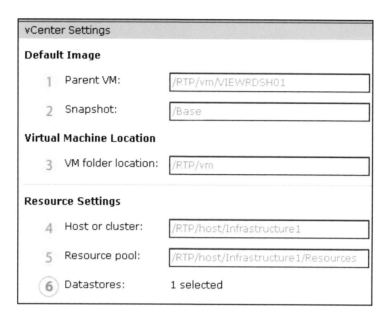

9. On the **Add Farm** | **Advanced Storage Options** page, make any changes that are desired and click on **Next >**.

10. On the **Add Farm** | **Guest Customization** page, select an **AD container** for the RDS server computer accounts, the Customization Specification created for the RDS servers under **Using a customization specification (Sysprep)**, and then click on **Next >**.

11. On the **Add Farm** | **Ready to Complete** page, review the configuration and click on **Finish** to create the farm.

12. Once created, the farm will be listed in the Horizon Administrator console under **Resources | Farms**; click on it to bring up the summary page as shown in the following screenshot:

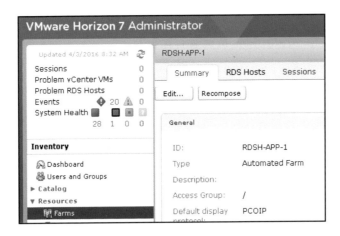

13. Click on the **RDS Host**s tab to bring up a list of RDS servers that were deployed as part of the farm as shown in the following screenshot:

Now that the RDS servers have been deployed, we can create **Horizon application pools** to stream their applications to our Horizon clients. This process is described in the next section.

# Creating a Horizon application pool

Horizon application pools are used to publish and entitle RDS-streamed applications to Horizon clients. We must create an application pool for each application that we want to publish and, as in the case of desktop pools, we must entitle users to each application pool individually. Fortunately, we can create and entitle multiple applications at once, which simplifies the initial creation process. In this section, we will configure application pools for each of the core Microsoft Office applications installed on our Windows RDS servers.

To create an application pool in Horizon, we need to have at least one RDS farm configured in our pod. Assuming that the RDS farm creation process completed successfully in the previous section, we should see the farm in the Farms menu, under Resources, of our Horizon Administrator console.

The following steps outline the procedure for creating an RDS application pool. An RDS farm is required before you can create an application pool; in this example, we are using the farm created in the previous section:

1. Log onto the Horizon Administrator console using an account that has administrative privileges.
2. Navigate to **Catalog** | **Application Pools** and click on **Add...** as shown in the following screenshot:

3. On the **Add Application Pools** page, shown in the following screenshot, use the **Select an RDS farm** drop-down menu to specify the RDS farm to be used, and then click on the checkbox to the left of the application **Name** to add it to the application pool. Multiple applications may be selected; when finished, click on **Next**:

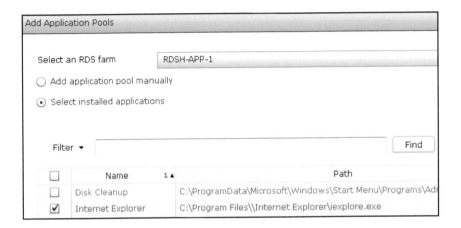

4. On the **Add Application Pools** page, shown in the following screenshot, make any desired changes to the application**ID** or **Display Name**, and click on **Finish** to create the application pools and return to the **Catalog** | **Application Pools** window.

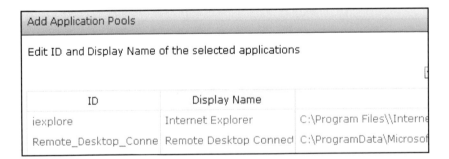

These settings may also be edited after the Application Pool is created, as with Desktop Pools. Refer to the section titled *Modifying a Horizon application pool* later on in this chapter for further details about how to modify existing Horizon application pools.

5. To entitle an Application Pool, click on it in the **Catalog | Application Pools** window, then click the **Entitlements…** drop down menu, and then click **Add entitlement…** to open the **Add Entitlements** window. The remainder of the entitlement process is similar to that described in Chapter 10, *Creating Horizon Desktop Pools*.

 You may also refer to the VMware document **Entitling Users and Groups** (http://pubs.vmware.com/horizon-7-view/topic/com.vmware.ho rizon-view.desktops.doc/GUID-B0C436DC-6B18-4F92-A0BB-8250 ECF8859D.html) for information about how to entitle desktop or application pools in Horizon.

The application pool has been created and entitled, and is now available to stream applications to Horizon clients.

# Using the Horizon client to access application pools

In this section, we will explore how RDS application streaming works from a Horizon client perspective. Unlike desktop pools, whose names are often created arbitrarily by the Horizon administrator, RDS applications appear much as they would in a Windows Explorer window.

The following steps outline how to use the Horizon Client to access application pools. In this example, we have already authenticated one of our Connection Servers using a user account that has been entitled to the application pool created in the previous section. Perform the following steps:

1. Use the Horizon Client to authenticate one of the Connection Servers in the pod.

2. Click on one of the applications from the list presented in the Horizon Client window. This is shown in the following screenshot:

3. The application will appear just as it would if it were launched from the client's device; when finished, simply close it as we normally would.

We have now verified that RDS application streaming is working as intended. While a given user can only have one active session on a given RDS host, Horizon allows users to stream multiple applications using a single client session.

# Monitoring the status of Horizon application pool clients and RDS servers

VMware Horizon includes multiple status pages for monitoring the status of Windows RDS servers and their client sessions. In this section, we will review the different status pages and review what each status page is used for. The following steps outline how to use the Horizon Administrator console to review the current status of our Windows RDS servers:

1. Log onto the Horizon Administrator console using an account that has administrative privileges.

2. Navigate to **Resources** | **Machines**, click on the **RDS Hosts** tab, and review the status of each Windows RDS host, including the agent version, number of active sessions, and server availability as shown in the following screenshot:

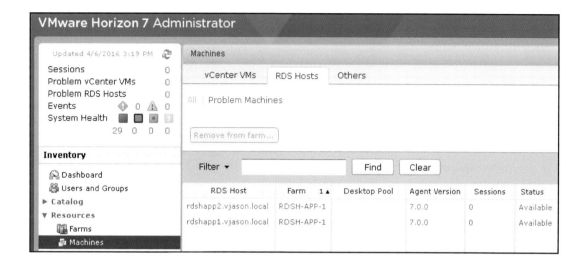

3. Navigate to **Monitoring** | **Sessions**, as shown in the following screenshot, and review the status of each client session. The **Desktop** and **Application** buttons can be used to control the types of clients that are displayed. Multiple pieces of information about the client connection are displayed, and other options are available, such as disconnecting or logging off the session.

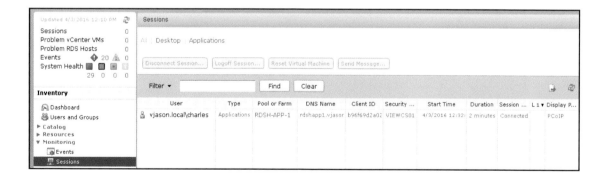

# Modifying or deleting a Horizon application pool

This section will discuss the steps that are required to modify the configuration of an existing Horizon application pool. Limited options exist at the Application Pool level, as settings that impact Horizon client connections are edited at the farm level as described in the next section.

The following steps outline the procedure used to modify a Horizon application pool. Note that each individual application in Horizon is considered an Application Pool and, as is the case with desktop pools they are managed independently of one another.

1. Log onto the Horizon Administrator console using an account that has administrative privileges.
2. Navigate to **Catalog** | **Application Pools** and click on the application pool that you wish to update or delete. From there, there are several actions that can be performed such as:
3. To remove an application pool, click on **Delete**. The RDS servers themselves will not be impacted by this change.
4. To edit the application pool settings, click on **Edit...** (highlighted in red), as shown in the following screenshot. Make changes as required to the fields shown, and then click on **OK**.

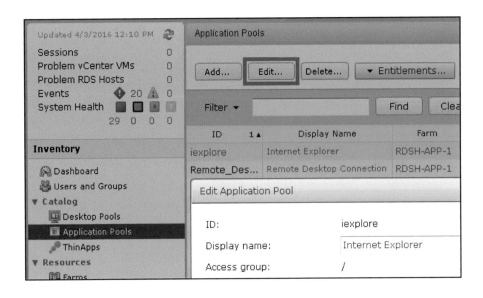

5. To add or remove an Application Pool entitlement, click on it in the **Catalog** | **Application Pools** window, then click the **Entitlements...** drop down menu, and then click **Add entitlement** or **Remove entitlement...** to open the associated entitlement management window. Perform the required changes and then click **OK**.

# Managing a Horizon RDS farm or server

This section will discuss the steps required to modify the configuration of an existing Horizon Windows RDS farm or individual RDS server. These include key configuration items that impact the Horizon client connection protocol, session handling, and many other common pool settings.

The following steps outline how to edit the settings of an existing RDS farm. Individual RDS servers can only be disabled or deleted; no other configuration options exist.

1. Log onto the Horizon Administrator console using an account that has administrative privileges.
2. Navigate to **Resources** | **Farms** and click on the RDS farm that needs to be updated.
3. Right-click on the farm and click on **Disable** to prevent additional clients from logging in; existing sessions will not be affected. This feature is typically used prior to performing a farm-wide maintenance. From there, there are several actions that can be performed such as:
    1. Click on a farm to open the farm **Summary** tab as shown in the following screenshot. Click **Recompose** to initiate a recompose of the RDS servers in the farm; this feature works just like it does for linked clone desktops, which is to say that it allows us to replace the underlying RDS master image with one we have updated or modified.

Note that unlike linked clone desktops, there is no option to perform a refresh, and RDS servers have no persistent data disk so any user data saved on the RDS server will be lost. User persona management features or folder redirection should be in place prior to using the recompose option.

2. From the **Resources** | **Farms** window, click on **Delete** to delete the RDS farm. Note that an RDS farm cannot be deleted unless any application pools it contains are deleted first.

3. From the **Resources** | **Farms** window, click on **Edit...** to open the **Edit Farm** window, as shown in the following screenshot. Update the farm settings as needed and click on **OK**. Note that most of these settings are identical to those seen when configuring desktop pools; a limited number of options such as **Max sessions per RDS Host** are unique to RDS farms. Consult the VMware document **Creating Farms** (`http://pubs.vmware.c om/horizon-7-view/topic/com.vmware.horizon-view.desktops.d oc/GUID-D1A45E90-1D77-4B28-B60E-83F89C28099A.html`) for further details about the different options available when creating RDS Farms.

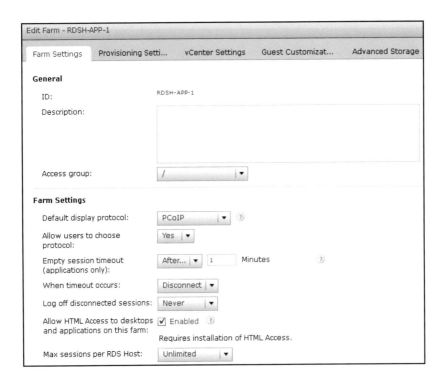

4. Click on a farm to open the farm **Summary** tab, and then click on the **RDS Hosts** tab as shown in the following screenshot to perform actions on individual RDS servers. Options include **Remove from farm…**, which will delete the selected server and force a new one to be created, and the **More Commands** drop down menu, which offers the ability to **Enable** or **Disable** hosts to perform maintenance. Actions performed here will not log off existing Horizon clients, but will prevent new sessions from connecting to the target RDS server.

# Summary

In this chapter, you have been introduced to Horizon application pools. You learnt what versions of Windows server are supported, basic sizing information, and what is required to configure a Windows RDS server master image for use with Horizon, including configuration of Windows and the installation of the Horizon Agent software.

We then discussed how to create a linked clone RDS farm, which functions like a linked clone desktop pool, in that each RDS server on a given datastore shares the same replica image.

Next, we discussed how to create and test Horizon application pools, which enable Horizon clients to stream applications instead of full desktop sessions. We also reviewed how to monitor RDS servers, as well as Horizon application pool client sessions.

Finally, we learnt how to manage existing RDS farms, and Application Pools, once they have been deployed.

In the next chapter, we will discuss how to create the different Horizon pool types, which include those that provide access to desktops as well as Windows RDS servers.

# 12
# Performing Horizon Desktop Pool Maintenance

Maintaining desktops, or Windows RDS servers deployed using VMware Horizon, requires a different approach depending on what desktop type you have selected. Full clone desktops are typically managed using the same techniques as traditional physical desktops, as each is a fully independent virtual machine with dedicated underlying virtual hard disks. Many organizations choose full clone desktops for this reason, as they can continue to manage them using tools and procedures that are already in place.

Linked clone desktops are an entirely different matter, especially if you wish to minimize the amount of per-desktop storage that is required. If an organization were to manage its linked clone desktops using the same traditional techniques used with physical or full clone desktops, they would find that over time those desktops used more and more storage space, negating the benefits of using linked clone desktops.

Instant clone desktops are natively non-persistent, so their maintenance is limited to updating the master image they are based on, or deleting individual desktops.

This chapter will focus primarily on managing linked clone and instant clone desktops using the various features of Horizon itself.

In this chapter you will learn:

- An overview of Horizon instant clone and linked clone maintenance
- How to recompose a Horizon linked clone desktop pool or single desktop
- How to refresh a linked clone desktop pool or single desktop
- How to rebalance a linked clone desktop pool or single desktop
- How to push a new parent image to an instant clone desktop pool

- How to recover an instant clone desktop
- How to manage Horizon Composer persistent disks

# An overview of instant and linked clone maintenance

To understand why a linked clone desktop requires different techniques from a physical or full clone desktop, we must again understand what makes it different. The following diagram shows the relationship between the linked clone disk and the shared replica disk:

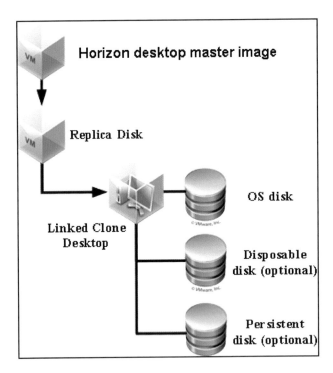

The replica disk is a read-only copy of the virtual desktop master image virtual hard disk; it is shared among as many as 1000 desktops within a given Horizon desktop pool. The linked clone disk is used by the virtual desktop when it needs to write data; one virtual desktop is created for each linked clone desktop.

One of the primary advantages of linked clone desktops is that they require far less storage space than full clone desktops; this is made possible by the shared replica disk. This reduced storage utilization is certainly useful at the time the desktops are deployed, but to maintain this advantage over time, you must use the Horizon native recompose or refresh features.

 Each of the maintenance operations described in this section requires the desktop to be powered off. Due to this, as well as the storage IO associated with each operation, it is recommended you perform these tasks during off-peak hours. Each of these tasks can be scheduled, making it easier for Horizon Administrators to accomplish this.

# Instant clone parent image update

An instant clone desktop is similar to a linked clone desktop in that it is dependent on a parent image, although as we know the desktops themselves function in two different ways. Instant clone desktop pools support a maintenance operation known as **Push Image**, which is similar to a linked clone recompose; however, instant clones also make use of the updated memory state of the new image. This is one of the characteristics of instant clone desktops that enables them to be deployed and configured much faster than linked clone desktops, albeit without the ability to maintain their state in between Horizon client sessions.

# Linked clone desktop refresh

A desktop refresh returns the desktop's linked clone disk, also known as the OS disk, to the original state and size as configured in the desktop pool options. If the desktop is configured with an optional persistent disk for storing user profile data, that data will be retained during the refresh operation. A refresh can be performed on either a desktop pool or an individual desktop. A desktop refresh provides several benefits:

- A quick way of reducing linked clone storage utilization
- If a desktop develops software problems, a refresh can be used to restore it to the original state

A refresh operation is also performed during linked clone recompose and rebalance operations. A refresh operation typically requires fewer than 10 minutes of downtime per desktop, although the time required may vary depending on the performance capabilities of the Horizon infrastructure and the specified number of concurrent refresh operations allowed. Horizon Composer performs up to 12 concurrent refresh operations at once by default. Instructions on how to perform a desktop refresh operation are provided later in this chapter.

Any maintenance task that includes a refresh operation will force the Windows desktop to reactivate the OS and Office software, if installed. Due to this, it is recommended that any organization that wishes to use linked clone desktops deploys a Windows KMS server to handle Windows and Office license activation. Windows MAK keys would be quickly exhausted in a linked clone desktop environment.

# Linked clone desktop recompose

A desktop recompose is used to replace the existing linked clone replica disk, usually in response to a configuration change, software installation, or software update. A desktop recompose is the preferred method of updating the linked clone desktop as the changes only affect the replica disk. Were the same updates or changes to be applied directly to the linked clone desktops themselves, each of the linked clone OS disks would increase in size by the amount needed to process the change.

The following example shows the difference between updating a virtual desktop master image and using a recompose to deploy an updated replica disk, versus installing the updates directly on the linked clone desktops.

In this example, it is determined that installing the updates on a single desktop requires 215 MB of additional space:

- If the virtual desktop master image is updated, and a recompose operation is performed, only 215 MB of additional space will be required to update all 1,000 desktops in the pool
- If the linked clone desktops are patched individually, a pool of 1,000 linked clone desktops would require an additional 210 GB of storage, or 215 MB for each linked clone desktop

In addition to the additional storage required to install the patches directly on the linked clone desktops, the patches or software installed would not persist if any maintenance that requires a refresh operation is performed.

A desktop recompose operation consists of the following steps:

1. The Horizon Administrator (or other responsible party) updates the virtual desktop master image with the required changes.
2. The Horizon Administrator takes a new snapshot of the updated virtual desktop master image.
3. The Horizon Administrator uses the Horizon Administrator console to initiate a recompose, selecting the updated snapshot. A new master image with a snapshot can also be selected, provided it is running on the same operating system.
4. Horizon Composer clones the selected virtual desktop master image and snapshot to a new replica disk. The original replica disk will remain until no more linked clones are associated with it.
5. Horizon Composer powers down the virtual desktop that will be recomposed.
6. Horizon Composer returns the existing linked clone OS disk to the original size and state (similar to a refresh operation), and associates it with the new replica disk. In addition, if the desktop has a persistent disk configured, it will be attached to the recomposed desktop at this point.
7. Horizon Composer powers on the recomposed linked clone and configures it using the Horizon Agent.
8. The Horizon Agent informs the Horizon Connection server that it is available for use.

A recompose operation typically requires fewer than 10 minutes of downtime per desktop and Horizon Composer performs up to 12 concurrent recompose operations at once by default. Instructions on how to perform a desktop recompose operation are provided later in this chapter.

# Linked clone desktop rebalance

A desktop rebalance is used to rebalance linked clone desktop storage across existing datastores, including any new datastores that were added to the desktop pool configuration. As mentioned previously, a rebalance operation will also refresh the desktop as part of the process, so a rebalance cannot be used as a way of balancing the linked clone OS disks.

A rebalance is typically most useful to balance persistent disk storage, as the persistent disk will remain in place until the desktop is deleted or the persistent disk is detached from the desktop and later deleted. Organizations that choose not to deploy a persistent disk may find that regular refresh or recompose operations are all that is required to maintain consistent desktop storage utilization throughout the life cycle of their linked-clone desktops.

# Managing Horizon maintenance tasks

Ongoing or scheduled refresh, recompose, or rebalance tasks can be paused, resumed from a pause, or canceled at any time using the Horizon Administrator console. When a maintenance task is canceled or paused, any operations currently underway will finish, but no new operations will start. When a paused task is resumed, the maintenance operation will continue.

- The resources required to perform Horizon maintenance tasks may impact the performance of the Horizon infrastructure. If Horizon maintenance tasks are causing performance problems for Horizon desktops currently in use, or for other resources that share the infrastructure, simply pause the maintenance task. Resume the maintenance task during a period of reduced infrastructure utilization.
- I do not recommend canceling maintenance tasks, as this may leave the desktops in an inconsistent state; if the maintenance operation is causing performance issues, simply pause until a more suitable time to resume can be identified.

The following steps outline how to manage a task assigned to a desktop pool or an individual desktop:

1. Log in to the Horizon Administrator console using an AD account that has administrative permissions within Horizon.
2. Go to **Catalog** | **Desktop Pools** within the console.
3. In the **Desktop Pools** window, click on the pool that has the task that you wish to cancel. In our example, we will click on the pool titled **AppVolumes-W10** to open the **AppVolumes-W10** window.

4. Under the **Tasks** tab of the **AppVolumes-W10** window (shown in the following screenshot), highlight the task that you wish to update and click on **Cancel task...**, **Pause task...**, or **Resume task...** as required. Since the sample task is not currently paused, the Resume task button is grayed out:

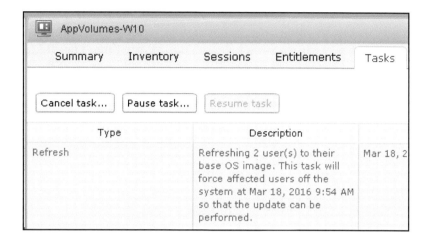

 The **Tasks** tab will show tasks assigned to individual desktops, as well as those assigned to the pool as a whole. The tasks are managed using the same process, regardless of their assignment.

# Global settings for Horizon maintenance

There are multiple configuration options within Horizon that affect Horizon refresh, recompose, and rebalance operations. This section will explain where those options can be found, and their purposes.

# Logoff warning and timeout

When a Horizon Administrator chooses to forcibly log off the user to perform a linked clone maintenance operation, the user is notified and the log off proceeds after five minutes. The notification message and the timeout value can both be configured in the **Global Settings** window.

If you choose to automatically log off users to perform desktop maintenance, your warning message will instruct them not to log in again until maintenance is complete. This will help prevent users from immediately trying to reconnect to their desktops after they have been logged off, which can interfere with the maintenance process.

The following steps outline how to update these global settings:

1. Log in to the Horizon Administrator console using an AD account that has administrative permissions within Horizon.
2. Open the **View Configuration | Global Settings** within the console. Click on the **Edit...** button in the **General** section, as shown in the following screenshot:

3. In the **General Settings** window, update the **Display warning before forced logoff** and **After warning, log off after** settings as needed. Click on **OK** to update the settings.

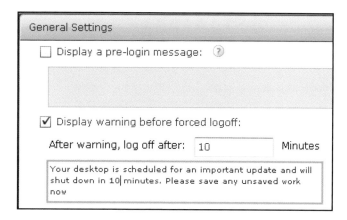

# Concurrent maintenance operations

By default, Horizon Composer will perform no more than 12 maintenance operations at one time. While this is considered the optimal setting for this option, it is possible to increase or decrease the number if required. This number is set on a per-vCenter Server basis, so if multiple vCenter Servers are being used, each one will need to be changed individually.

The following steps outline how to update the number of concurrent maintenance operations that Horizon Composer will perform:

1. Log in to the Horizon Administrator console using an AD account that has administrative permissions within Horizon.
2. Open the **View Configuration** | **Servers** window within the console.

3. In the **vCenter Servers** tab of the **Servers** window (shown in the following screenshot), highlight the vCenter Server you wish to update and click on the **Edit** button.

4. In the **Edit vCenter Server** window, click on the **Edit** button underneath the **vCenter Server Settings** section.
5. In the second **Edit vCenter Server** window, under the **Advanced Settings** section (shown in the following screenshot), update the **Max concurrent View Composer maintenance operations** value as needed. Click on **OK** twice to close both **Edit vCenter Server** windows and update the settings.

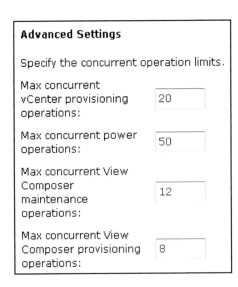

The **Edit vCenter Server** window also allows you to change other settings that affect the speed at which Horizon desktops and Windows RDS servers are provisioned, deployed, and powered on. For each of these settings, the default value is considered optional and changes are not recommended.

# Storage overcommit

Storage overcommit levels are configured on a per-datastore basis and affect how many linked clones Horizon Composer will provision on each datastore. Storage overcommit is typically configured when the desktop pool is created, but the settings can be updated at any time.

The following are the five different storage overcommit levels supported by Horizon. Each is calculated based on the size of the parent virtual machine:

- **None**: Storage is not overcommitted
- **Conservative**: The default; storage will be overcommitted up to four times the size of the datastore
- **Moderate**: Storage will be overcommitted up to seven times the size of the datastore
- **Aggressive**: Storage will be overcommitted up to fifteen times the size of the datastore
- **Unbound**: Storage will be overcommitted without any limits, even if the datastore is filled to capacity

Consider an example where the overcommit level is set to Conservative, the parent virtual machine uses a disk that is 12 GB in size, and linked clones will be configured on datastores that are 240 GB in size:

- *120 GB (datastore) X 4 (overcommit level) = 480 GB*
- *480 GB / 12 GB (parent virtual machine size) = 40 linked clones*

Based on these figures, when using the default storage overcommit level, Horizon Composer will place up to 40 linked clones on each datastore at the time of linked clone deployment or the rebalance operation.

# Updating datastore storage overcommit settings

The following steps outlines how to update the storage overcommit levels of an existing desktop pool:

1. Log in to the Horizon Administrator console using an AD account that has administrative permissions within Horizon.
2. Open the **Catalog** | **Desktop Pools** window within the console.
3. In the **Desktop Pools** window, highlight the linked clone pool you wish to refresh. In our example, we will highlight the pool titled **AppVolumes-W10**. Click on the **Edit** button shown in the following screenshot to open the **AppVolumes-W10** window:

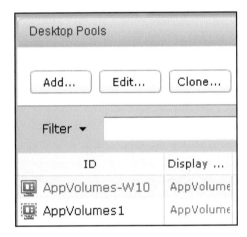

4. In the **AppVolumes-W10** window, click on the **vCenter Settings** tab.
5. In the **vCenter Settings** tab, click on the **Browse...** button next to the **Datastores** setting shown in the following screenshot. This will open the **Select Linked Clone Datastores** window.

6. In the **Select Linked Clone Datastores** window (shown in the following screenshot), open the **Storage Overcommit** drop-down menu next to each datastore to set the storage overcommit level. The level can only be changed for the datastores that are in use by the pool.

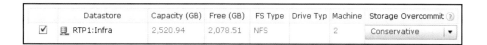

| | Datastore | Capacity (GB) | Free (GB) | FS Type | Drive Typ | Machine | Storage Overcommit ⑦ |
|---|---|---|---|---|---|---|---|
| ☑ | 🖳 RTP1:Infra | 2,520.94 | 2,078.51 | NFS | | 2 | Conservative ▼ |

7. Click **OK** twice to close the **Select Linked Clone Datastores** and **Edit AppVolumes-W10** windows and implement the changes.

Changing the storage overcommit settings does not, by itself, initiate any desktop maintenance activities. To enforce the updated storage overcommit policies on an existing desktop pool, simply perform a desktop rebalance using the procedure described later in this chapter.

# Performing linked clone desktop maintenance

In this section, we will look at the different techniques used to perform maintenance on linked clone desktop pools, or individual linked clone desktops themselves.

# Refreshing linked clone desktops

The following steps outline how to refresh a linked clone desktop pool using the Horizon Administrator console:

1. Log in to the Horizon Administrator console using an AD account that has administrative permissions within Horizon.
2. Open the **Catalog | Desktop Pools** window within the console.

3.  In the **Desktop Pools** window (shown in the following screenshot), click on the linked clone pool you wish to refresh. In our example, we will click on the pool titled **AppVolumes-W10** to open the **AppVolumes-W10** window:

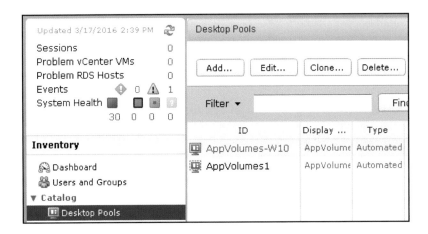

4.  On the right side of the **AppVolumes-W10** window (shown in the following screenshot), open the **View Composer** drop-down menu and click on **Refresh** to open the **Refresh** window:

5.  In the **Refresh | Scheduling** window (shown in the following screenshot), accept the default settings and click on **Next** to continue. If no changes are made, the refresh operation will begin immediately and users will be logged off from their desktops automatically after 5 minutes. The following are the optional settings:
    *   The date and time the refresh should start
    *   Whether to force the users to log off or wait for them to log off
    *   Whether to stop the refresh if an error occurs

- Updates to the warning and grace period settings must be made in Horizon's global settings

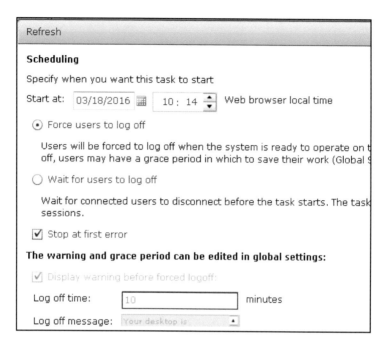

6. Review the options in the **Refresh | Scheduling** window. If changes are required, click on the **Back** button to return to the previous screen. Click on **Finish** to begin or schedule the refresh operation, depending on what was configured in the previous step.

The time required to complete a linked-clone desktop refresh operation varies, based on a number of different factors beyond that of the Horizon configuration itself. Generally speaking, under average circumstances it will take no more than 10 minutes per desktop, starting from the time that Horizon Composer performs the initial power down of the desktop.

The status of the refresh operation can be viewed in the **Tasks** tab of the desktop pool.

# Refreshing individual desktops

A refresh can also be performed on an individual desktop. This is often done in response to an event, such as problems with the guest OS, that affects only the desktop that is to be refreshed. The following steps outline how to refresh a single linked clone desktop using the Horizon Administrator console:

1. Log in to the Horizon Administrator console using an AD account that has administrative permissions within Horizon.
2. Open the **Catalog** | **Desktop Pools** window within the console.
3. In the **Desktop Pools** window, click on the pool that contains the linked clone desktop you wish to refresh.
4. In the window for the desktop pool you selected, click the **Inventory** tab.

5. Click on the linked clone desktop that you wish to refresh. In our example, we will click on the desktop named **APPV10-2** to open the **APPV10-2** window.
6. In the **APPV10-2** window, open the **View Composer** drop-down menu and then click on **Refresh** to open the **Refresh** window.
7. Complete the remaining steps to initiate the refresh operation.

# Recomposing linked clone desktops

The following steps outline how to recompose a linked clone desktop pool using the Horizon Administrator console:

1. Log in to the Horizon Administrator console using an AD account that has administrative permissions within Horizon.
2. Open the **Catalog** | **Desktop Pools** window within the console.
3. In the **Desktop Pools** window, click on the linked clone pool you wish to recompose. In our example, we will click on the pool titled **AppVolumes-W10** to open the **AppVolumes-W10** window.
4. On the right side of the **AppVolumes-W10** window, open the **View Composer** drop-down menu and click on **Recompose** to open the **Recompose** window.

5. On the **Image** page of the **Recompose** window (shown in the following screenshot), highlight the updated snapshot that you wish to use with your desktops. You may also select a different parent VM and accompanying snapshot by clicking on the **Change…** button, as long as they use the same OS as the existing desktops. In our example, we have chosen a new snapshot of the existing parent VM. Click on **Next** to move to the next step.

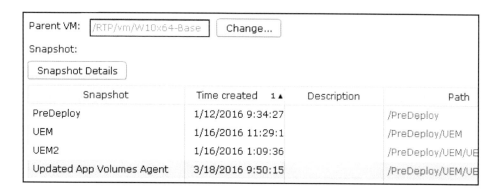

By default, Horizon will use the selected snapshot when deploying new desktops within the desktop pool. Uncheck the **Change the default image for new desktops** checkbox to change this behavior and force new desktops to use the existing image.

6. On the **Scheduling** page of the **Recompose** window, select the desired scheduling options and click on **Next**. These are the same scheduling options that appear when performing a desktop refresh.
7. Review the options in the **Ready to Complete** page of the **Recompose** window. If changes are required, click on the **Back** button to return to the previous screen. Click on **Finish** to begin or schedule the recompose operation, depending on what was configured in the previous step.

The time required to complete a linked clone desktop recompose operation varies based on a number of different factors beyond that of the Horizon configuration itself. Generally speaking, under average circumstances, it will take no more than 15 minutes per desktop, starting from the time that Horizon Composer performs the initial power down of the desktop.

If a desktop pool is configured to use Windows Sysprep for machine customization, a new Windows Machine **System Identifier (SID)** will be generated during a recompose operation. Consider any potential issues this may cause within your environment. The only alternative is to redeploy the desktops using VMware QuickPrep instead of Windows Sysprep. For more information about the differences between QuickPrep and System, consult the *Choosing QuickPrep or Sysprep to Customize Linked-Clone Machines* section of the VMware document **Setting Up Desktop and Application Pools in View** (https://www.vmware.com/support/pubs /view_pubs.html).

The status of the recompose operation can be viewed in the **Tasks** tab of the desktop pool window.

# Recomposing individual desktops

A recompose can also be performed on an individual desktop. Reasons to do this might include the need to test out an updated desktop configuration on a small number of users prior to recomposing all the desktops. The following steps outline how to recompose a single linked clone desktop using the Horizon Administrator console:

1. Log in to the Horizon Administrator console using an AD account that has administrative permissions within Horizon.
2. Open the **Catalog | Desktop Pools** window within the console.
3. In the **Desktop Pools** window, click on the pool that contains the linked clone desktop you wish to recompose.
4. In the window for the desktop pool you selected, click the **Inventory** tab.
5. Click on the linked clone desktop that you wish to recompose. In our example, we will click on the desktop named **APPV10-2** to open the **APPV10-2** window.
6. In the **APPV10-2** window, open the **View Composer** drop-down menu and then click on **Recompose** to open the **Recompose** window.
7. Complete the remaining steps to initiate the recompose operation.

# Rebalancing linked clone desktops

The following steps outline how to rebalance a desktop pool using the Horizon Administrator console. In this example, we will be adding additional datastores to our desktop pool prior to the rebalance operation. These datastores will then be used for the rebalance:

1. Log in to the Horizon Administrator console using an AD account that has administrative permissions within Horizon.
2. Open the **Catalog | Desktop Pools** window within the console.
3. In the **Desktop Pools** window, highlight the pool to which you wish to add the datastores and then rebalance. In our example, we will highlight the pool titled **AppVolumes-W10**. Click on the **Edit** button to open the **Edit AppVolumes-W10** window.
4. In the **Edit AppVolumes-W10** window, click on the **vCenter Settings** tab.
5. In the **vCenter Settings** tab, click on the **Browse** button next to the **Datastores** setting. This will open the **Select Linked Clone Datastores** window.
6. In the **Select Linked Clone Datastores** window (shown in the following screenshot), click on the checkboxes next to the datastores you wish to add to the desktop pool. In our example, we will check the box next to the **RTP1:Infra2** datastore:

| | Datastore | Capacity (GB) | Free (GB) | FS Type | Drive Typ | Machine | Storage Overcommit ⓘ |
|---|---|---|---|---|---|---|---|
| ☑ | 🖳 RTP1:Infra | 2,520.94 | 2,076.40 | NFS | | 2 | Conservative ▾ |
| ☐ | 🖳 RTP1:Infra2 | 1,008.37 | 769.88 | NFS | | 0 | |

By default, only datastores accessible to all hosts in the vSphere cluster will be shown.

7. Click on **OK** twice to close the **Select Linked Clone Datastores** and **Edit AppVolumes-W10** windows, implement the changes, and return to the **AppVolumes-W10** window.

8. On the right side of the **AppVolumes-W10** window (shown in the following screenshot), open the **View Composer** drop-down menu and click on **Rebalance** to open the **Rebalance** window:

9. On the **Rebalance** page of the **Rebalance** window, review the message and click on **Next**.
10. On the **Scheduling** page of the **Rebalance** window, select the desired scheduling options and click on **Next**. These are the same scheduling options that appear when performing a desktop refresh or recompose.
11. Review the options in the **Scheduling** page of the **Rebalance** window. If changes are required, click on the **Back** button to return to the previous screen. Click on **Finish** to begin or schedule the rebalance operation, depending on what was configured in the previous step.

As with other Horizon maintenance operations, the time required to complete a linked clone desktop rebalance operation varies. Generally speaking, under average circumstances it will take no more than 15 minutes per desktop, starting from the time that Horizon Composer performs the initial power down of the desktop.

The status of the rebalance operation can be viewed in the **Tasks** tab of the target desktop pool window.

# Rebalancing individual desktops

A rebalance can also be performed on an individual desktop. This can be helpful in scenarios where only a small number of desktops need to be rebalanced, and not the entire desktop pool. The following steps outline how to rebalance a single desktop using the Horizon Administrator console:

1. Log in to the Horizon Administrator console using an AD account that has administrative permissions within Horizon.
2. Open the **Catalog | Desktop Pools** window within the console.
3. In the **Desktop Pools** window, click on the pool that contains the desktop you wish to rebalance.
4. In the window for the desktop pool you selected, click the **Inventory** tab.
5. Click on the linked clone desktop that you wish to recompose. In our example, we will click on the desktop named **APPV10-2** to open the **APPV10-2** window.
6. In the **APPV10-2** window, open the **View Composer** drop-down menu and then click on **Rebalance** to open the **Rebalance** window.
7. Complete the remaining steps to initiate the rebalance operation.

# Performing instant clone desktop maintenance

In this section, we will look at the different techniques used to perform maintenance on instant clone desktop pools, or individual instant clone desktops themselves.

# Updating the instant clone desktop parent image

Due to the stateless nature of instant clone desktops, the process used to replace their base images is called Push Image rather than recompose. Since instant clone desktops do not save their state, all that is really performed during a push image operation is that the base VM the desktops are dependent on is replaced with an updated version.

A Push Image operation does require that the desktops be briefly powered off, but the operation can be delayed until the current user session ends. The following steps outline how to perform a push image operation on an instant clone desktop pool using the Horizon Administrator console.

Prior to performing these steps, you should update the desktop master image and take a new snapshot, the same as is typically done prior to recomposing a linked clone desktop pool.

1. Log in to the Horizon Administrator console using an AD account that has administrative permissions within Horizon.
2. Open the **Catalog | Desktop Pools** window within the console.
3. In the **Desktop Pools** window, click on the instant clone pool you wish to push a new image to. In our example, we will click on the pool titled **InstantClone1** to open the **InstantClone1** window.
4. On the right side of the **InstantClone1** window, open the **Push Image** drop-down menu as shown in the following screenshot, and click on **Schedule** to open the **Schedule Push Image** window:

5. In the **Schedule Push Image – Image** window shown in the following screenshot, click on the updated snapshot and then click **Next**:

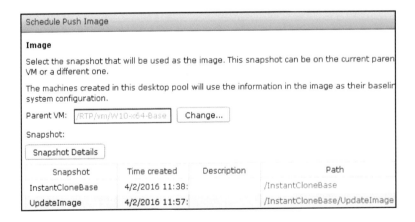

6. In the **Schedule Push Image | Scheduling** window, update the settings as needed and then click **Next**. This is the same screen that is displayed when performing any of the linked clone maintenance operations.

7. In the **Schedule Push Image | Ready to Complete** window, review the operation that will be performed, make changes if needed by clicking the **Back** button, and when ready click **Finish** to begin the push image operation.

The time required to complete an instant clone desktop push image operation varies based on a number of different factors beyond that of the Horizon configuration itself. That being said, once the updated replica disks have finished being cloned, the desktops themselves take only a few seconds to update. The status of the push image operation can be viewed in the **Tasks** tab of the target desktop pool window.

# Recover an individual instant clone desktop

Instant clone desktops have one additional maintenance operation that can be performed, known as **Recover**. A recover operation deletes the desktop, at which point it is immediately replaced with a new one. This is the same operation that is performed when a user logs off a desktop session, but in some cases it may be necessary to perform this operation as part of troubleshooting Horizon, or for some other reason.

The following steps outline how to recover an individual instant clone desktop:

1. Log in to the Horizon Administrator console using an AD account that has administrative permissions within Horizon.

2. Open the **Catalog | Desktop Pools** window within the console.

3. In the **Desktop Pools** window, click on the pool that contains the instant clone desktop you wish to recover.

4. In the window for the desktop pool you selected, click the **Inventory** tab.

5. Click on the instant clone desktop that you wish to refresh. In our example, we will click on the desktop named **IC2** to open the **IC2** window.

6. In the **IC2** window, click the **Recover** button to open the **Recover Virtual Machine** window, shown in the following screenshot:

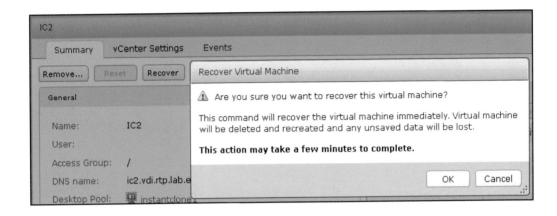

7. In the **Recover Virtual Machine** window, click **OK** to begin the Recover operation.

The status of the Recover operation can be viewed in the **Tasks** tab of the target desktop pool window. Due to the unique architecture of instant clone desktops, it should typically take less than a minute to recover a single desktop.

# Managing Horizon Composer persistent disks

Horizon Composer persistent disks are used to store user profile data, and enable it to persist during the Horizon Composer maintenance tasks described in this chapter. A linked clone is not required to have a persistent disk; features such as user profile folder redirection and User Environment Manager enable a linked clone desktop to appear to be persistent, even if it lacks a persistent disk.

Organizations that rely on Horizon Composer persistent disks to store critical user data should be familiar with how to manage them using the native features of Horizon. This section will provide examples of the different Horizon maintenance operations that involve Horizon Composer persistent disks.

Persistent disks will work only with the operating system version with which they were deployed. In the event that the original operating system is unavailable, and the data on the disk must be accessed, the persistent disks will need to be manually attached to a new virtual desktop and an assigned Windows drive letter. When attached this way, the persistent disks will simply appear as another hard drive.

# Detaching persistent disks

Detaching the persistent disk from a desktop allows it to remain managed by Horizon, while discarding the linked clone files that are no longer required. If the persistent disk is needed again at a later date, a desktop can quickly be deployed, and the persistent disk is associated with it.

The following steps outline how to detach a persistent disk using the Horizon Administrator console:

1. Log in to the Horizon Administrator console using an AD account that has administrative permissions within Horizon.
2. Open the **Resources** | **Persistent Disks** window within the console.
3. Highlight the persistent disk that you wish to detach. In the following example, we have highlighted the persistent disk associated with the desktop **APPV10-1**, belonging to the user **vjason.local\Charles**. Click on the **Detach** button to open the **Detach Persistent Disk** window.

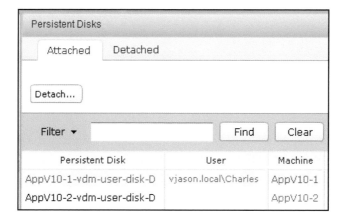

4. In the **Detach Persistent Disk** window (shown in the following screenshot), select where to store the persistent disk. In this example, we will leave it on the current datastore, although organizations may choose to move the disk elsewhere for organizational or archival purposes. Click on **OK** to detach the disk.

The persistent disk will be detached from the linked clone it was associated with, the linked clone will be deleted, and a new unassigned one will be deployed in its place. The detached persistent disk can be found under the **Persistent Disks** window – **Detached** tab, as shown in the following screenshot:

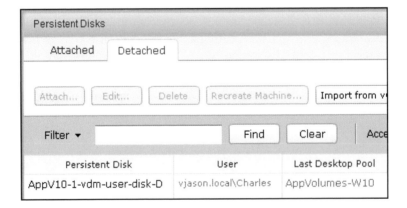

Horizon maintains the information required to quickly recreate the linked clone desktop, including the desktop pool and user it was assigned to.

# Recreating a desktop using a persistent disk

The following steps outline how to recreate a linked clone desktop using a previously detached persistent disk:

1. Log in to the Horizon Administrator console using an AD account that has administrative permissions within Horizon.
2. Open the **Resources** | **Persistent Disks** window within the console, and click on the **Detached** tab.
3. Highlight the persistent disk you wish to use and click on the **Recreate Machine** button, as shown in the following screenshot:

4. In the **Recreate Desktop** window, review the information and click on **OK**.

Since Horizon retained information about the desktop pool to which the persistent disk was previously assigned, no further information is required in order to recreate the desktop.

# Attaching a detached persistent disk to an existing desktop

Horizon provides the ability to attach a detached persistent disk to an existing desktop, enabling the user of that desktop to have access to that persistent disk, as well as his/ her own disk. This can be useful in scenarios where someone needs quick access to the data of a departed user, and you want to accomplish the task using only the Horizon Administrator console.

Remember that linked clone virtual machines should never have their storage configuration changed from within vCenter, as this can render the desktop or Windows RDS server unmanageable by Horizon. Always use the Horizon Administrator console to make changes that affect the linked clone storage configuration.

The following steps outline how to attach the detached persistent disk to an existing desktop:

1. Log in to the Horizon Administrator console using an AD account that has administrative permissions within Horizon.
2. Open the **Resources | Persistent Disks** window within the console, and click on the **Detached** tab.
3. Highlight the persistent disk that you wish to use and click on the **Attach...** button. This button is shown in the screenshot provided with step 3 of the previous section of this chapter.
4. In the **Attach Persistent Disk** window, select the desktop that you wish to assign the disk to and click on **OK**. Only desktops with assigned users will appear in the list of choices.

The persistent disk will be attached to the existing desktop and the contents will be accessible to the user whose desktop it was assigned to.

# Importing a persistent disk

To support a wider range of recovery scenarios, Horizon supports importing persistent disks and using them to create a new desktop. An imported persistent disk will not have any owner or desktop pool information, so the Horizon Administrator will have to choose a new owner and desktop pool. This can be useful in scenarios where an organization wishes to retain persistent disks offline, or on secondary storage that is not attached to the Horizon infrastructure.

The following steps outline how to import persistent disks and use them to create a new desktop:

1. Log in to the Horizon Administrator console using an AD account that has administrative permissions within Horizon.
2. Open the **Resources | Persistent Disks** window within the console, and click on the **Detached** tab.

3. Click on the **Import from vCenter...** button, as shown in the following screenshot:

4. In the **Import Persistent Disk From vCenter** window (shown in the following screenshot), select the appropriate resources, including:
   - **vCenter Server**: Target vCenter Server
   - **Datacenter**: Target vCenter datacenter object
   - **Linked clone pool**: Pool where the linked clone will be created
   - **View Folder**: Optional; destination folder for the virtual machine object
   - **Persistent Disk File**: The file you will be importing
   - **User**: The user who will be assigned the desktop that will use the persistent disk

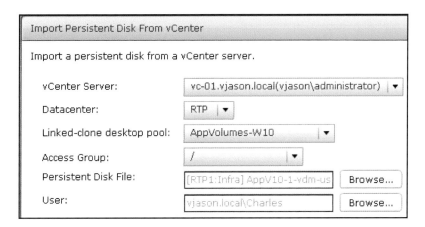

5. Click on **OK** to import the persistent disk and associate it with the linked clone desktop.

To access the data on the imported persistent disk, the user it was assigned to will need to log in to the newly configured desktop.

# Summary

In this chapter, we have learned about different Horizon Composer Instant and linked clone maintenance operations. We discussed each of these maintenance tasks and went through the examples of how they are used.

We learned about updating the Instant clone parent image, and linked clone refresh, recompose, and rebalance operations. We learned what they are for and what to be aware of concerning their use; we then went through the operation of each. We also learned about persistent disk maintenance, including how to detach them from existing desktops, how to reattach them, and how to use them to recreate a new linked clone desktop.

In the next chapter, we will discuss how to create a virtual desktop master image, an important task that requires careful consideration and planning.

# 13
# Creating a Master Horizon Desktop Image

When designing your VMware Horizon infrastructure, creating a Master Horizon desktop image is second only to infrastructure design in terms of importance. The reason for this is simple: as ubiquitous as Microsoft Windows is, by default, it is not optimized for use as a virtual desktop.

The good news is that, with a careful bit of planning and a thorough understanding of what your end users need, you can build a Windows desktop that serves all your needs, while requiring the bare minimum of infrastructure resources.

A default installation of Windows contains many optional components and configuration settings that are either unsuitable for, or likely not needed in, a Horizon environment. Understanding the impact of these items and settings plays an important part in keeping the performance of the Horizon infrastructure consistent over time.

Uninstalling unnecessary components, and disabling services or scheduled tasks that are not required will help reduce the amount of resources the desktop requires and ensure that the Horizon infrastructure can properly support the planned number of desktops, even as resources are oversubscribed.

Oversubscription is defined as having assigned more resources than what is physically available. This is most commonly done with processor resources in virtualized environments, where a single server processor core may be shared between multiple virtual machines. As the average desktop does not require 100 percent of its assigned resources at all times, we can share those resources between multiple desktops without affecting their performance.

This chapter will focus on a number of different topics related to the planning and creation of a Master Horizon desktop image.

In this chapter we will learn:

- The importance of optimizing a Master Horizon desktop image
- Sample Windows OS optimization results
- How to customize the master image filesystem cluster size
- Tasks to perform before optimizing Windows
- How to disable unwanted application-specific update features
- How to permanently remove Windows Store applications
- How to optimize the Windows OS
- The importance of customizing the default Windows-user local profile

# The importance of desktop optimization

While nothing stops you from using a default installation of any OS or software package in a virtualized environment, you may find it difficult to maintain consistent levels of performance in Horizon environments where many of the resources are shared, and, in almost every case, oversubscribed in some manner. In this section, we will examine a sample of the CPU and disk IO resources that could be recovered were you to optimize the Master Horizon desktop image.

Due to the technological diversity that exists from one organization to the next, optimizing your Master Horizon desktop image is not an exact science. The optimization techniques used and their end results will likely vary from one organization to the next, due to factors unrelated to Horizon or vSphere.

# Optimization results – Horizon desktop IOPS

Desktop optimization benefits one infrastructure component more than any other: storage. Until all flash storage arrays achieve price parity with the traditional spinning disk arrays many of us use today, reducing the per-desktop **input/output operations per second (IOPS)** required will continue to be an important part of any Horizon deployment.

On a per-disk basis, a flash drive can accommodate more than 15 times the IOPS of an enterprise SAS or SCSI disk, or 30 times the IOPS of a traditional desktop SATA disk. Organizations that choose an all-flash array may find that they have more than sufficient IOPS capacity, even without doing any optimization.

The following graph shows the reduction in IOPS that occurred after performing the optimization techniques described later in this chapter. This measurement was observed while testing the desktop using a user workload simulator:

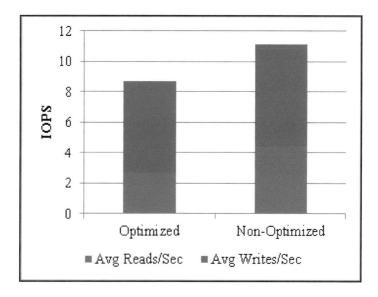

The optimized desktop generated 15 percent fewer IOPS during the user workload simulation. By itself, that may not seem like a significant reduction, but, when multiplied by hundreds or thousands of desktops, the savings become more significant.

In an era where the cost of flash-based storage systems and flash-based or dependent **Software Designed Storage(SDS)** used in **Hyper Converged Infrastructure(HCI)** appliances seems to continually decrease, there is less of a concern to consider measures that focus on decreasing Windows desktop IOPS. Just know that optimizing your Horizon desktop master image is about decreasing the total infrastructure resources it requires, and not just the storage itself.

# Optimization results – CPU utilization

Horizon recommends a maximum of 8 to 10 desktops per physical CPU core. There is no guarantee that your Horizon implementation will be able to attain this high consolidation ratio, though, as desktop workloads will vary from one type of user to another. The optimization techniques described in this chapter will help maximize the number of desktops you can run per server core.

The following graph shows the reduction in ESXi server **% Processor Time** that occurred after performing the optimization techniques described later in this chapter:

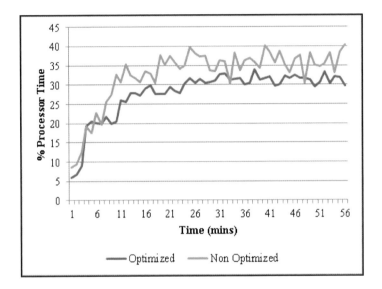

 **% Processor Time** is one of the metrics that can be used to measure server processor utilization within vSphere. The statistics in the preceding graph were captured using the vSphere ESXTOP command line utility, which provides a number of performance statistics that the vCenter performance tabs do not offer in a raw format that is more suited for independent analysis.

The optimized desktop required between 5 and 10 percent less processor time during the user workload simulation. As was the case with the IOPS reduction, the savings are significant when multiplied by large numbers of desktops.

# Customizing the Windows desktop OS cluster size

Microsoft Windows uses a default cluster size, also known as allocation unit size, of 4 KB when creating the boot volume during a new installation of Windows. The cluster size is the smallest amount of disk space that will be used to hold a file, which affects how many disk writes must be made to commit a file to disk. For example, when a file is 12 KB in size, and the cluster size is 4 KB it will take three write operations to write the file to disk.

The default 4 KB cluster size will work with any storage option that you choose to use with your environment, but that does not mean it is the best option. Storage vendors frequently do performance testing to determine which cluster size is optimal for their platforms, and it is possible that some of them will recommend that the Windows cluster size should be changed to ensure optimal performance.

## Customizing the Windows cluster size during the installation process

The following steps outline how to change the Windows cluster size during the installation process; the process is the same for both **Windows 7** and **Windows 8.1**. In this example, we will be using an 8 KB cluster size, although any size can be used, based on the recommendation from your storage vendor.

The cluster size can only be changed during the Windows installation, not after. If your storage vendor recommends the 4 KB Windows cluster size, the default Windows settings are acceptable.

1. Boot from the Windows OS installer ISO image or physical CD, and proceed through the install steps until the **Where do you want to install Windows?** window appears.
2. Press *Shift+ F10* to bring up a command window.
3. In the command window, enter the following commands:

```
diskpart
select disk 0
create partition primary size=100
active
format fs=ntfs label="System Reserve" quick
create partition primary
```

```
format fs=ntfs label=OS_8k unit=8192 quick
assign
exit
exit
```

4. Click on **Refresh** to refresh the **Where do you want to install Windows?** window.
5. Select **Drive 0 Partition 2: OS_8k**, as shown in the following screenshot, and click on **Next** to begin the installation:

| Where do you want to install Windows? | | | |
| --- | --- | --- | --- |
| Name | Total size | Free space | Type |
| Drive 0 Partition 1: System Reserve | 100.0 MB | 88.0 MB | System |
| Drive 0 Partition 2: OS_8k | 31.9 GB | 31.8 GB | Primary |

The System Reserve partition is used by Windows to store files critical to the boot process and will not be visible to the end user. These files must reside on a volume that uses a 4 KB cluster size, so we created a small partition solely for that purpose. Windows will automatically detect this partition and use it when performing the Windows installation.

Once Windows is installed, it is possible to move the boot files to the partition Windows was installed on and then remove the System Reserve partition, but only if the following four items are all true: the Windows partition is formatted using a **GUID Partition Table(GPT)** rather than **Master Boot Record(MBR)**, the Windows partition uses a 4 KB cluster size, Windows BitLocker encryption is not enabled, and the Windows partition is a primary partition. If any of these items are untrue, the System Reserve partition must be left as is.

In the event that your storage vendor recommends a different cluster size from that shown in the previous example, replace the 8192 in the sample command in step 3 with whatever value the vendor recommends, in bytes, without any punctuation.

# Permanently removing Windows Store applications

Windows 8.1 and later include a number of applications that may not be required in a Horizon environment. These applications are referred to as **Metro Apps** in Windows 8.1, but have since been renamed to **Modern Apps** with the release of Windows 10.

Some of these applications, such as ones that are weather- and news-related, are active even if they are not being used by the end user. The resources required to operate these applications place unnecessary load on the Horizon infrastructure, which is why the applications should be removed unless explicitly required.

The following procedure outlines how to remove some or all of the *Online* Windows Store packages, which are those that will be installed for all new users of the desktop image:

1. Open an elevated Windows PowerShell prompt.
2. To review the Windows store applications that will be installed for all users of the desktop image, as shown in the following screenshot, use the following PowerShell command:

```
Get-AppxProvisionedPackage -Online | Select DisplayName,
PackageName
```

```
PS C:\> Get-AppxProvisionedPackage -Online | Select DisplayName, PackageName

DisplayName                                          PackageName
-----------                                          -----------
Microsoft.BingFinance                                Microsoft.BingFinance_2014.
Microsoft.BingFoodAndDrink                           Microsoft.BingFoodAndDrink_
Microsoft.BingHealthAndFitness                       Microsoft.BingHealthAndFitn
Microsoft.BingMaps                                   Microsoft.BingMaps_2014.130
Microsoft.BingNews                                   Microsoft.BingNews_2014.221
```

3. To remove *all* Windows Store applications except the Windows Store itself, execute the following command, as shown in the following screenshot:

```
Get-AppxProvisionedPackage -Online | Where-Object
{$_.PackageName -notlike "*store*"} | Remove-
AppxProvisionedPackage -Online
```

```
PS C:\> Get-AppxProvisionedPackage -Online | Where-Object {$_.PackageName -notlike "*store*"} | Remove-AppxProvisionedPa
ckage -Online

Path            :
Online          : True
Restart Needed  : False

Path            :
Online          : True
Restart Needed  : False
```

Removing the Windows Store is not recommended, as it is required for some features of Windows to function properly.

4. To remove *a single* Windows Store application, using the information obtained in step *1* for the application **PackageName**, execute the following command:

```
Get-AppxProvisionedPackage -Online | Where-Object
{$_.PackageName -like "*BingFinance*"} | Remove-
AppxProvisionedPackage -Online
```

When using the -like switch, along with wildcards, you can also use switches similar to -like "*Bing*" **to remove all applications with "Bing" in the title.**

Refer to the following Microsoft TechNet links for information about these and other PowerShell commands used to manage Windows Store applications:

- *Get-AppxPackage* (https://technet.microsoft.com/en-us/library/hh856 044.aspx)
- *Remove-AppxPackage* (https://technet.microsoft.com/en-us/library/dn 448374.aspx)

- *Get-AppxProvisionedPackage* (`https://technet.microsoft.com/en-us/library/hh852131.aspx`)
- *Remove-AppxProvisionedPackage* (`https://technet.microsoft.com/en-us/library/hh852174.aspx`)

# Windows OS pre-deployment tasks

The following tasks are unrelated to the other optimization tasks that are described in this chapter, but they should be completed prior to placing the desktop into production.

## Installing VMware Tools

VMware Tools should be installed prior to the installation of the Horizon Agent software. To ensure that the master image has the latest version of the VMware Tools software, apply the latest updates to the host ESXi server prior to installing the tools package on the desktop.

 The same applies if you are updating your VMware Tools software. The Horizon Agent software should be reinstalled after the VMware Tools software is updated to ensure that the appropriate Horizon drivers are installed in place of the versions included with VMware Tools.

# Removing unwanted application – native update features

A number of applications install their own updater utility, including the almost ubiquitous Adobe Acrobat Reader and the Oracle Java Runtime Environment. If linked clone or instant clone desktops are being used, and regular updates of the desktop master image are made, these updater utilities should be disabled to reduce the growth of the desktop OS disk. Full clone desktops, you may wish to leave these updaters enabled, unless the software will be updated by other methods.

The procedure used to disable or remove these components will vary based on the architecture of the individual application. The following are examples of how to disable the Adobe Acrobat Reader and the Java Runtime Environment application updaters. For other applications, consult with their vendors for instructions on how to control or otherwise disable similar features with their software packages.

# Disabling the Adobe Acrobat Reader DC update feature

The following steps outline how to disable the Adobe Acrobat automatic updater:

 In the following instructions, the **Product Name**, **Product Version**, and **Product Code** registry keys will differ based on the version of Acrobat Reader that is installed. Simply select the installed version and make the remaining changes as instructed.

1. From an elevated Windows command prompt, load the `regedit.exe` application.
2. Navigate to **HKLM** | **SOFTWARE** | **Policies** | **Adobe** | `Product Name` | `Product Version` | **FeatureLockdown**.
3. Update the **bUpdater** DWORD value to a value of 0, as shown in the following screenshot, which disables the updater and removes the updater-related user interface items. If this registry entry does not exist, create it as a DWORD value.

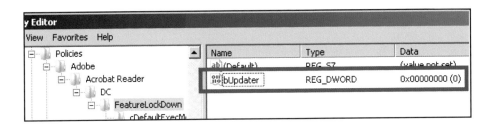

4. Navigate to **HKLM** | **SOFTWARE** | **Wow6432Node** | **Adobe** | **Adobe ARM** | **Legacy** | `Product Name` | `Product Code`.

5. Update the **Mode** DWORD value to a value of 0, as shown in the following screenshot, which prevents the download or installation of software updates. If this registry entry does not exist, create it as a DWORD value.

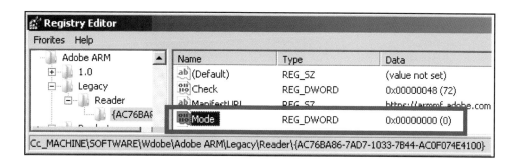

Step 4 is optional, and primarily used to configure the default updater settings, rather than disable them entirely using the procedure outlined in step 3. When configuring Horizon full clone desktops, you may wish to skip step 3 and set the value of **Mode** to 4 in step 5, which automatically downloads and installs updates.

If you wish to prevent users from performing manual updates within the Acrobat Reader application itself, use the Adobe Acrobat Group Policy templates mentioned in the *Adobe Acrobat Enterprise Administration Guide* located at http://www.adobe.com/devnet-docs/acrobatetk/tools/AdminGuide/index.html. These Group Policy objects enable you to completely disable the ability to update Acrobat Reader using the application menus.

# Disabling the Java updater utility

The following steps outline how to disable the Java updater utility:

1. From an elevated Windows command prompt, load the regedit.exe application.
2. For 32-bit Windows versions, navigate to **HKLM | SOFTWARE | JavaSoft | Java Update | Policy**; for 64-bit Windows versions, navigate to **HKLM | SOFTWARE | Wow6432Node | JavaSoft | Java Update | Policy**.

3. Update the **EnableJavaUpdate** DWORD value to the value of 0, as shown in the following screenshot, which disables the updater:

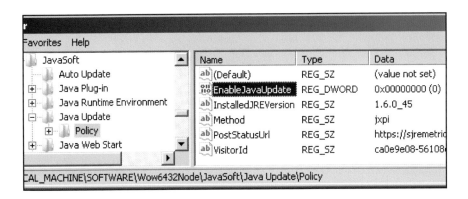

# Windows OS optimizations

A default installation of Microsoft Windows contains a number of configuration settings, components, and scheduled tasks that may not be required or are not desirable in a Horizon environment. This section will detail these settings, and provide instructions on how to make the recommended changes.

A team of VMware engineers have created a tool that can be used to automatically apply (or remove) a number of different Windows desktop and server OS optimizations. The **VMware OS Optimization Tool** (`https://labs.vmware.com/flings/vmware-os-optimization-tool`). This tool may be used to perform many of the optimizations detailed throughout the rest of this chapter, as well as additional ones not listed.

Many of these optimizations are implemented using Windows Group Policies, which can be applied to the Master Horizon desktop image prior to deployment, or by using domain-enforced Active Directory Group Policies. It is recommended to apply the majority of the policies directly to the master image when using linked clone and instant clone desktops. Doing this allows the Horizon pool maintenance operation to proceed more quickly, as the majority of the settings the desktop requires will already have been applied. Were the necessary policies to be applied using only domain-based Group Policy templates, a Horizon desktop or RDS server maintenance operation would be likely to take more time and resources to complete as each desktop must process the policy updates and make the necessary configuration changes. In addition, the desktops may require a reboot to fully implement the policy changes.

Most of the information in this section applies to Windows 7, 8.1, and 10. If a specific recommendation applies only to Windows 8.1 or 10, it will be identified.

# Disabling Windows Error Reporting

Windows Error Reporting compiles error reports that occur when an application crashes and, if configured to, forwards the information on to Microsoft. Linked clone and instant clone desktops are less likely to require this feature, as the underlying OS is likely to be updated on a regular basis. This feature may be needed when using full clone desktops, though, as those desktops generally have a much longer life cycle that may require occasional application troubleshooting. The following steps outline how to disable Windows Error Reporting:

1. Using the Group Policy console, edit the local desktop or domain-based Group Policy.
2. Select the **Computer Configuration** | **Administrative Templates** | **Windows Components** | **Windows Error Reporting** policy object.
3. Set **Disable Windows Error Reporting** to **Enabled**.

# Disabling automatic updates

Linked clone and instant clone desktops are typically updated using a Horizon pool maintenance operation, which negates the need for the Windows update service. To prevent these desktops from installing updates, which would significantly increase the OS disk size, this Windows feature should be disabled.

If your environment uses full clone Horizon desktops, which are deployed using a vSphere template, you should regularly update the template with the latest Windows patches or other required configuration changes. This ensures that new desktops will require little or no additional configuration upon deployment.

The following steps outline how to disable Windows Update:

1. Using the Group Policy console, edit the local desktop or domain-based Group Policy.
2. Select the **Computer Configuration** | **Administrative Templates** | **Windows Components** | **Windows Update** policy object.
3. Set the **Configure Automatic Updates** to **Disabled**.

Delete the `C:\Windows\SoftwareDistribution\Download` folder to remove any update packages that may have already been downloaded to the desktop.

Do not disable Automatic Updates if you are using `System Center Configuration Manager (SCCM)`; SCCM requires it to install Windows updates.

# Removing unnecessary Windows components

There are a number of Windows components that are installed by default that may not be needed in a Horizon environment. To further reduce the resources required by the desktop, remove any Windows components that are not required. Some components that may not be required include the Indexing Service, Internet Printing Client, Media Features, Tablet PC Components, and Windows Search.

The following steps outline how to remove unnecessary Windows components:

1. Open the Windows Control Panel.
2. Navigate to **Programs** | **Turn Windows features on or off**.
3. Remove any unnecessary components.

# Pre-compiling Microsoft .NET Framework assemblies

Microsoft .NET compiles framework assemblies on an as-needed basis when .NET-dependent programs are launched for the first time. This process can be both CPU- and disk-intensive, so you should pre-compile all .NET Framework assemblies on the Master Horizon desktop image prior to deployment.

> Microsoft .NET 3.5 is not installed by default on Windows 7 and later. If it is required, it should be installed prior to completing the following procedure. Microsoft .NET 3.5 can be installed using the **Control Panel** entry **Programs | Turn Windows features on or off**.

The following steps outline how to pre-compile all versions of the .NET Framework assemblies:

1. Use Windows Update to download and install all available .NET updates, and reboot as needed.
2. Open an elevated Windows command prompt.
3. On 32-bit Windows computers, navigate to the `C:\Windows\Microsoft.NET\Framework\v4.0.30319`; on 64-bit Windows computers, navigate to `C:\Windows\Microsoft.NET\Framework64\v4.0.30319`.
4. Type `ngen.exe executequeueditems` and hit *Enter*, as shown in the following screenshot. This process may require several minutes to complete; in the example provided there were no additional assemblies to pre-compile.

> In some cases, a newer .NET Framework may be installed that has a higher version number than 4.0.30319. If step 4 fails, repeat step 3, but navigate to the directory created for that version and complete step 4 again.

```
Administrator: C:\Windows\System32\cmd.exe

C:\Windows\Microsoft.NET\Framework64\v4.0.30319>ngen executequeueditems
Microsoft (R) CLR Native Image Generator - Version 4.0.30319.34209
Copyright (c) Microsoft Corporation.  All rights reserved.
All compilation targets are up to date.

C:\Windows\Microsoft.NET\Framework64\v4.0.30319>
```

# Disabling Windows hibernation

When the Windows OS goes into hibernation mode, a significant amount of write storage I/O is required to write the contents of the system's RAM to the `hiberfil.sys` file. An equivalent amount of storage read I/O is needed to resume the desktop from hibernation. During periods of heavy use, this additional I/O may affect the performance of other desktops that share the same storage. In addition to that, the `hiberfile.sys` file requires disk space equivalent to that of the desktops, configured RAM, which further increases the amount of per-desktop space required. To reduce desktop storage utilization, hibernation should be disabled.

To disable hibernation, execute the following command from an elevated Windows command prompt:

```
powercfg /hibernate off
```

If required, Horizon can manage workstation power states using native vSphere features. Desktops can be powered down or suspended as required, based on the configuration of the desktop pool. These settings are discussed further in `Chapter 10`, *Creating Horizon Desktop Pools*.

# Disabling Windows System Restore

**Windows System Restore** is used to restore a Windows desktop to a previous state, a useful feature when using a traditional physical desktop. This feature is generally not required when using linked clone and instant clone desktops, though, as those desktops can be restored to their original state using Horizon maintenance operations.

vSphere snapshots can be used in place of System Restore if you need the ability to quickly undo changes made to your Master Horizon desktop images or full clone desktops. vSphere snapshots should not be used with linked clone and instant clone desktops, as the snapshot would prevent Horizon maintenance operations from completing successfully.

Generating Windows System Restore snapshots generates intermittent spikes in storage I/O, and also requires additional disk space. To minimize the per-desktop storage utilization, this feature should be disabled on all linked clone and instant clone desktops, as well as full clone desktops unless the feature is explicitly required. The following steps outline how to disable system restore:

1. Right-click on **My Computer** (Windows 7) or **This PC** (Windows 8.1 and newer) and select **Properties**.
2. Select **Advanced system settings | System Protection**.
3. Click on the **Configure** button to open the **System Protection** window.
4. Under the **Restore Settings** section, click on the **Turn off system protection** (Windows 7) or **Disable system protection** (Windows 8.1 or newer) radio button.

# Sizing virtual machine RAM properly

The amount of RAM used for the desktop affects both the amount of storage space required and the likelihood that it will need to swap memory into the Windows page file.

Windows initially sizes the `C:\pagefile.sys` system file based on the amount of RAM the virtual machine is granted. From that point forward, the file expands as needed in response to Windows OS virtual memory requirements. The page file will also increase in size when the desktop RAM is increased.

The amount of RAM assigned to the virtual machine affects whether it is likely to need to utilize the Windows page file. Using the page file generates additional storage I/O, which we prefer to avoid in a Horizon environment where the storage is shared among multiple desktops. Using the techniques described in `Chapter 1`, *VMware Horizon Infrastructure Overview*, the desktop should be assigned sufficient RAM so that, under normal circumstances, it will not need to use the page file.

The Microsoft TechNet article **Pushing the Limits of Windows: Virtual Memory** (`http://blogs.technet.com/b/markrussinovich/archive/2008/11/17/3155406.aspx`) contains additional guidance about how to properly size Windows system RAM.

# Setting the Windows page file to a fixed size

By default, Windows dynamically expands and shrinks the Windows page file as required. This leads to fragmentation of the page file and additional storage I/O. To minimize the storage I/O associated with page file operations, set the page file to a fixed size.

 Not every desktop configuration will require a page file. If you determine that a desktop pool has low per-desktop memory requirements, common when minimal applications are being used, you can disable the page file entirely.

The following steps outline how to configure a fixed-size page file:

1. Right-click on **My Computer** (Windows 7) or **This PC** (Windows 8.1 and newer) and select **Properties**.
2. Select **Advanced system settings | Advanced**.
3. Click on the **Settings...** button under **Performance** to open the **Performance Options** window.
4. In the **Performance Options** window, click on the **Advanced** tab.
5. In the **Advanced** tab, click on the **Change...** button.
6. Uncheck the **Automatically manage paging file size for all drives** checkbox.
7. Click on the **Custom size** radio button, and populate the **Initial size** and **Maximum size** fields with the same value in MB.
8. Click on the **Set** button to implement the changes, and then click on **OK** three times to complete the action. Reboot the desktop if prompted.

Refer to the Microsoft TechNet article *Pushing the Limits of Windows: Virtual Memory* for additional guidance about how to determine the fixed page file size.

# Disabling paging the executive

By default, Windows writes kernel-mode drivers and system code to the Windows page file when not in use, which leaves more RAM available for the system. This action generates additional storage I/O, which we prefer to limit in a Horizon environment.

If the virtual machine is assigned sufficient memory, this feature is unnecessary and therefore should be disabled to reduce the per-desktop storage I/O. The following steps outline how to disable paging of the executive:

1. From an elevated Windows command prompt, load the `regedit.exe` application.
2. Navigate to **HKLM | System | CurrentControlSet | Control | Session Manager | Memory Management**.
3. Update the **Disable Paging Executive** DWORD to a value of 1 (from 0) to disable the feature.

# Disabling Content Indexing of the desktop drive

Content Indexing creates storage I/O overhead as it builds the content index cache for the desktop filesystems. If Content Indexing is not required, or if the desktop is a linked clone or instant clone, this feature should be disabled to reduce desktop storage I/O.

 Linked clone and instant clone desktops would require a Content Index after each Horizon pool maintenance operation, significantly increasing the storage I/O required to complete these operations. Content Indexing should be disabled when using these types of desktop.

The following steps outline how to disable indexing of the local disk:

1. Open the **My Computer** (Windows 7) or **This PC** (Windows 8.1 and newer) window, right-click on **C:**, and click on **Properties**.
2. On the **General** tab, clear the **Allow files on this drive to have contents indexed in addition to file properties** checkbox.
3. Click on **OK** to initiate the change, and click on OK again to update the indexing settings using the default option (**Apply changes to Drive C:\, subfolders and files**).

During the application of the new indexing settings, an error message stating that a file is in use may occur. If this happens, select **Ignore All**. If the desktop has additional hard disks, repeat this process for each of those disks.

# Disabling Content Indexing for the remaining file locations

Windows indexes a number of system and user-specific folders by default. To reduce the storage I/O overhead associated with these indexing operations, remove any unnecessary folder locations from the index list.

When using linked clone and instant clone desktops, it is suggested to uncheck all file locations from the **Indexed Locations** window.

The following steps outline how to disable the indexing of the remaining default locations:

1. Open the Windows **Control Panel**.
2. Navigate to **Indexing Options**.
3. Click on the **Modify** button to open the **Indexed Locations** window.
4. Deselect any locations or folders in the list that you do not want indexed and click on **OK**.

# Disabling unnecessary services

There are multiple Windows services that are typically not useful in a Horizon environment and can be disabled to reduce desktop resource requirements. These services, a sample of which is listed in this section, can be disabled using the Windows Services MMC plugin. A description of each of these services is provided in the Services MMC plugin:

- Diagnostic Policy Service
- IP Helper
- Network Location Awareness
- Security Center
- Shell Hardware Detection
- SSDP Discovery
- SuperFetch (disable only when using non-persistent desktops; additional information about SuperFetch follows this section)
- Telephony
- Themes
- Touch Keyboard and Handwriting Panel Service

- Windows Defender Service (disable only when using alternative antivirus or anti-malware platforms)
- Windows Audio
- Windows Connect Now (Config Registrar; Windows 8.1 and newer only)
- Windows Update (optional for full clones; it should be disabled in linked and instant clones)
- WLAN AutoConfig
- WWAN AutoConfig

For a more detailed list of Windows services and configuration options, consult the *Windows 7 Service Configurations*, *Windows 8.1 Service Configurations*, and *Windows 10 Service Configurations* guides at `www.blackviper.com`.

## SuperFetch

SuperFetch analyzes desktop usage patterns and pre-populates system RAM with the programs the user is most likely to use. When using non-persistent desktops, this results in unnecessary storage I/O as the optimizations will not persist and will be repeated each time the desktop is used. Additionally, SuperFetch also allocates additional system RAM for its use, which increases the amount of per-desktop RAM required.

For persistent Horizon desktops that also have larger amounts of RAM, you should leave SuperFetch enabled so that Windows can optimize the disk layout of the prefetch data and proactively load user binaries into RAM. This will make the desktop more responsive, and, since the desktop is persistent, the SuperFetch optimizations will persist across Horizon client sessions.

# Removing unnecessary scheduled tasks

Windows has a number of scheduled tasks that are either undesirable or not required in a Horizon environment. These tasks can be removed or disabled using the Windows **Control Panel | Schedule tasks** utility or an elevated command prompt. The following is a list of some of the tasks that should be reviewed to determine if they are required within your Horizon environment; if not, they should be disabled or removed. Details about each task are available in the **Schedule tasks** Windows Control Panel utility.

- `\Microsoft\Windows\Application Experience\ProgramDataUpdater`
- `\Microsoft\Windows\Application Experience\StartupAppTask`—Windows 8.1 and newer only

- `\Microsoft\Windows\Autochk\Proxy`
- `\Microsoft\Windows\Bluetooth\UninstallDeviceTask`
- `\Microsoft\Windows\Customer Experience Improvement Program\Consolidator`
- `\Microsoft\Windows\Customer Experience Improvement Program\KernelCeipTask`
- `\Microsoft\Windows\Customer Experience Improvement Program\UsbCeip`
- `\Microsoft\Windows\Defrag\ScheduledDefrag`
- `\Microsoft\Windows\DiskDiagnostic\Microsoft-Windows-DiskDiagnosticDataCollector`
- `\Microsoft\Windows\FileHistory\File History (maintenance mode)` âøøWindows 8.1 and newer only
- `\Microsoft\Windows\Maintenance\WinSAT`âøøWindows 8.1 and newer only
- `\Microsoft\Windows\Mobile Broadband Accounts\MNO Metadata Parser`âøøWindows 8.1 and newer only
- `\Microsoft\Windows\Power Efficiency Diagnostics\AnalyzeSystem`
- `\Microsoft\Windows\Ras\MobilityManager`
- `\Microsoft\Windows\SpacePort\SpaceAgentTask`âøøWindows 8.1 and newer only
- `\Microsoft\Windows\SpacePort\SpaceManagerTask`âøøWindows 8.1 and newer only
- `\Microsoft\Windows\SystemRestore\SR`
- `\Microsoft\Windows\UPnP\UPnPHostConfig`
- `\Microsoft\Windows\Windows Error Reporting\QueueReporting`
- `\Microsoft\Windows\Windows Media Sharing\UpdateLibrary`

To remove a task using an elevated Windows command prompt, use a command similar to the following example:

```
SCHTASKS /Delete /TN \Microsoft\Windows\Autochk\Proxy" /F
```

# Changing the Group Policy refresh interval

By default, all computers in an Active Directory domain attempt to refresh their Group Policy settings every 90 minutes, with a 30-minute offset. This is extended to limit the peak amount of network bandwidth that is consumed when refreshing the Group Policies. By default, the Group Policy is also updated at every boot of the OS. The following steps outline how to change the Group Policy refresh interval:

1. Using the Group Policy console, edit the local desktop or domain-based Group Policy.
2. Select the **Computer Configuration** | **Administrative Templates** | **System** | **Group Policy** policy object.
3. Double-click on the **Group Policy refresh internal for computers** policy to open the policy properties window.
4. Click on the **Enabled** radio button to enable the policy.
5. In the **Options** area, configure how often the Group Policy will be applied to the computer by providing a value for the **Minutes** field.
6. In the same area, set the amount of random time to be added to the Group Policy refresh interval by providing a value for the **Minutes** field. This randomizes the policy refresh interval to prevent the desktops from refreshing the policies at the same time.

# Disabling the Windows boot animation

Windows displays a start-up animation during the Windows portion of the boot process. This animation can only be seen when you are connected to the virtual machine console, and requires additional vSphere resources to display, which is why it should be disabled. The following steps outline how to disable the Windows boot animation:

1. From an elevated Windows command prompt, load the `msconfig.exe` application.
2. Select the **Boot** tab.

3. Under **Boot options**, check the **No GUI boot** and **Base video** checkboxes, as shown in the following screenshot. Click on **OK** to finalize the changes.

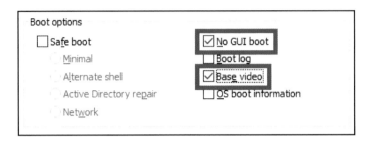

# Optimizing the Windows profile

There are various Windows settings that cannot be changed using normal Group Policies or other post-installation customizations, such as those we have already described in this chapter. To implement these additional settings, we can customize the default Windows local user profile, implementing changes that will be applied to all users who log in to the desktop for the first time.

In most cases, it is possible to create customized scripts or Group Policies that make these changes after a user has already logged in to the account. This generally requires changes to the desktop system registry, and an in-depth understanding of how the settings are recorded and updated within Windows.

As we discussed earlier, and this is particularly the case with linked clone and instant clone desktops, it is preferable to apply as much of your customization as you can to the Master Horizon desktop image. This ensures that the desktops are prepared using the minimum system resources required and are fully configured prior to their use. Policies that apply after the desktops are deployed may require an additional reboot to fully implement, which is not ideal for a Horizon environment. The process used to customize the default local user profile is outlined in the Microsoft KB article **Customize the default local user profile when preparing an image of Windows** (http://support.microsoft.com/kb/973289). The following settings, each of which helps reduce desktop resource utilization, are recommended to be made to the default local user profile.

The changes in this section will only apply to other desktop users if they are applied using the default user profile. The changes will not affect any profiles that are already present on the desktop image.

# Adjusting for best performance

Some of the more advanced UI features, such as menu fading and animations, require additional desktop CPU and memory resources. The following steps outline how to disable these effects:

1. Right-click on **My Computer** (Windows 7) or **This PC** (Windows 8.1 and newer) and click on **Properties**.
2. Click on **Advanced system settings** to open the **System Properties** window.
3. In the **System Properties** window, click on the **Advanced** tab.
4. Under **Performance**, click on the **Settings** button.
5. Click on the **Adjust for best performance** radio button, and then click on **OK** twice to close the window and update the settings.

# Turning off system sounds

System sounds require additional server and network resources and may not be required in every Horizon environment. If sounds are required, the Horizon administrator may want to configure a custom sound scheme based on the specific needs of the organization. The following steps outline how to turn off the system sounds:

1. Navigate to **Control Panel | Sound | Sounds**.
2. Set **Sound Scheme:** to **No Sounds**, or create and then select a custom sound scheme.

# Disabling the Windows background and screen saver

Displaying a custom Windows wallpaper or screen saver requires additional server and network resources. The Windows wallpaper should be changed to either none or a solid color by choosing the appropriate option based on the version of Windows being used. The screen saver should be disabled, or set to a blank screen, by choosing the appropriate option based on the version of Windows being used.

# Summary

In this chapter, we have learned about how to configure the Master Horizon desktop image and about what makes it different from configuring a traditional desktop.

We have discussed how to customize the Windows file system cluster size before beginning the installation process, how to permanently remove Windows store apps, disabling application native updaters, Windows optimizations that can reduce the desktop resource requirements, and when to use a custom Windows default user profile.

In Chapter 14, *Managing Horizon SSL Certificates*, we will discuss how to manage and replace the default Horizon self-signed SSL certificates.

# 14
# Managing Horizon SSL Certificates

VMware Horizon, similar to many other applications that require SSL-based encryption, installs self-signed SSL certificates by default. A self-signed certificate is one that is signed by the creator, in this case the VMware Horizon component that is being installed. While self-signed certificates do enable secure communications, by default they will not be trusted by any client or server who connects to them. An untrusted certificate leads to the familiar *There is a problem with this website's security certificate* message in Microsoft Internet Explorer, or the *The host name in the certificate is invalid or does not match* message in the VMware Horizon client.

In addition, the default self-signed SSL certificates may have a smaller key length than what is required within your organization; this is something that can only be addressed by replacing them after the installation has completed.

While it is possible to add exceptions that will make the default Horizon SSL certificates trusted by the different components of the Horizon infrastructure, and the Horizon clients themselves, it is preferable to replace the certificates with those signed by a commercial or private certificate authority. A number of commercial certificate authorities are supported by many OS's by default, and organizations can distribute their own root certificate from a private certificate authority, which will enable trusted connections to any resource, using certificates issued by that authority.

This chapter will show how to replace the default SSL certificates installed by each of the components of Horizon. We will use Microsoft **Active Directory (AD)** Certificate Services to issue the certificates, although the process is similar if you were to use a commercial certificate authority.

By the end of this chapter, we will have learned:

- How to create a Local Computer Certificates console
- How to request a certificate using Microsoft AD Certificate Services
- How to request a certificate with Subject Alternative Names using Microsoft AD Certificate Services
- How to replace the Horizon Connection Server certificate
- How to replace the Horizon Security Server certificate
- How to replace the Horizon Composer certificate
- How to replace the Horizon Access Point appliance certificate
- How to replace the App Volumes Manager appliance certificate

# Creating a Local Computer Certificates console

The Local Computer Certificates **Microsoft Management Console** (**MMC**) will be used to replace the certificate on the Horizon Connection, Security, and Composer servers.

 It is not necessary to create this console on each of the Horizon servers. The same console can be created on a remote server and, in step 5 in the following procedure, a remote connection is made rather than a local one.

1. From the Windows Start menu, open the MMC by searching for and opening the `mmc.exe` application.
2. In the MMC console window, open the **File** menu and select **Add/Remove Snap-in…** to open the **Add or Remove Snap-ins** window.
3. In the **Available snap-ins:** section of the **Add or Remove Snap-ins** window, select **Certificates** and click on **Add >** to open the **Certificates snap-in** selection window.

4. In the **Certificates** snap-in window, click the **Computer account** radio button, and then click on **Next >** to move to the **Select Computer** window:

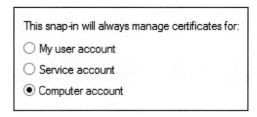

 Note the option to select **My user account**; we will use that option in the next section of this chapter to export newly created certificates.

5. In the **Select Computer** window shown in the following screenshot, if the computer is not already selected, click on the **Local computer:** (the computer this console is running on) radio button, and then click on **Finish** to return to the **Add or Remove Snap-ins** window.

6. Click on **OK** to close the **Add or Remove Snap-ins** window and return to the MMC console window. The console will now include the **Certificates (Local Computer)** snap-in, as shown in the following screenshot:

7.  If you also wish to add a certificate manager snap-in for your logged on user account, repeat steps 2 through 6, this time selecting **My user account** in step 4. This will create a single console that can be used to manage certificates for both the local computer and currently logged on user, as shown in the following screenshot:

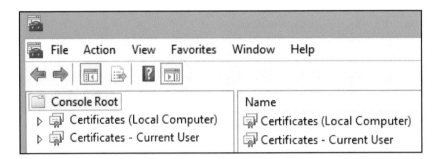

The **Local Computer Certificates** console is now ready for use. To create a shortcut for the console, open the **File** menu and click on **Save As** to open the **Save As** window. Provide a name and location for the shortcut and click on **Save**. This shortcut can be used to access the console without having to reconfigure it again.

# Requesting a certificate using Microsoft Active Directory Certificate Services

**Microsoft Active Directory Certificate Services** is an optional component of the Windows Server operating system which enables organizations to create their own private certificate authority. Similar functionality is available with alternative operating systems, but many organizations that have a large Windows infrastructure often already rely on AD Certificate Services to provide a number of different client and server certificates.

We will use AD Certificate Services to request certificates for each of the Horizon components. The process is the same for each, although App Volumes Manager servers, Horizon Security Servers, and Horizon Access Points may require additional information to be provided in step 5 in the following procedure. Consult the next section of this chapter for instructions on how to add additional DNS names and IP addresses, known as **Subject Alternative Names (SAN)**, to a certificate request.

If you wish to configure a certificate suitable for multiple private or public FQDN (or both), or one that includes IP addresses, and intend to use Microsoft AD Certificate Services to issue the certificate, you will need to enable support for SAN on an AD Certificate Services server. Review Microsoft KB article 931351 (`http://support.microsoft.com/kb/931 351`) for instructions on how to enable SAN support on an AD Certificate Services server.

In this section, we are focusing on using the AD Certificate Services website to request a certificate, rather than using the Certificate MMC we configured in the preceding section. The advantage of using the console is that you can use it from the Horizon Connection Server, and the certificate will be placed directly in the appropriate certificate store. This differs from using the Certificate Services website, which places it in the logged on user's Personal certificate store, which requires us to export the certificate and then import it into the local computer's Personal store.

You cannot use the Certificate console to request a certificate on a Horizon Security Server because those servers are typically not a member of a domain that has Microsoft AD Certificate Services installed.

The reason we use the website in this chapter is because we can use it to request certificates for all Horizon components, not just the Connection Servers. If you are interested in using the Certificates MMC console to request a certificate, the Microsoft TechNet Wiki article titled *Create a Certificate Request using the Microsoft Management Console (MMC)* (`http://soc ial.technet.microsoft.com/wiki/contents/articles/10377.create-a-certifi cate-request-using-microsoft-management-console-mmc.aspx`) details the procedure used to do so.

The following steps may be performed from any available computer that has access to the AD Certificate Services website. We will export the certificate when we are finished with the request, which is required for later import in the destination server:

1. From a web browser, open the Microsoft AD Certificate Services website. The URL for the site is typically in the format `https://FQDN of the server/certsrv`. If prompted, provide credentials for a user with the ability to request certificates from the certificate authority.

To access the Microsoft AD Certificate Services website remotely, it must be configured with an SSL certificate. If your Certificate Services server has not been configured with an SSL certificate, you can only access the Certificate Services website from a web browser on the Certificate Services server itself, using HTTP instead of HTTPS. This section assumes that you can access the Certificate Services server remotely.

2. In the **Welcome** page shown in the following screenshot, click on **Request a certificate**:

> **Select a task:**
> Request a certificate
> View the status of a pending certificate request
> Download a CA certificate, certificate chain, or CRL

3. In the **Request a Certificate** page shown in the following screenshot, click on **advanced certificate request**:

> **Request a Certificate**
>
> Select the certificate type:
>   User Certificate
>
> Or, submit an advanced certificate request.

4. In the **Advanced Certificate Request** window (shown in the following screenshot), click on **Create and submit a request to this CA**:

> **Advanced Certificate Request**
>
> The policy of the CA determines the types of cert
>
>   Create and submit a request to this CA.
>
>   Submit a certificate request by using a base-6
>   using a base-64-encoded PKCS #7 file.

5. In the **Advanced Certificate Request** window (shown in the following screenshot), use the **Certificate Template:** drop-down menu if required to select a web server template that allows the certificate keys to be exported, provide any remaining information needed to complete the request, and click **Submit >**:

 The **Name:** field must always be populated with the FQDN of the target server. This field is the same as the **Common Name** field you see when using the Certificates MMC to request a certificate, and is also used in various other SSL certificate-related resources.

6. In the **Web Access Confirmation** window, review the message and click on **Yes** to complete the certificate request.

 If Microsoft AD Certificate Services is configured to approve web server requests automatically, the certificate will be available immediately. If not, the certificate administrator must approve the request to create the certificate.

 This section assumes that the certificate request will automatically be approved and available for immediate download. If you need to wait for the certificate administrator to approve the certificate request, simply return to the certificate services website after the request has been approved, and select **View the status of a pending certificate request to download the certificate**.

7. In the **Certificate Issued** page, click on **Install this certificate** to install the certificate in the logged on users **Personal** certificate store, as shown in the following screenshot:

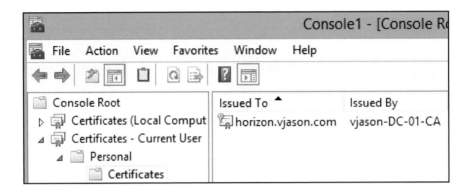

8. Right-click on the certificate shown in the following screenshot and click **Export...** to open the **Certificate Export Wizard**:

9. In the **Certificate Export Wizard** welcome screen, click **Next**.
10. In the **Certificate Export Wizard | Export Private Key** screen shown in the following screenshot, click the **Yes, export the private key** radio button and then click **Next**:

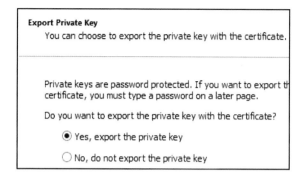

11. In the **Certificate Export Wizard** | **Export File Format** screen shown in the following screenshot, uncheck all options under **Personal Information Exchange – PKCS #12 (.PFX)** and then click **Next**:

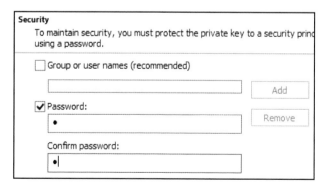

12. In the **Certificate Export Wizard** | **Security** screen shown in the following screenshot, click the **Password:** check box, provide a password for the certificate, and then click **Next**:

13. In the **Certificate Export Wizard | File to Export** screen, provide a name and destination location for the exported PFX file and then click **Next**.

14. In the **Certificate Export Wizard | Completing the Certificate Export Wizard** screen, review the settings and then click **Finish** to complete the export process.

New certificates should be copied and archived to a secure location, prior to being imported into their destination certificate stores. This enables the certificates to be reused if any of the Horizon servers ever need to be rebuilt.

# Requesting a certificate with Subject Alternative Names

A certificate's Subject Alternative Name (SAN) is often used on servers that have only one web service running, but are accessed from multiple DNS names. A Horizon Security Server or Access Point are examples of this, as they are often accessed using a publicly known name such as `horizon.vjason.com`, as well as a private (internal) name such as `viewsec-01.vjason.local`, and even their IP address. Additionally, App Volumes Manager servers require their FQDN, server name, and IP address in their certificates.

While a certificate will work regardless of what DNS name was used to connect to it, if the DNS name or IP address used to access it is not present as a SAN in the certificate, the client will receive an error that the certificate name does not match. To prevent these errors from occurring when requesting the certificate, we simply need to provide a list of the different DNS names or IP addresses that will be used to connect to the server.

In this section, we will request a certificate with SAN from our AD Certificate Services server. As mentioned previously, you will need to enable support for SAN on your AD Certificate Services server or the SAN will not be added to the certificate.

To request a certificate with SAN, all that is needed is to provide additional information in step 5 of the preceding section, *Requesting a certificate using Microsoft Active Directory Certificate Services*. As shown in the following screenshot, we will use the Attributes: section of the **Advanced Certificate Request** window to request the SAN:

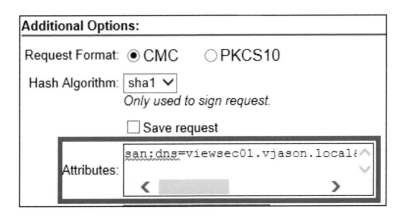

Using the examples provided in this chapter, the following text should be added to the **Attributes:** field to add SAN to the certificate request. You must add all possible alternative server names to this option, including the name used with the certificate request:

```
san:dns=viewsec01.vjason.local&dns=horizon.vjason.com&ipaddress=172.16.100.
15
```

If additional SAN are required, simply append the text with an ampersand (&), and then the additional DNS names or IP addresses in the format `dns=my.domain.com` or `ipaddress=1.2.3.4`. Do not insert spaces in any part of the string of text. You can also add just the host name itself, without the domain name, such as `dns=servername`.

The following screenshot shows the properties of a certificate that has multiple SAN, which was created using the example text provided earlier. When SAN are added to a certificate, a new property **Subject Alternative Name** is created under **Field** in **Details** tab, and the additional DNS names or IP addresses are added. This certificate enables the destination server to be accessed using any of the four DNS names shown, without any errors about a certificate to host name mismatch (were the DNS name used not listed among the SAN).

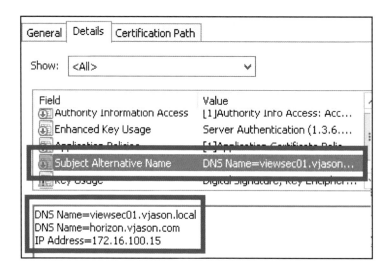

The rest of the certificate request process is the same; once the request has been approved, save the certificate to the local computer for later import into the Windows certificate store.

# Converting a certificate from PFX to PEM format

Replacing the certificate on either an App Volumes Manager Server or Horizon Access Point appliance requires a certificate in the PEM format, which necessitates a different procedure when using the AD Certificate Services certificate authority. The following items are needed to convert a certificate in the PFX format to the PEM format:

- A computer with the open source OpenSSL software installed, which is available at `www.openssl.org`. OpenSSL is used to convert the certificate into the format needed by the Apache Web Server used with the Horizon Access Point. In our example, OpenSSL was installed on a Windows computer.

- A certificate with an exportable private key, which is not allowed with the default AD Certificate Services web server template. To use certificates issued by AD Certificate Services, review the Microsoft TechNet article *cc725621* (`http://tech net.microsoft.com/en-us/library/cc725621(v=ws.10).aspx`) for instructions on how to create a new certificate template that allows exportable private keys.

The following steps must be completed on a computer that has OpenSSL installed. For the purpose of this exercise, we have already copied the exported PFX file with private key included to the computer we will perform the conversion on:

1. Execute each of the following commands in turn, providing the password created when the certificate was exported, when prompted. These commands are executed on a computer with OpenSSL installed, from within the `OpenSSL-Win32\bin` directory:

```
openssl.exe pkcs12 -in e:\Horizon\horap01.pfx -out
e:\Horizon\key.pem -nodes
openssl rsa -in e:\Horizon\key.pem -out e:\Horizon\server.key
openssl.exe pkcs12 -in e:\Horizon\horap01.pfx -clcerts -nokeys -out
e:\Horizon\horap01.crt
```

Replace the file and path name in the `-in` and `-out` switches in the preceding commands with the name and location of your files.

- The following screenshot shows the execution of these commands and their expected output. Three files are generated during the conversion process: `key.pem`, `server.key`, and `server.crt`:

```
c:\OpenSSL-Win32\bin>openssl.exe pkcs12 -in e:\Horizon\horap01.pfx -out e:\Horiz
on\key.pem -nodes
Enter Import Password:
MAC verified OK

c:\OpenSSL-Win32\bin>openssl.exe rsa -in e:\Horizon\key.pem -out e:\Horizon\serv
er.key
writing RSA key

c:\OpenSSL-Win32\bin>openssl.exe pkcs12 -in e:\Horizon\horap01.pfx -clcerts -nok
eys -out e:\Horizon\horap01.crt
Enter Import Password:
MAC verified OK
```

2. Retain the `server.key` file; it will be used during the installation of the Horizon Access Point.

3. From a web browser, open the Microsoft AD Certificate Services website. The URL for the site is typically in the format `https://FQDN of the server/certsrv`.

4. In the **Welcome** page, click on **Download a CA certificate, certificate chain, or CRL**.

5. In the **Download a CA Certificate, Certificate Chain, or CRL** page shown in the following screenshot, click the **Base 64** radio button, and then click **Download CA certificate** to download the root certificate for the certificate server. Copy the downloaded file, named `certnew.cer` by default, to the same location as the files created in step 1.

6. Using Notepad, or another similar text editor, open both the `certnew.cer` root certificate and the `horap01.crt` server certificate.

7. Copy the contents of both files into a new text file in the order of server certificate first, then the root certificate, retaining only the contents that are bracketed by the `-----BEGIN CERTIFICATE-----` and `-----END CERTIFICATE-----` text blocks. The following sample screenshot is abbreviated; your file will likely have significantly more lines in between the brackets:

```
-----BEGIN CERTIFICATE-----
MIIFvjCCBKagAwIBAgITLgAAAB11czz52VRZDwABAAAAHTANBgkqhkiG9w0BAQsF
-----END CERTIFICATE-----
-----BEGIN CERTIFICATE-----
MIID1DCCAnygAwIBAgIQSsToIsb9waNGuNFjY8/GdjANBgkqhkiG9w0BAQsFADBJ
-----END CERTIFICATE-----
```

If your environment includes intermediate certificate authorities, the certificates for those would need inserting in between the root and server certificates. Insert the certificates in order, starting with the server certificate first, then the next intermediate certificate in the chain, and so on, until all certificates in the chain are present.

8. Save the new file with a `.crt` extension. For recovery purposes, retain a backup of both the original certificates and files created during the conversion, being careful to secure them as they contain the certificate private keys.

Your certificates are now converted to PEM format for use by either App Volumes Manager servers or Horizon Access Point appliances.

# Replacing a Horizon Connection Server certificate

The following steps outline how to replace the certificate on the Horizon Connection Server, and assume that you have already obtained the replacement certificate using the steps outlined in *Requesting a certificate using Microsoft Active Directory Certificate Services*. The Horizon Connection Server will be unavailable while the certificate is being replaced, so plan for downtime accordingly:

1. Using the Services MMC, stop the **VMware Horizon View Connection Server** service. This will also stop other Horizon-related services.

2. Open the Local Computer Certificates MMC you created in the *Creating a Local Computer Certificates console* section.

3. Right-click on the existing Horizon Connection Server certificate (shown in the following screenshot) and click on **Properties** to open the **Properties** window. This certificate is easily identified as it has a **Friendly Name** of **vdm**:

4. In the certificate's Properties window, append the friendly name of the certificate with -original, as shown in the following screenshot, and click on **OK** to return to the Local Computer Certificates MMC:

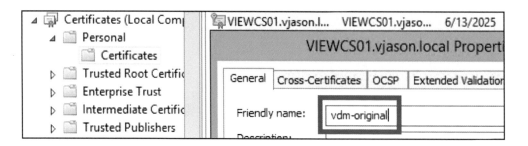

5. In the **Local Computer Certificates** MMC, go to **Certificates (Local Computer)** | **Personal**. Then, right-click on the **Certificates** folder and click on **All Tasks** | **Import…** as shown in the following screenshot. This will open the **Welcome to the Certificate Import Wizard** window.

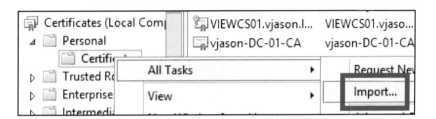

6. In the **Certificate Import Wizard** window, click on **Next**.
7. In the **Certificate Import Wizard** | **File to Import** window, click on the **Browse…** button, use the file type drop-down menu to show **All Files (*.*)**, select the certificate file that you obtained from your certificate authority, and click on **Next**.
8. In the **Certificate Import Wizard** | **Private key protection** window, type the certificate password used when the certificate was exported, and then click **Next**.
9. In the **Certificate Import Wizard** | **Certificate Store** window (shown in the following screenshot), the **Place all certificates in the following store** radio button should already be checked. Select the **Personal** store and click on **Next**.

10. In the **Certificate Import Wizard | Completing the Certificate Import Wizard** window, review the settings and click on **Finish** to close the **Certificate Import Wizard** window. If changes are required, click on the **Back** button and make the changes where necessary.

11. The **Certificate Import Wizard** will open an additional window to confirm the successful import of the certificate. Click on **OK** to close this window.

12. The new certificate will appear alongside the existing certificate, as shown in the following screenshot. Note that the certificate was issued by our internal certificate authority, and not the local server itself like the default certificate:

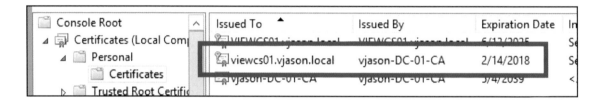

13. Right-click on the new certificate and click on **Properties** to open the **Properties** window. This certificate is easily identified as it has no friendly name.

14. In the certificate's **Properties** window, set the friendly name of the certificate to vdm and click on **OK** to return to the Local Computer Certificates MMC.

The Horizon Connection and Security Server software identifies which certificate to use by the value of the friendly name, which should be **vdm**.

15. Using the Services MMC, start the **VMware Horizon View Connection Server** service.

16. From a web browser, access the Horizon Connection Server using HTTPS and the FQDN. As shown in the following screenshot, verify that no SSL errors are shown, the new certificate is being used, and the certificate is trusted:

The same process should be repeated for any additional Horizon Connection Servers, using unique certificates for each one.

# Replacing a Horizon Security Server certificate

The process used to replace the certificate on a Horizon Security Server is nearly identical to that of the Horizon Connection Server. This section will detail which steps from the preceding section differ when replacing the certificate on a Horizon Security Server. The Horizon Security Server will be unavailable while the certificate is being replaced, so plan for downtime accordingly.

These updated steps assume that you have already obtained the replacement certificate using the steps outlined in *Requesting a certificate using Microsoft Active Directory Certificate Services*. Follow the steps outlined in the replacing the certificate in a Horizon Connection Server section, replacing steps 1, 14, and 15 with updated ones as follows:

- **Step 1**: Using the Services MMC, stop the **VMware Horizon View Security Server** service. This will also stop other View-related services.
- **Step 14**: Using the Services MMC console, start the **VMware Horizon View Security Server** service.
- **Step 15**: From a web browser, access the Horizon Security Server using HTTPS and all of the FQDN that are defined in the SAN certificate. Verify that no SSL errors are shown, the new certificate is being used, the certificate is trusted, and that the expected SAN are present.

The same process should be repeated on any additional Horizon Security Servers, using unique certificates for each one.

# Replacing a Horizon Composer certificate

Horizon Composer uses a default certificate that is not trusted by the Horizon Connection Server. While an exception can be made to trust this certificate when Composer is enabled, replacing the certificate with one that is trusted is straightforward, and enables Composer to be trusted without an exception being made.

The following steps outline how to replace the Horizon Composer SSL certificate, and assume that you have already obtained the replacement certificate using the steps outlined in *Requesting a certificate using Microsoft Active Directory Certificate Services*. Horizon Composer will be unavailable while the certificate is being replaced, so plan for downtime accordingly.

This process should be done before any linked-clone desktops are deployed. This isn't a requirement; however, if any problems occur with Horizon Composer, it is much easier to rebuild if no linked-clone desktops are deployed.

1. Open the Local Computer Certificates MMC.
2. In the Local Computer Certificates MMC, go to **Certificates (Local Computer)** | **Personal**, right-click on the Certificates folder, and click on **All Tasks** | **Import...**. Complete the steps to import the certificate.
3. The new certificate will appear alongside the existing certificate. Unlike the certificates for the Horizon Connection and Security Servers, you do not need to change the certificate's Friendly Name.
4. Open the Services MMC and stop the **VMware Horizon 6 Composer** service.

5. Open a Windows command prompt and change to the `\Program Files (x86)\VMware\VMware View Composer` directory, as shown in the following screenshot:

```
c:\Program Files (x86)\VMware\VMware View Composer>dir *.exe
 Volume in drive C has no label.
 Volume Serial Number is 0217-149C

 Directory of c:\Program Files (x86)\VMware\VMware View Composer

11/29/2015  10:34 PM           327,384 SviConfig.exe
11/29/2015  10:34 PM            40,664 SviWebService.exe
11/29/2015  10:34 PM            81,920 zip.exe
               3 File(s)        449,968 bytes
               0 Dir(s)  27,883,098,112 bytes free

c:\Program Files (x86)\VMware\VMware View Composer>_
```

6. Enter the following command and press Enter. The `delete=false` option leaves the existing certificate in place, allowing us to use it again if ever required:

```
SviConfig -operation=replacecertificate -delete=false
```

7. Type in the number for the new certificate from the list provided and press Enter. As shown in the following screenshot, we will select certificate **2** as that is the newly issued certificate that we wish to enable. The output of the `SviConfig` command should verify that the operation completed successfully:

```
c:\Program Files (x86)\VMware\VMware View Composer>SviConfig.exe -operation=repl
acecertificate -delete=false

Select a certificate:

 1. Subject: C=US, S=CA, L=CA, O=VMware Inc., OU=VMware Inc., CN=VIEWCOMP01, E=s
upport@vmware.com
     Valid from: 12/23/2015 9:37:42 AM
     Valid to: 12/23/2017 9:37:42 AM
     Thumbprint: 6ABE570CCBA8861593EB939CC5F6BDE788A21568

 2. Subject: CN=viewcomp01.vjason.local
     Valid from: 2/15/2016 7:59:44 AM
     Valid to: 2/14/2018 7:59:44 AM
     Thumbprint: 54FD4F386DD73986CCED2F9D2AC34012065DACAE

Enter choice (0-2, 0 to abort):_
```

8. Open the Services MMC and start the **VMware Horizon 6 Composer** service.
9. To verify that the certificate is trusted by the Horizon Connection Servers, open the Horizon Administrator console.
10. In the Horizon Administrator console's dashboard, under **System Health**, expand the **View Composer Servers** object.
11. Click on the Horizon Composer Server you wish to check, to open the **View Composer Server Detail**s window as shown in the following screenshot. Verify that the SSL Certificate field is shown as **Valid**:

| View Composer Server Details | |
| --- | --- |
| Name: | ■ https://viewcomp01.vjason.local:18443 |
| Version: | 6.2.0.17889 |
| Status: | No problem detected. |
| SSL Certificate: | Valid |

The same process should be repeated on any additional servers that host Horizon Composer, using unique certificates for each.

# Replacing a Horizon Access Point certificate

Horizon Access Points differ from other Horizon components and App Volumes Manager servers in how you replace their certificate. The Horizon Access Point configuration is modified using **JSON** requests to the Access Point **REST API**, the syntax for which is provided in the VMware document *Deploying and Configuring Access Point* (`https://www.v mware.com/support/pubs/view_pubs.html`).

Horizon Access Points require a certificate with SAN that include the FQDN of the individual Access Point, the FQDN used on any load balancers in front of the Access Point (if applicable), and the Access Point IP address. Using the method outlined in *Requesting a certificate with Subject Alternative Names*, that would require a certificate attributes string similar to:

```
san:dns=horap01.vjason.local&dns= horizon.vjason.com&ipaddress=172.16.100.5
```

Using the **VMware Access Point Deployment Utility** shown in `Chapter 5`, *Implementing a Horizon Access Point*, you may find it much faster to simply deploy a new appliance than replace the certificate. However, if you have never worked with JSON requests and REST APIs, you may find this a good learning experience, which is something I always encourage. Regardless of which method you choose, I recommend installing a permanent certificate when the appliance is deployed, rather than updating it after the fact, as it adds very little time to the deployment process.

The following process outlines the steps required to replace the certificate on a Horizon Access Point, and assumes that you have already obtained the replacement certificate with the appropriate SAN. Additionally, you will need to download and install Notepad++ (`https://notepad-plus-plus.org`) in order to modify the format of the certificate and key files so that the contents are all located on one single line:

1. Use the process outlined in *Converting a certificate from PFX to PEM format* to convert the PFX certificate into separate **CRT** and **KEY** files. The CRT file must contain all certificates in the chain.
2. Using Notepad++, open the `horap01.crt` and `horap01.key` files. Look at the bottom of the window for each file as shown in the following screenshot and note the file format; it may be different for each file. Two instances of the program were opened here so both formats can be shown; the options are **UNIX** and **Dos\Windows**:

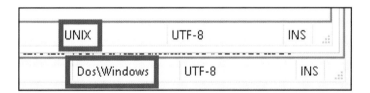

3. If the file is in **Dos\Windows** format, open the Notepad++ **Edit** menu, click **EOL Conversion**, and then click **UNIX/OSX Format**, as shown in the following screenshot:

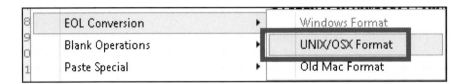

4. Open the Notepad++ **Search** menu and click **Replace…**.
5. For each file, in the **Replace** window**Find what :** field, type \n, and in the **Replace with :** field, type \\n as shown in the following screenshot, and then click **Replace All**:

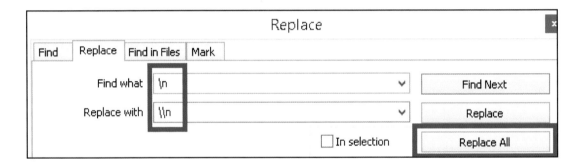

6. Confirm the contents of both files are now located on a single line, as shown in the following screenshot:

7. In a separate Notepad++ window, create a third file for the JSON request in the following format, replacing the values for **string** with the contents of the `horap01.key` and `horap01.crt` files, respectively:

```
{
  "privateKeyPem": "string",
  "certChainPem": "string"
}
```

8. Verify the JSON request looks similar the following screenshot:

9. Use a REST API client such as Postman for Google Chrome (`https://chrome.g oogle.com/webstore/detail/postman/fhbjgbiflinjbdggehcddcbncdddo mop`) to connect to the Horizon Access Point, as shown in the following screenshot. Configure the **GET** address with the Access Point management interface IP in the format `https://x.x.x.x:9443/rest/v1/config/certs/ssl`, set the **Authorization** drop-down to **Basic Auth**, type the **Username** as `admin`, and in the **Password** field, enter the Access Point admin password configured during appliance deployment, then set the drop-down to the left of the appliance URL to **PUT** as shown. Click **Update Request** when the settings have been configured:

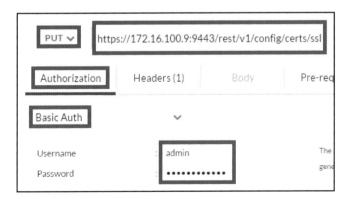

10. Click on the **Body** tab, click the **raw** radio button, select **JSON (application/json)** in the drop-down menu to the right of the **binary** radio button, paste in the contents of the JSON request created in step 7, and then click **Send**. The following screenshot highlights each of the items used in this step:

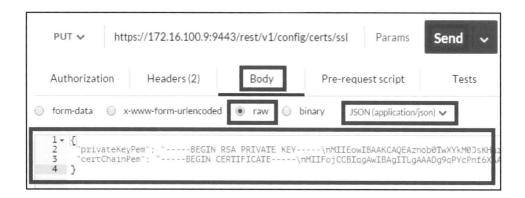

11. Verify that a status of **200 OK** is returned, as shown in the following screenshot; this confirms that the certificate was successfully installed:

12. Access the Horizon Access Point web interface and verify that the certificate is working:

The Horizon Access Point appliance is now updated with the new certificate.

# Replacing an App Volumes Manager server certificate

App Volumes Manager servers require a certificate with SAN that include the server name, the FQDN of the server, and the server IP address. Using the method outlined in *Requesting a certificate with Subject Alternative Names*, that would require a certificate attributes string similar to:

```
san:dns=appvolmgr01.vjason.local&dns=appvolmgr01&ipaddress=172.16.100.20
```

The following process outlines the steps required to replace the certificate on an App Volumes Manager appliance, and assume that you have already obtained the replacement certificate with the appropriate SAN:

1. Use the process outlined in *Converting a certificate from PFX to PEM format* to convert the PFX certificate into separate **CRT** and **KEY** files. The CRT file must contain all certificates in the chain.
2. Rename the files to `appvol_self_vmware.com.crt` and `appvol_self_vmware.com.key`, and copy them to a computer capable of accepting inbound **Secure Copy (SCP)** connections.

 An ESXi host can accept inbound SCP connections if its security policies allow it.

3. Use the vSphere Web Client to access the App Volumes Manager appliance console, log on using the appliance `root` account, and navigate to the `/etc/nginx` directory.
4. Make copies of or rename the existing `appvol_self_vmware.com.crt` and `appvol_self_vmware.com.key` files contained in that directory.

5. Use the `scp` command to copy the files uploaded to a remote server in step 2 to the local App Volumes appliance. The syntax is `scp root@`*IPofHostToCopyFrom*`:/path/appvol_self_vmware.com.crt /etc/nginx/appvol_self_vmware.com.crt`. The following screenshot shows this command being used to copy the two certificate files to the local App Volumes appliance; since this was the first connection to the remote server, we were prompted to accept the RSA key fingerprint:

```
root@rtpappv01:/etc/nginx# scp root@172.16.100.27:/tmp/appvol_self_vmware.com.crt /etc/nginx/appvol_
self_vmware.com.crt
The authenticity of host '172.16.100.27 (172.16.100.27)' can't be established.
RSA key fingerprint is a7:9a:c0:b3:1f:df:ac:b1:a3:a7:8b:2c:82:f2:be:70.
Are you sure you want to continue connecting (yes/no)? yes
Warning: Permanently added '172.16.100.27' (RSA) to the list of known hosts.
Password:
appvol_self_vmware.com.crt                          100% 3850     3.8KB/s   00:00
root@rtpappv01:/etc/nginx# scp root@172.16.100.27:/tmp/appvol_self_vmware.com.key /etc/nginx/appvol_
self_vmware.com.key
Password:
appvol_self_vmware.com.key                          100% 1675     1.6KB/s   00:00
root@rtpappv01:/etc/nginx#
```

6. Execute the command `service nginx restart` to load the new SSL certificate and private key.

7. Access the App Volumes Manager web portal using HTTPS and verify that the certificate is trusted, as shown in the following screenshot. Note that since we used SAN to add both the server name and IP address to the certificate, we can access it using either of those without any host mismatch errors being displayed.

8. Repeat this procedure as needed for the remaining App Volumes Manager appliances, using a unique certificate and private key file for each.

# Summary

In this chapter, we discussed how to use native Windows OS features to create certificate requests and generate certificates, and how the new certificates are imported and enabled.

We also learned how to request a certificate with SAN, which allows us to add additional DNS names and even IP addresses to a certificate, an option typically required for Horizon Security Servers, Access Points, and App Volumes Manager servers.

Next we learned how to convert a certificate from PFX to PEM format, which is required when you wish to use it with Horizon Access Point and App Volumes Manager appliances.

Finally, we learned how to replace the SSL certificates in each of the Horizon servers, as well as the App Volumes Manager appliances.

In the next chapter, we will discuss how to use Horizon PowerCLI to perform administrative tasks, and configuration tasks, using the command line, which is useful for customers who have a desire to automate as much of their infrastructure as they can.

# 15
# Using Horizon PowerCLI

In this chapter, we will review how to enable remote management of our Horizon Connection Servers using PowerCLI, and then how to use PowerCLI to perform various tasks related to Horizon configuration, administration, and troubleshooting. The topics we will cover include:

- Enabling remote management on a Horizon Connection Server so that PowerCLI can be used remotely
- Establishing a remote PowerCLI session
- Viewing all the PowerCLI commands and their options
- Configuring the Horizon infrastructure
- Administering Horizon Desktop pools
- Managing Horizon Client entitlements and sessions
- Working with Horizon network label specifications
- Retrieving information about the Horizon infrastructure

VMware Horizon provides a number of different PowerShell commands that you can use to configure, manage, and monitor the Horizon environment. These commands are known as Horizon PowerCLI, and they enable Horizon administrators to do everything from automating repetitive operations to using existing IT infrastructure management platforms in order to perform common Horizon tasks. While not every aspect of the Horizon environment can be managed or configured using Horizon PowerCLI, most of the common settings can.

Horizon PowerCLI commands can only be executed against a single Horizon pod at a time; if you have multiple distinct Horizon pods, you must use separate PowerShell sessions for each. While each of these commands uses capital letters to identify individual words within the command, PowerCLI itself is not case-sensitive. You do not need to capitalize any part of the PowerCLI commands or the command options.

Using the information provided in this chapter, you should be able to reduce the time you spend in the Horizon Administrator console by building scripts that can perform the actions more quickly, even automating tasks if you wish.

# Enabling remote management on Windows

Unlike vSphere PowerCLI, VMware Horizon does not include a standalone installer that is used to remotely manage Horizon using PowerCLI. The Horizon PowerCLI commands will only work when executed from a Horizon Connection Server. To enable remote management, we must enable **Windows Remote Management** (**WinRM**) on at least one Horizon Connection Server in each Horizon pod that we want to manage.

WinRM is based on the WS-Management Protocol, which is a SOAP-based protocol that is used to enable interoperability between hardware and OSes from different vendors. We will use WinRM to establish remote PowerShell connections to a Horizon Connection Server; this will enable us to run commands from that server without actually having to log in to the server console.

# Enabling WinRM

In this section, we will configure WinRM to use HTTPS for an added measure of security. This ensures that, if we need to pass sensitive information over a WinRM session, it cannot be read in clear text. Consult Microsoft KB article 2019527 (`http://support.microsoft.com/kb/2019527`) for information on how to obtain the SSL certificate required to enable WinRM HTTPS connections.

The following steps outline how to enable WinRM in Windows in the event that it has not been previously enabled:

1. Log in to the Horizon Connection Server that you will use for your remote sessions.
2. Enable and start the **Windows Remote Management (WS-Management)** service. This service should be set to start automatically.
3. From an elevated Windows command prompt on the server, execute the following command in order to enable inbound WinRM requests over HTTPS:

```
winrm quickconfig -transport:https
```

4. When prompted, answer y to approve the operation, and verify that the operation succeeded, as shown in the following screenshot:

```
C:\>winrm quickconfig -transport:https
WinRM service is already running on this machine.
WinRM is not set up to allow remote access to this machine for management.
The following changes must be made:

Create a WinRM listener on HTTPS://* to accept WS-Man requests to any IP on this
 machine.
Configure CertificateThumbprint setting for the service, to be used for CredSSP
authentication.

Make these changes [y/n]? y

WinRM has been updated for remote management.

Created a WinRM listener on HTTPS://* to accept WS-Man requests to any IP on thi
s machine.
Configured required settings for the service.
```

5. If the Windows firewall is enabled on the Horizon Connection Server, create a firewall rule that allows TCP port `5986` inbound. This is the port that is used when connecting to WinRM over SSL. If you wish to block WinRM over HTTP to ensure that only HTTPS can be used, block TCP port `5985` inbound, using an additional firewall rule.

WinRM is now configured and is available to any users with local administrative access to the server.

# Establishing a remote Horizon PowerCLI session

Once WinRM is enabled, you can connect to the Horizon Connection Server remotely over a PowerShell session. The following steps outline how to establish a remote PowerShell session, and then enable the Horizon PowerCLI commands:

1. Open a PowerShell window on the computer that you will use to remotely manage VMware Horizon.
2. Use the following command to initiate a remote PowerShell session. You will need to provide the FQDN of the Horizon Connection Server, a user ID that has administrative access to both the Horizon and the Connection Server, and include the `-UseSSL` option:

```
Enter-PSSession -ComputerName "ConnectionServerFQDN" -UseSSL
Credential "domain\username"
```

The following screenshot shows an example of this command in our test environment:

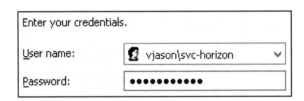

```
PS C:\> Enter-PSSession -ComputerName "viewcs03.vjason.local" -UseSSL -Credentia
l "vjason\svc-horizon"
```

3. A **Windows PowerShell credential request** window will open, as shown in the following screenshot; provide the password for the user account specified in the -Credential option of the previous step and click on **OK**:

4. The PowerShell window will now display a command prompt that includes the name of the Horizon Connection Server, as shown in the following figure. You are now running a PowerShell session on this server from the local drive indicated in the console. You can change drives by selecting another drive letter exactly as you would if you were logged on directly using the console on the Horizon Connection Server:

```
[viewcs03.vjason.local]: PS C:\> _
```

5. Switch to the following directory on the Horizon Connection Server; this folder path assumes that the Horizon Connection Server was installed in the default `Program Files\VMware\VMware View\Server\extras\PowerShell` directory.

6. Execute the following command to run the script that will load the Horizon PowerCLI commands:

```
.\Add-snapin.ps1
```

Once the script has run completely, `Welcome to VMware View PowerCLI` should appear, as shown in the following figure. You are now able to use PowerCLI to remotely manage the Horizon Connection Server.

```
[viewcs03.vjason.local]: PS C:\Program Files\VM
werShell> .\add-snapin.ps1
Loading VMware View PowerCLI

          Welcome to VMware View PowerCLI


[viewcs03.vjason.local]: PS C:\Program Files\VM
werShell>
```

# Viewing all the PowerCLI commands and their options

In this section, we will review all of the current VMware Horizon PowerCLI commands and provide examples of how they are used. The Horizon PowerCLI commands must be enumerated using either a local, or remote, PowerCLI session. To establish a remote session, refer to the *Establishing a Remote Horizon PowerCLI Session* section found earlier in this chapter.

## Listing all Horizon PowerCLI commands

The `Get-Command` PowerShellcommand is used to display all of the commands available in the specified PowerShell snap-in. To display a current list of PowerCLI commands available in the version of Horizon you are working with, use the following command:

```
Get-Command -PSSnapin VMware.View.Broker | more
```

VMware has not yet updated Horizon PowerCLI to include support for newer features such as **Instant Clone** desktops, Windows RDS **Application Pools**, or **Cloud Pods**. When a new version of Horizon is released, in addition to reviewing the product documentation you can run this command to see what, if any, PowerCLI commands have been added.

# Displaying the options for a single PowerCLI command

The `Get-Help` PowerShellcommand is used to display the command-line options for the specified PowerShell or Horizon PowerCLI command. To display a list of command options and examples, use the following command:

```
Get-Help command | more
```

To display more detailed information about any of the Horizon PowerCLI commands, append the `Get-Help` command with either of the following switches:

- The `-detailed` switch: This displays additional information about the command
- The `-examples` switch: This displays examples of how the command is used
- The `-full` switch: This displays additional technical information about the command

The following is an example of how these switches are used with the `Get-Help` command; replace *command* with the PowerCLI command you wish to get information about:

```
Get-Help command -full | more
```

# Sample data for Horizon PowerCLI commands

The following values will be used to complete our sample Horizon PowerCLI commands. Some portions of the text are in **bold**; these represent objects that are created automatically within vCenter, but are not visible to the end user (such as **vm** or **Resources**) or objects that are unique to each environment (such as **host**, referring to a ESXi server hostname). These objects must be included in the PowerCLI command or it will not work:

| Configuration object | Sample value |
|---|---|
| The AD domain name | vjason.local |
| The AD group used for example commands | Engineering_Horizon_Users |
| The AD user used for example commands | Charles Xavier (vjason\charles) |
| The destination vCenter folder for Horizon desktops, including the path | /RTP/Desktops |
| The linked clone OS disk storage | /RTP/**host**/HOR-Cluster1/VSAN1 |
| The linked clone persistent (user) data disk storage | /RTP/**host**/HOR-Cluster1/VSAN2 |
| The linked clone replica disk storage | /RTP/**host**/HOR-Cluster1/VSAN3 |
| For full clone desktops, each datastore serves the same role. We still need to specify a destination datastore for our desktops, but only one is explicitly required with full clones. | |
| Linked clone desktop parent VM, including the path | /RTP/**vm**/Master/Win10x32-LC |
| The vCenter datacenter | RTP |
| The vCenter server name | Vc-01.vjason.local |
| The Horizon vCenter AD service account | vjason\svc-horizon |
| The Horizon Composer Server AD account | vjason\svc-composer |
| The Horizon Composer AD domain | vjason.local |
| The Horizon Connection Server used | Viewcs03.vjason.local |
| Horizon Engineering Users AD Group | Engineering_Horizon_Users |
| The Horizon folder for the Engineering Desktop Pool | Engineering |
| Virtual machine snapshot 1 name | 0222 |
| Virtual machine snapshot 2 name | 0225 |
| The virtual machine template for full clone desktops with the path | /RTP/**vm**/Master/Win10x32-FC |
| The vSphere cluster for desktops with the path | /RTP/**host**/HOR-Cluster1 |
| The vSphere resource pool for desktops with the path | /RTP/**host**/HOR-Cluster1/**Resources** |
| vSphere Windows customization specification | Hor_Full_Clones |

# Horizon PowerCLI commands not covered in this chapter

The following commands will not be covered in this chapter, as they are used to create and manage desktops, and desktop pools, for vSphere VMs that are managed by vCenter Servers, which are not linked to Horizon, VMs deployed on third-party virtualization platforms, or even physical computers. As such, these commands are not used in the majority of Horizon environments. Regardless, the syntax for these commands is very similar to the commands we will review, and any other information needed can be obtained using the PowerCLI `Get-Help` command.

- `Add-ManualUnmanagedPool`: Used with VMs from any source, or even physical computers. The Horizon agent must be installed on these computers.
- `Get-DesktopPhysicalMachine`: Return a list of physical desktops registered with Horizon that were added to a manual unmanaged pool.
- `Update-ManualUnmanagedPool`: Update the configuration of a manual unmanaged Horizon desktop pool.

The following commands will not be covered in this chapter as they are no longer supported by Horizon. Refer to VMware KB article 2124209 (`https://kb.vmware.com/selfservice/microsites/search.do?language=en_US&cmd=displayKC&externalId=2124209`) for further details:

- `Add-TerminalServerPool`
- `Get-TerminalServer`
- `Update-TerminalServerPool`

# Configuring the Horizon infrastructure

In this section, we will review several different commands that can be used to configure the Horizon infrastructure. These commands include those used for an initial configuration, as well as those used to modify existing settings.

# Adding a vCenter Server to Horizon

The `Add-ViewVC` command is used to add a VMware vCenter Server to Horizon so that it can be used to manage and provision the Horizon desktops. The following example links the `Vc-01.vjason.local` vCenter Server to Horizon:

```
Add-ViewVC -ServerName "Vc-01.vjason.local" -Username "vjason\svc-
horizon" -Password "Password123" -CreateRampFactor 8 -UseComposer $true
```

The `Add-ViewVC` command requires several options to be specified in order to link a vCenter Server to the Horizon environment. These include the following:

- `CreateRampFactor`: Maximum of concurrent vCenter desktop provisioning operations.
- `Password`: Password for the `-Username` account. The password should be contained within quotes.
- `ServerName` or `Name`: FQDN of the vCenter Server. Either option can be specified.
- `Username` or `User`: The user who has appropriate permissions within vCenter in the `domain\username` format. Either option can be specified.

Additional options can be specified. These include the following:

- `ComposerPort`: Port that needs to be used with the Horizon Composer Server.
- `DeleteRampFactor`: Maximum number of concurrent desktop power operations.
- `Description`: Description for vCenter Server in the Horizon console. This value should be contained within quotes.
- `DisplayName`: Display name for vCenter Server in the Horizon Administrator console. This value should be contained within quotes.
- `Port`: Port to be used with vCenter Server.
- `UseComposer`: Used when the Horizon Composer Server is installed on vCenter Server. The options are `$true` or `$false` (the default).
- UseComposerSsl: Enable SSL for the connection to the Horizon Composer Server. The options are `$true` (the default) or `$false`.
- `UseSpaceReclamation`: Enable SeSparse space reclamation on ESXi servers managed by the vCenter Server. The options are `$true` or `$false` (the default).
- UseSsl: Enable SSL for the connection to the vCenter Server. The options are `$true` (the default) or `$false`.

Options such as port numbers and whether or not to use SSL (enabled by default) will use their default values if not specified and should not be changed under most circumstances.

A number of vCenter options cannot be configured when linking a vCenter Server using PowerCLI. These include Horizon Storage Accelerator, standalone Horizon Composer Servers, dedicated users for the Horizon Composer, the Horizon Composer domains, and others. These options must be configured after using the Horizon Administrator console.

> If your vCenter Server or Horizon Composer Server SSL certificate is not trusted by the Horizon Connection Servers, the Add-ViewVC operation will fail. This is different from adding a vCenter Server using the Horizon Administrator console, which allows you to accept an untrusted certificate. To use this command, you must replace the default vCenter Server SSL certificate with one signed by a trusted certificate authority.

# Updating the settings of vCenter Server that is linked to Horizon

The Update-ViewVC command can be used to update the settings of a vCenter Server that is currently linked to Horizon. The following example command updates the DeleteRampFactor value, as well as the description of the vCenter Server named Vc-01.vjason.local:

```
Update-ViewVC -ServerName "Vc-01.vjason.local" -DeleteRampFactor 10 -
Description "VC-01 vCenter Server"
```

This command supports the same options as the Add-ViewVC command. Specify the vCenter Server to be updated using the ServerName or Name option, and then update the options as required.

# Removing a vCenter Server from Horizon

The Remove-ViewVC command can be used to remove a vCenter Server that is currently linked to Horizon. The Remove-ViewVC requires only the vCenter Server name in order to unlink it from Horizon. The vCenter Server cannot be removed if desktops are currently deployed. The following example command will remove the Vc-01.vjason.local vCenter Server from Horizon:

```
Remove-ViewVC -ServerName "Vc-01.vjason.local"
```

# Updating the Horizon connection broker settings

The `Update-ConnectionBroker` command supports a number of options in order to configure Horizon Connection brokers, which include both Connection Servers and Security Servers. The following example command updates the external PCoIP URL of the Horizon Security Server named `VIEWSEC-01`:

```
Update-ConnectionBroker -Broker_id "VIEWSEC-01" -ExternalPCoIPUrl
"192.168.0.1:4172"
```

The following options are supported when using the `Update-ConnectionBroker` command:

- `Broker_id`: Name of the Horizon connection broker.
- `DirectConnect`: Enable direct connections to the Horizon desktops. The options are `$true` or `$false` (the default).
- `DirectPCoIP`: Enable direct PCoIP connections to the Horizon desktops. The options are `$true` (the default) or `$false`.
- `ClearNodeSecret`: Clear the existing RSA SecurID node secret (if in use).
- `ExternalURL`: External URL for the Connection Server home page.
- `ExternalPCoIPUrl`: External URL for PCoIP access using the secure gateway.
- `LdapBackupFolder`: Folder that is used for the Horizon LDAP backups.
- `LdapBackupFrequency`: Frequency of LDAP backups. The options are `EveryHour`, `Every6Hour`, `Every12Hour`, `EveryDay` (the default), `Every2Day`, `EveryWeek`, `Every2Week`, and `Never`.
- `LdapBackupMaxNumber`: Maximum number of LDAP backups that need to be retained. The default is `10`.
- `LogoffWhenRemoveSmartCard`: Log off the Horizon Client sessions when the client's smart card is removed. The options are `$true` or `$false` (the default).
- `NameMapping`: Enforce RSA SecurID and Windows name matching. The options are `$true` or `$false` (the default).
- `SecureIDEnabled`: Enable RSA SecurID authentication. The options are `$true` or `$false` (the default).
- `SmartCardSetting`: Enable smart card authentication. The options are `Required`, `Off`, or `Optional` (the default).

- `Tags`: Set Connection Server tags, used to restrict connections to desktop pools to specific Connection Servers.
- `PCoIPBandwidthLimit`: Configure the per-session PCoIP bandwidth limit in Kbps.

# Updating the Horizon global settings

The `Update-GlobalSetting` command can be used to update a number of different Horizon global settings. The following example command enables and configures the **Force Logoff** and **Pre Login** messages:

```
Update-GlobalSetting –DisplayPreLogin $true –PreLoginMessage
"Unauthorized users prohibited" –DisplayLogoffWarning $true –
ForcedLogoffMessage "You will be logged off"
```

The following settings can be set using the `Update-GlobalSetting` command:

- `DisplayLogoffWarning`: Displays a warning to the Horizon Client prior to a forced logoff; this value should be contained within quotes.
- `DisplayPreLogin`: Displays a login message prior to the Horizon Client logging into the Connection Server; this value should be contained within quotes.
- `ForceLogoffAfter`: Sets how long you need to wait in minutes after the warning message appears to force logoff the Horizon Client.
- `ForceLogoffMessage`: The text for the force logoff message; this value should be contained within quotes.
- `MessageSecurityMode`: Sets the security level for communication between Horizon components. The options include `Disabled`, `Mixed`, and `Enabled` (the default).
- `PreLoginMessage`: The text for the pre-login message; this value should be contained within quotes.
- `ReauthenticateOnInterrupt`: Forces the Horizon Client to re-authenticate after connection interruption. The options are `$true` or `$false` (the default).
- `SessionTimeout`: The timeout value in minutes for inactive Horizon Client sessions.
- `UseSslClient`: Forces SSL Horizon Client connections. The options are `$true` or `$false` (the default).
- `WidgetPolling`: Enables automatic status updates in the Horizon Administrator. The options are `$true` (the default) or `$false`.

## Configuring the Horizon license

The `Set-License` command is used to license a Horizon pod. The `Set-License` command requires only one option: `-key`. Do not remove the dashes from the license key, for example:

```
Set-License -Key "AAAAA-BBBBB-CCCCC-DDDDD-EEEEE"
```

# Administering Horizon desktop pools

In this section, we will review the PowerCLI commands that are used to create Horizon desktop pools. This section assumes you are familiar with Horizon pool configuration options, some of which are described in `Chapter 10`, *Creating Horizon Desktop Pools*. As mentioned earlier in this chapter, if you need more information about a specific command, you can use the PowerCLI `Get-Help` command in the format: `Get-Help command -full | more`, replacing X with the `command` in question.

When creating linked clone desktop pools, you must specify the vCenter and Horizon Composer domain in separate commands prior to beginning the command that actually creates the pool. This is done in the sample commands provided, and the required text is shown below:

```
Get-ViewVC -serverName "Vc-01.vjason.local" | Get-
ComposerDomain -domain "vjason.local" -username
"vjason\svc-composer" | ...
```

The `|` character is used to feed the results of one PowerCLI command into the next command provided, which is an operation known as **piping**.

# Create a dedicated assignment persistent linked clone pool

In this section, we will create a dedicated assignment persistent linked clone Horizon desktop pool.

Not all of the values in the following example command are mandatory; the `FolderId`, `DataDiskLetter`, `DataDiskSize`, `TempDiskSize`, `VmFolderPath`, and `NetworkLabelConfigFile` values can all be omitted and the Horizon defaults will be used. The remaining values are all required in order to create a linked clone pool using the `Add-AutomaticLinkedClonePool` PowerCLI command:

```
Get-ViewVC -serverName "Vc-01.vjason.local" | Get-ComposerDomain -
domain "vjason.local" -username "vjason\svc-composer" | Add-
AutomaticLinkedClonePool -Pool_id "EngineeringLC1" -DisplayName
"Engineering Desktops" -NamePrefix "EngineeringLC{n:fixed=4}" -VmFolderPath
"/RTP/vm/Desktops" -ResourcePoolPath "/RTP/host/HOR-Cluster1/Resources" -
ParentVmPath "/RTP/vm/Master/Win10x32-LC" -ParentSnapshotPath "/0222" -
DatastoreSpecs "[Aggressive,OS]/RTP/host/HOR-
Cluster1/VSAN1;[Aggressive,data]/RTP/host/HOR-
Cluster1/VSAN2;[Aggressive,replica]/RTP/host/HOR-Cluster1/VSAN3" -
MaximumCount 100 -MinProvisionedDesktops 25 -HeadroomCount 90 -MinimumCount
100 -DataDiskLetter D -DataDiskSize 1536 -TempDiskSize 3072 -FolderId
"Engineering" -NetworkLabelConfigFile "d:\LCConfigFile"
```

# Create a floating assignment (non-persistent) linked clone pool

To create a linked clone desktop pool floating assignment (non-persistent), the following changes would need to be made to the example command from the previous section of this recipe:

- Omit the options for `DataDiskLetter` and `DataDiskSize`
- The OS and data disks must be placed on the same datastore, so adjust the datastore specifications to read `[Aggressive,data,OS]`
- Add the `-Persistence NonPersistent` option

Based on these requirements, the updated command is as follows. The items that were added or changed are in bold; the items that were removed are not shown:

```
Get-ViewVC -serverName "Vc-01.vjason.local" | Get-ComposerDomain -
domain "vjason.local" -username "vjason\svc-composer" | Add-
AutomaticLinkedClonePool -Pool_id "EngineeringLC1" -DisplayName
"EngineeringDesktops" -NamePrefix "EngineeringLC{n:fixed=4}" -VmFolderPath
"/RTP/vm/Desktops" -ResourcePoolPath "/RTP/host/HOR-Cluster1/Resources" -
ParentVmPath "/RTP/vm/Master/Win10x32-LC" -ParentSnapshotPath "/0222" -
DatastoreSpecs
"[Aggressive,data,OS]/RTP/host/DTCluster1/VSAN1;[Aggressive,data,OS]/RTP/ho
st/HOR-Cluster1/VSAN2;[Aggressive,replica]/RTP/host/HOR-Cluster1/VSAN3" -
```

```
MaximumCount 100 -MinProvisionedDesktops 25 -HeadroomCount 90 -MinimumCount
100 -TempDiskSize 3072 -FolderId "Engineering" -Persistence NonPersistent
```

# Creating an automatically provisioned full clone desktop pool

The `Add-AutomaticPool` command can be used to create Horizon full clone desktop pools. Some desktop pool options, such as **Horizon Storage Accelerator**, cannot be configured using PowerCLI. These settings must be configured after the pool has been created using the Horizon Administrator console.

Not all of the values in the following example command are mandatory; the `FolderID` and `CustomizationSpecName` values can both be omitted, and the Horizon defaults can be used. The remaining values are all required in order to create a full clone pool using the `Add-AutomaticPool` PowerCLI command:

```
Get-ViewVC -serverName "Vc-01.vjason.local" | Get-ComposerDomain -
domain vjason.local" -username vjason\svc-composer" | Add-AutomaticPool -
Pool_id "EngineeringFC1" -DisplayName "Engineering Desktops" -NamePrefix
"EngineeringFC{n:fixed=4}" -VmFolderPath "/RTP/vm/Desktops" -
ResourcePoolPath "/RTP/host/HOR-Cluster1/Resources" -TemplatePath
"/RTP/vm/Master/ Win10x32-FC" -DatastorePaths "/RTP/host/HOR-
Cluster1/VSAN1;/ RTP/host/HOR-Cluster1/VSAN2;/RTP/host/HOR-Cluster1/VSAN3"
-MaximumCount 100 -HeadroomCount 90 -MinimumCount 100 -FolderId
"Engineering" -CustomizationSpecName "Hor_Full_Clones"
```

# Creating a manually provisioned desktop pool

Manually provisioned desktop pools are typically used when the Horizon desktops are created outside the Horizon environment using tools such as vSphere or an array-based virtual machine cloning tool. These manually provisioned desktops must be available in vCenter in order for them to be added to the manually provisioned desktop pool.

 VMware Horizon cannot deploy Linux desktops, so if you intend to use them as Horizon desktops you will need to provision them manually and place them in a manually provisioned desktop pool.

Prior to creating the manually provisioned desktop pool, at least one supported virtual machine with the Horizon agent installed must be available within vCenter. This desktop must not be assigned to any existing Horizon desktop pools, as it will be added to the new manually provisioned desktop pool during the pool-creation process.

The following example command will create a manually provisioned desktop pool and add the virtual machine named `LinuxDT-01` to it:

```
Add-ManualPool -Pool_id "Manual1" -Id (Get-DesktopVM -Name
"LinuxDT-01").id -Vc_name "Vc-01.vjason.local"
```

 The `Get-DesktopVM` option was run within the command in order to obtain the value for the virtual machine ID (id). By placing the command within parentheses, and appending it with `.id`, it returns the value we require in order to complete our `Add-ManualPool` command.

Manual desktop pools support most of the same configuration options as linked clone or full clone pools. As well as the following additional options:

- `Id`: vCenter machine ID for the virtual machine to be added to the pool
- `VC_name`: Hostname of the vCenter Server that manages the pool VMs
- `Vm_id_list`: ID for multiple virtual machines to be added to the pool, separated by semicolons

The `Add-ManualPool` command requires at least these options to be specified in order to create a pool: `Pool_id`, `VC_name` or `Vc_id`, and `Id`.

# Updating the configuration of a Horizon desktop pool

There are two different Horizon PowerCLI commands used to update the configuration of a Horizon desktop pool that we will review in this section:

- `Update-AutomaticLinkedClonePool`: Used to update the configuration of an existing Horizon linked clone pool
- `Update-AutomaticPool`: Used to update the configuration of an existing Horizon full clone pool

The majority of the Horizon pool configuration options can be modified after the pool has been deployed, regardless of whether they were specified during deployment or not. If you are unable to update a given configuration option, use the `Get-Help command -full | more` command to verify if the parameter in question is able to be updated. One example of this is the Horizon pool `Pool_id` value, which can only be set when the pool is first configured.

# Updating a linked clone pool

In this example, we will update the linked clone desktop pool configuration using the `Update- AutomaticLinkedClonePool` command. The only option required is the value for `Pool_id`, as well as any other options you wish to change:

```
Update-AutomaticLinkedClonePool -Pool_id "EngineeringLC1" -
AllowProtocolOverride $true
```

# Updating an automatically provisioned full clone pool

In this example, we will update the full clone desktop pool configuration using the `Update- AutomaticPool` command. The only option required is the value for `Pool_id`, as well as any other options you wish to change:

```
Update-AutomaticPool -Pool_id "EngineeringFC1" -DefaultProtocol PCOIP
```

# Updating a manually provisioned pool

In the following example, we will update the manually provisioned pool configuration using the `Update-ManualPool` command. The only option required is the value for `Pool_id`, as well as any other options you wish to change:

```
Update-ManualPool -Pool_id "Manual1" -FlashQuality HIGH
```

# Refreshing a linked clone desktop or pool

The `Send-LinkedCloneRefresh` command is used to refresh either a specific Horizon linked clone desktop or an entire desktop pool. The following demonstrates two different ways the command is used:

- The following example command selects all the desktops in the `EngineeringLC1` pool and schedules them to refresh at the indicated time. In addition, the operation will continue even if an error occurs but will not force users to log off:

```
Get-Pool -Pool_id "EngineeringLC1" | Get-DesktopVM | Send-
LinkedCloneRefresh -schedule "2016-02-25 22:00" -StopOnError $false -
ForceLogoff $false
```

- To refresh just a single desktop, you can use a simpler version of the command that requires only the machine ID and the schedule. This command will refresh only the desktop named `HorLC0001`:

```
Send-LinkedCloneRefresh -Machine_id (Get-DesktopVM -Name
"HorLC0001").machine_id -schedule "2016-02-25 22:00"
```

When using the `Send-LinkedCloneRefresh` command to refresh an entire pool, the command requires us to specify each desktop within the pool, so we will be piping the output of the `Get-Pool` and `Get-DesktopVM` commands into the `Send-LinkedCloneRefresh` command.

We must also specify the time to begin the refresh using the `-schedule` option in the `YYYY-MM-DD HH:MM` format, using a 24-hour format for the hour. We must remember that any time specified will be executed based on the time on the Horizon Connection Server itself.

Other options for the command include `StopOnError`, which is enabled by default and halts the refresh if errors occur, and `ForceLogoff`, which is disabled by default and will force users to log off. Both of these options accept either `$true` or `$false` as options.

# Recomposing a linked clone desktop pool

The `Send-LinkedCloneRecompose` command is used to recompose either a specific Horizon linked clone desktop or the entire desktop pool.

In the following example, we will be recomposing to a new snapshot of the same parent VM; the snapshot is named `0225`. Since this VM now has two snapshots, the `ParentSnapshotPath` will now be in the `/0222/0225`, format, where `0222` is the name of the original snapshot used to create the pool. The remainder of the command follows a format that is similar to the `Send-LinkedCloneRefresh` command:

```
Get-Pool -Pool_id "EngineeringLC1" | Get-DesktopVM | Send-
LinkedCloneRecompose -ParentVMPath "/RTP/vm/Master/Win10x32-LC" -
ParentSnapshotPath "/0222/0225" -schedule "2016-02-25 22:00"
```

The command will recompose all desktops in the pool to the snapshot named `0225` at the indicated time. You can also select a different parent VM when performing a recompose, but remember that the VM must be running the same OS as the existing desktops.

You can also recompose a single desktop using the `-machine_id` option and the `Get-DesktopVM` command:

```
Send-LinkedCloneRecompose (Get-DesktopVM -Name "HorLC0001").machine_id
-ParentVMPath "/RTP/vm/Master/Win10x32-LC" -ParentSnapshotPath "/0222/0225"
-schedule "2016-02-25 22:00"
```

The `Send-LinkedCloneRecompose` command requires you to specify multiple options, including `Schedule`, `ParentVMPath`, and `ParentSnapshotPath`. The command also supports the `StopOnError` and `ForceLogoff` options.

# Rebalancing a linked clone desktop pool

The `Send-LinkedCloneRebalance` command is used to rebalance either a specific Horizon linked clone desktop or an entire desktop pool. The following demonstrates two different ways the command is used:

- The following example command selects all the desktops in the `EngineeringLC1` pool and schedules them to rebalance at the indicated time:

```
Get-Pool -Pool_id "EngineeringLC1" | Get-DesktopVM | Send-
LinkedCloneRebalance -schedule "2016-02-25 22:00"
```

- To rebalance just a single desktop, you can use a simpler version of the command that requires only the machine ID and the schedule. This command will rebalance only the desktop named `HorLC0001`:

```
Send-LinkedCloneRebalance -Machine_id (Get-DesktopVM -Name
"HorLC0001").machine_id -schedule "2016-02-25 22:00"
```

The `Send-LinkedCloneRebalance` command uses the same format as the other linked clone maintenance commands. All that is required is the desktop pool ID and the schedule. The command also supports the `StopOnError` and `ForceLogoff` options.

## Resetting a Horizon desktop

The `Send-VMReset` command can be used to reset a Horizon desktop, for example, when it is in an unresponsive state. The following example command will reset the Horizon desktop named `HorLC0001`:

```
Send-VMReset -Machine_id (Get-DesktopVM -Name "HorLC0001").machine_id
```

The `Send-VMReset` command requires the machine ID in order to identify the desktop.

# Managing Horizon Client entitlements and sessions

In this section, we will review several different commands that can be used to manage Horizon Client entitlements and sessions.

# Adding desktop pool entitlements

Entitling is the act of granting AD users, or groups, access to the Horizon pools. In this section we will review how to entitle individual users as well as AD security groups:

- The following `Add-PoolEntitlement` command will entitle the `Engineering_Horizon_Users` group to the `EngineeringLC1` desktop pool:

```
Add-PoolEntitlement -Pool_id EngineeringLC1 -sid (Get-User -Name
"Engineering_Horizon_Users").sid
```

- To entitle individual users, simply provide the first and last name of the user:

```
Add-PoolEntitlement -Pool_id EngineeringLC1 -sid (Get-User -Name
"Charles Xavier").sid
```

The `Get-User` command accepts wildcards, but be careful when using them, as the wrong user might be returned. If in doubt, use the `Get-User` command by itself to verify that you are selecting the correct user.

# Removing desktop pool entitlements

The `Remove-PoolEntitlement` command uses the same format as the `Add-PoolEntitlement` command; however, if you are removing the last entitlements from the desktop pool, you must add the `-ForceRemove $true` option for the command to succeed. This prevents you from accidentally removing all entitlements from a desktop pool, for example:

```
Remove-PoolEntitlement -Pool_id "EngineeringLC1" -sid (Get-User -Name
"Engineering_Horizon_Users").sid -ForceRemove $true
```

The `Add-PoolEntitlement` and `Remove-PoolEntitlement` commands require you to specify the user or group AD **system identifier** (**SID**) in order to add or remove desktop pool entitlements. For this, use the `Get-User` command within the `Remove-PoolEntitlement` command. Despite the name, the `Get-User` name is used to obtain both AD users and groups.

# Entitling or un-entitling an individual desktop

Entitling an individual desktop is similar to entitling a desktop pool, except that, in this case, we need both the user SID as well as the machine ID. For the following example command, we will nest two commands, `Get-DesktopVM` and `Get-User`, within the two different `UserOwnership` commands:

```
Update-UserOwnership -Machine_id (Get-DesktopVM -Name
"HorLC0001").machine_id -Sid (Get-User -Name "Jason Ventresco").sid
```

The `Get-User` command accepts wildcards, but be careful when using them, as the wrong user might be returned. If in doubt, use the `Get-User` command by itself to verify that you are selecting the correct user.

The `Remove-UserOwnership` command requires only the desktop machine ID:

```
Remove-UserOwnership -Machine_id (Get-DesktopVM -Name
"HorLC0001").machine_id
```

# Disconnecting the Horizon Client session

The `Send-SessionDisconnect` commanddisconnects users based on the Horizon session ID. The following example command will disconnect the session belonging to the `vjason.local\charles` AD user:

```
Send-SessionDisconnect -Session_id (Get-RemoteSession -Username
"vjason.local\charles").session_id
```

The Horizon session ID is a really long value that is difficult to work with, so we will use the `Get-RemoteSession` command within the `Send-SessionDisconnect` command instead in order to disconnect the target user.

# Logging off the Horizon Client session

The `Send-SessionLogoff` commanddisconnects users based on the Horizon session ID. The `Send-SessionLogoff` command uses the same format as the `Send-SessionDisconnect` command. The following example command will log off the session belonging to the AD user `vjason.local\charles`:

```
Send-SessionLogoff -Session_id (Get-RemoteSession -Username
"vjason.local\charles").session_id
```

# Working with Horizon desktop network label Specifications

A network label specification is used to configure desktop pools that need to automatically place desktops on one of multiple available virtual machine networks, often for network capacity reasons. This feature is currently available only when using Horizon PowerCLI.

In the example provided, the vSphere cluster where your Horizon desktops will be deployed has two virtual machine networks named VLAN500 and VLAN510, and each virtual machine network can support no more than 250 desktops. We are going to create a desktop pool that has 500 desktops. To do this using the Horizon Administrator console, we will need two virtual desktop master images, one connected to each virtual machine network. You will then need to create two desktop pools, one for each virtual desktop master image.

When you use Horizon network label specification files, you need only one virtual desktop master image and one desktop pool. In this recipe, we will create network label specification files that we can use when creating desktop pools.

 While it is possible to manually create a network label specifications file, the recommended method for the created file is to export it from an existing Horizon desktop master image. The export process is described in the next two sections in this chapter.

# Sample network label specification file

The following code shows you the contents of a network label configuration file that will create 250 desktops at most in each of the two virtual machine networks (VLAN500 and VLAN510):

```
#Network Label Configuration Spec
#WARNING! Setting enabled flag to false will
#turn off the automatic network label assignment
#for newly provisioned desktops.
enabled=true
#Parameter Definition for NIC
nic1=Network adapter 1
#Parameter Definition for Network
network01=VLAN500
network02=VLAN510
#Network Label Attribute Definition
#Expected format:
#<nic_param>.<network_param>.maxvm=<max vm for network label>
nic1.network01.maxvm=250
nic1.network02.maxvm=250
```

The network label specification file contains the following fields, that should be edited based on the needs of our Horizon desktop pool and infrastructure configuration:

- The `enabled` field: This can be set to `true` or `false`; it is used to enable or disable the network label configuration for new desktops.
- The `maxvm` field: This defines the maximum number of Horizon desktops that will be placed in the specified virtual machine network.
- The `nic1` field: This defines the network adapter of the Horizon desktop that will be configured.
- The `networkXX` field: This defines each of the vSphere virtual machine networks where the desktops will be placed. One parameter will be created for each virtual machine network used, and the network name should match the name of the virtual machine network on the ESXi server where the desktop will be deployed.

Once all of these fields have been defined, they are combined to create network label attribute definitions using the following format:

```
nic1.network01.maxvm=250
nic1.network02.maxvm=250
```

Once the network label specification file has been configured, use the `-NetworkLabelConfigFile` option to import it when creating the Horizon desktop pool.

# Export a linked clone network label specification

To export the network label specification file that will be used to create Horizon linked clone pools, we need a virtual desktop master image that is configured with our desired virtual machine network settings. The virtual machine should also have a snapshot taken, as this is a prerequisite for images that will be used to create linked clone desktop pools.

The following example command reads the network labels of the virtual machine networks for the specified linked clone parent VM, which is located in the specified vSphere cluster and vCenter Server. The maximum number of VMs that will be created per network label is 250, and the network label specification file will be created on the D drive:

```
Export-NetworkLabelSpecForLinkedClone -ClusterPath "/RTP/host/HOR-
Cluster1" -vc_id (Get-ViewVC -ServerName "Vc-01.vjason.local").vc_id -
ParentVmPath "/RTP/vm/Master/Win10x32-LC" -ParentSnapshotPath "/0222" -
MaxVMsPerNetworkLabel 250 -NetworkLabelConfigFile "d:\LCConfigFile"
```

The `Get-ViewVC` command is run within the preceding command to obtain the `vc_id` value. You can also add the `FailIfNoNetworkFound` command option, which will cause the command to fail if no suitable network labels are found in the vSphere cluster. The options are `$false` and `$true` (the default).

 Since we are running a PowerCLI command on a remote system, the network label specification file will actually be created on the `D` drive of the Horizon Connection Server.

# Exporting a full clone network label specification

To export the network label specification file, that will be used to create Horizon full clone pools, we need a virtual desktop master image that is configured with our desired virtual machine network settings. The virtual machine should also be converted into the vSphere template format, as this is a prerequisite for images that will be used to create full clone desktop pools.

The following example command uses the same parameters as the `Export-NetworkLabelSpecForLinkedClone` command:

```
Export-NetworkLabelSpecForFullClone -ClusterPath "/RTP/host/HOR-
Cluster1" -vc_id (Get-ViewVC -ServerName "Vc-01.vjason.local").vc_id -
TemplatePath "/RTP/vm/Master/Win10x32-FC" -MaxVMsPerNetworkLabel 250 -
NetworkLabelConfigFile "d:\FCConfigFile"
```

# Retrieving information about the Horizon infrastructure

In this section, we will review several different commands that can be used to display information about the Horizon infrastructure.

# Retrieving Horizon Composer server information

The Get-ComposerDomain commandcan be used to obtain Horizon Composer information using the Vc_id, Domain, or Username options.

The following example command retrieves Horizon Composer information based on which vCenter the Server Composer is linked to:

```
Get-ComposerDomain -Vc_id (Get-ViewVC -Name "Vc-01.vjason.local").vc_id
```

The Get-ViewVC command is run within the command to obtain the vc_id value, which is easier than attempting to type in the value manually, as it is a series of random letters and numbers. This technique will be used in many of the examples for this chapter, as it makes working with certain values much easier. Omit the options in order to retrieve a list of all Horizon Composer server information.

# Retrieving a list of the Horizon desktop pools

The Get-Pool commandcan be used to retrieve a list of all the Horizon pools, or simply those that match the supplied specifications. The following command will retrieve a list of the Horizon pools that have the PCoIP protocol enabled:

```
Get-Pool -Enabled $true -Protocol PCOIP
```

Omit the options to retrieve a list of all the Horizon desktop pools. The Get-Pool command can be used to obtain information on desktop pools based on these options: Description, DisplayName, Enabled ($true or $false), Pool_id, PoolType, Protocol, and VcServerName. The VcServerName option is simply the name of the vCenter Server that hosts the desktop pools' virtual machines.

# Retrieving the global Horizon configuration data

The Get-GlobalSetting command is used to retrieve information about the Horizon global settings. The command has no options; simply execute the command by itself in order to obtain the configuration data.

# Retrieving the Horizon connection broker information

The `Get-ConnectionBroker` command is used to retrieve information about Horizon connection brokers, which include both Connection Servers and Security Servers. The following example command retrieves information about the `VIEWCS01` Connection Server:

```
Get-ConnectionBroker -Broker_id "VIEWCS01"
```

# Retrieving a list of virtual machines managed by Horizon

The `Get-DesktopVM` PowerCLIcommand can be used to return a list of the Horizon virtual desktops that meet the specified criteria. The following example command retrieves a list of desktops that currently have a refresh operation scheduled:

```
Get-DesktopVM -ComposerTask refresh
```

Omit the options in order to retrieve a list of all virtual machines. The `Get-DesktopVM` command supports multiple options that enable you to return desktops based on very specific criteria. The criteria include the following:

- The `ComposerTask` option: This retrieves desktops with the specified scheduled composer tasks. The options are `attachUdd`, `detachUdd`, `mkChkPoint`, `rebalance`, `refresh`, `replaceUdd`, and `resync`. The `Udd` term stands for user data disk.

A full description of each of these options is available in the VMware document View Integration (`https://www.vmware.com/support/pubs/view_pubs.html`).

- `GetNetworkLabel`: Retrieves the network label settings. The options are `$true` or `$false`.
- `IsInPool`: Retrieves desktops based on whether they are in a desktop pool. The options are `$true` or `$false`.

- `IsLinkedClone`: Retrieves desktops based on whether they are linked clones. The options are `$true` or `$false`.
- `Name`: Displays the name of the desktop in vCenter.
- `Pool_id`: Desktop pool ID.
- `PoolType`: Lists VMs that will work with the specified pool type; the only option is Manual.
- `Vc_id`: vCenter Server ID.

# Retrieving the AD user or group information

The `Get-User` command is typically used to pipe user or group names into other Horizon PowerCLI commands. The following example returns only those AD groups that start with Horizon:

```
Get-User -IncludeUser $false -Name "Horizon"
```

Omit the options to retrieve a list of all users and groups. The following options are available when using the `Get-User` command:

- `IncludeUser`: Specified whether the results include AD user accounts. The options are `$False` and `$True` (the default).
- `IncludeGroup` option: This sets whether the results include AD groups. The options are `$False` and `$True` (the default).
- `Name`: Name of the user or group to be returned. This value should be contained within quotes. If quotes are not used, partial matches are allowed based on the start of the name.
- `Domain`: Return users or groups from a specific domain.

# Retrieving information about user persistent data disks

The `Get-ProfileDisk` command can be used to retrieve information about the Horizon desktop persistent data disks that are registered with Horizon. The following example command will retrieve information about the persistent disk that belongs to the specified user:

```
Get-ProfileDisk -Username "vjason.local\charles"
```

Omit the -Username option in order to retrieve details about all of the persistent data disks registered with Horizon. The Get-ProfileDisk command supports several options in order to retrieve information about the persistent disks registered with Horizon:

- Name: Name of the persistent disk.
- Username: Full domain\username of the owner of the persistent disk.
- VmName: Name of the VM that is using the persistent disk.
- LastPool: Desktop pool that contains the persistent disk.
- DataStore: Datastore where the persistent disk is stored.
- Status: Status of the persistent disk. The options include In Use, Archiving, and Detached.

# Retrieving the Horizon event reports and their descriptions

The Get-EventReportList command is used to retrieve a list of Horizon event report names and their descriptions. The Get-EventReportList command has no options; simply execute the command by itself.

# Retrieving the Horizon event reports

The Get-EventReport command is used to retrieve a list of Horizon events from the specified event report. The following example command retrieves all event data about user events:

```
Get-EventReport -ViewName user_events
```

# Retrieving the Horizon infrastructure health monitors and their statuses

The Get-Monitor command is used to retrieve Horizon health-monitoring data from all or specific Horizon monitors. The following example command retrieves all the Horizon health-monitoring data for the VIEWCS01 Horizon Connection Server:

```
Get-Monitor -Monitor_id "VIEWCS01"
```

Omit the options to retrieve a list of all of the Horizon monitoring data. The `Get-Monitor` command supports two different options:

- `Monitor_id` option: This is the ID of the monitor. You can provide the specific monitor ID itself, as obtained from the `Get-Monitor` command, or you can specify a Horizon server name; all monitors for that server will be returned.
- `Monitor` option: This is the name of the monitor. The possible values include the following:
  - `CBMonitor`: Connection Server monitor
  - `DBMonitor`: Horizon event database monitor
  - `DomainMonitor`: Domain connection monitor
  - `SGMonitor`: Security Server monitor
  - `VCMonitor`: vCenter Server monitor

# Retrieving information about remote Horizon sessions

The `Get-RemoteSession` command is used to obtain information about any current Horizon sessions. The command supports several options that can be used to return only those sessions that match the specified criteria. The following example command retrieves all the remote Horizon sessions for the `EngineeringLC1` desktop pool:

```
Get-RemoteSession -Pool_id EngineeringLC1
```

The `Get-RemoteSession` command supports multiple options for listing client connections. Only one option is required in order to retrieve session information. The options include the following:

- `Username`: Username is in the FullDomainName\username format, for example, `vjason.local\charles`
- `Pool_id`: Desktop pool ID, for example, `EngineeringLC1`
- `Session_id`: Horizon session ID
- `Duration`: Duration in the format "dd day(s) hh hour(s) mm minute(s) ss second(s)", for example, `2 days 1 hour 15 minutes 1 second`
- `DnsName`: DNS name of the virtual desktop

- `State`: State of the desktop (`Connected` or `Disconnected`)
- `Protocol`: Protocol being used in the session (`PCOIP` or `RDP`)
- `StartTime`: Time at which the session was started, including the day, time, time zone, and year, for example, `Mon Feb 25 22:00:15 EST 2016`

# Retrieving a list of the vCenter Servers linked to the Horizon environment

The `Get-ViewVC` commandretrieves the Horizon Composer Server information for the specified Horizon Composer server. The following is an example of how the `Get-ViewVC` command is used:

```
Get-ViewVC -Name "Vc-01.vjason.local"
```

Omit the `-Name` option in order to retrieve a list of all vCenter Servers.

# Retrieving the Horizon license information

The `Get-License` command is used to retrieve the Horizon license status. The `Get-License` command has no options; simply execute the command by itself.

# Reviewing the desktop pool entitlement

The `Get-PoolEntitlement` command can be used to review the AD users and groups that have been granted access to the specified pool ID. The `Get-PoolEntitlement` command supports only one option: `Pool_id`. The following example command retrieves the entitlement settings for the desktop pool with the `EngineeringLC1` ID:

```
Get-PoolEntitlement -Pool_id "EngineeringLC1"
```

Omit the options in order to retrieve a list of user entitlements for all desktop pools. If the pool does not have an entitlement, the command will return an exception.

# Summary

In this chapter, we reviewed how to use Horizon PowerCLI to configure and administer VMware Horizon using the command line, which provides us the capability to script or automate various tasks.

We started out by learning how to enable SSL-encrypted remote management on our Horizon Connection Servers, which enables us to use Horizon PowerCLI remotely rather than needing to log in to the Horizon Connection Servers.

We continued by reviewing each of the Horizon PowerCLI commands, seeing examples of how those commands are used to configure and manage the Horizon infrastructure, including the desktops, desktop pools, and the Horizon Connection Servers themselves.

# Index

# W

# X

Printed in Great Britain
by Amazon